FRED BASSET YEARBOOK 2020

An Hachette UK Company
www.hachette.co.uk

Summersdale Publishers Ltd
Part of Octopus Publishing Group Limited
Carmelite House
50 Victoria Embankment
LONDON
EC4Y 0DZ
UK

www.summersdale.com

Printed and bound in the Czech Republic

ISBN: 978-1-78685-986-0

Substantial discounts on bulk quantities of Summersdale books are available to corporations, professional associations and other organizations.
For details contact general enquiries: telephone: +44 (0) 1243 771107 or email: enquiries@summersdale.com.

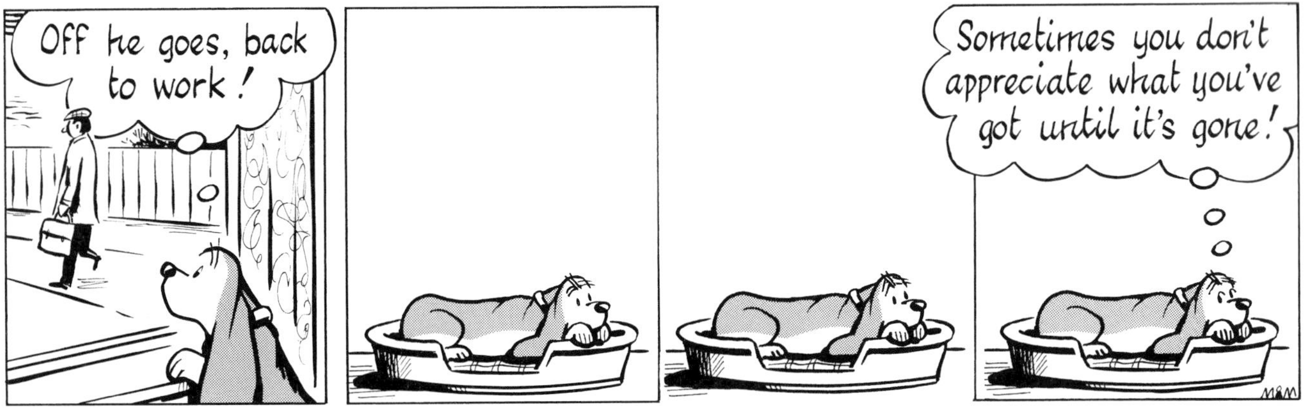
Off he goes, back to work!
Sometimes you don't appreciate what you've got until it's gone!

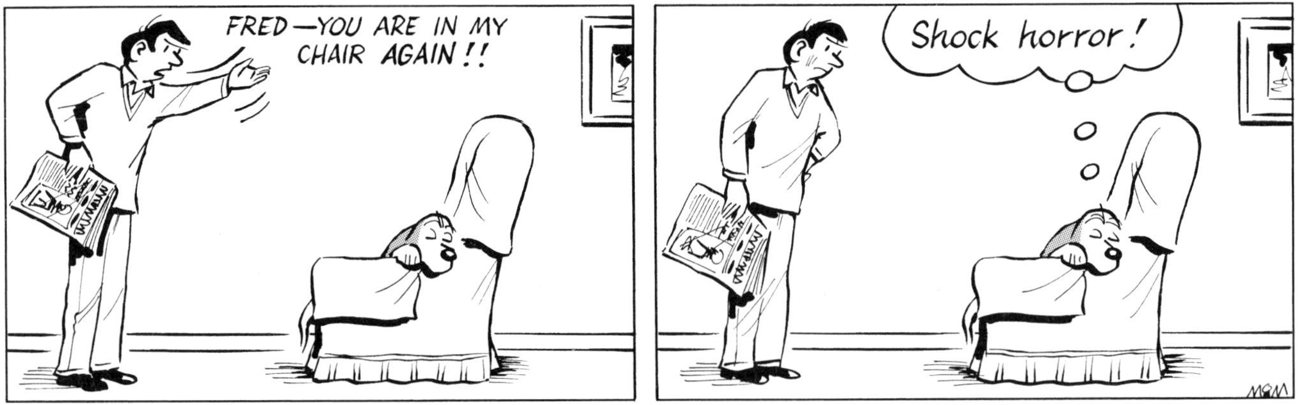
FRED—YOU ARE IN MY CHAIR AGAIN!!
Shock horror!

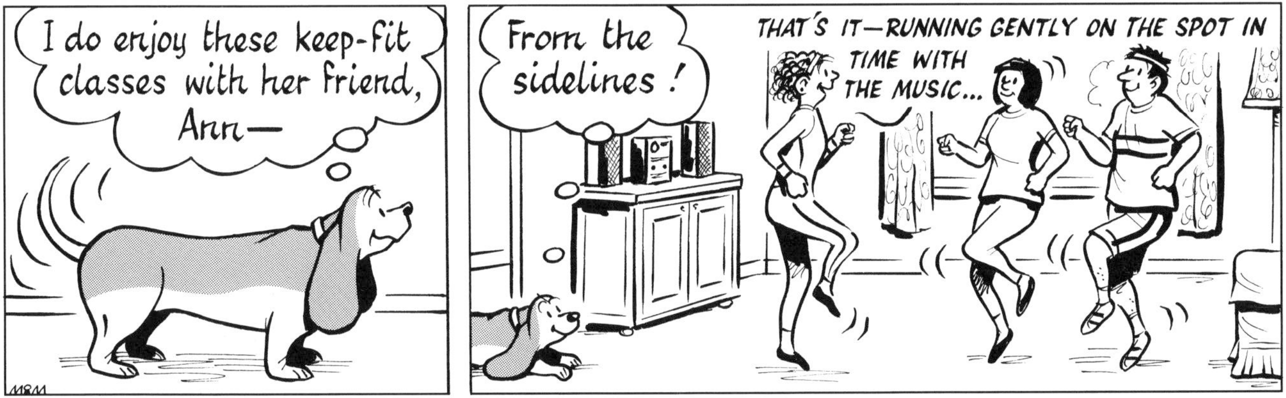
I do enjoy these keep-fit classes with her friend, Ann—
From the sidelines !
THAT'S IT—RUNNING GENTLY ON THE SPOT IN TIME WITH THE MUSIC...

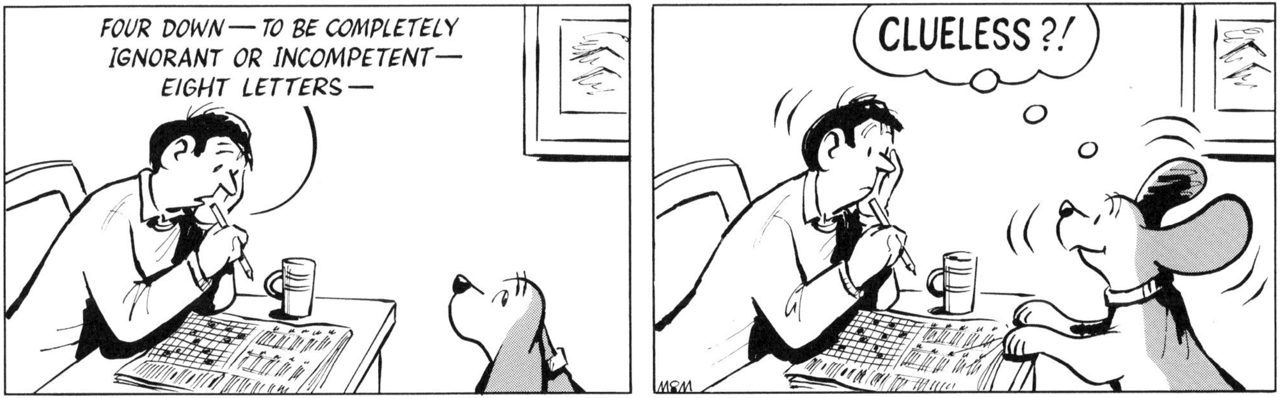
FOUR DOWN—TO BE COMPLETELY IGNORANT OR INCOMPETENT—EIGHT LETTERS—
CLUELESS ?!

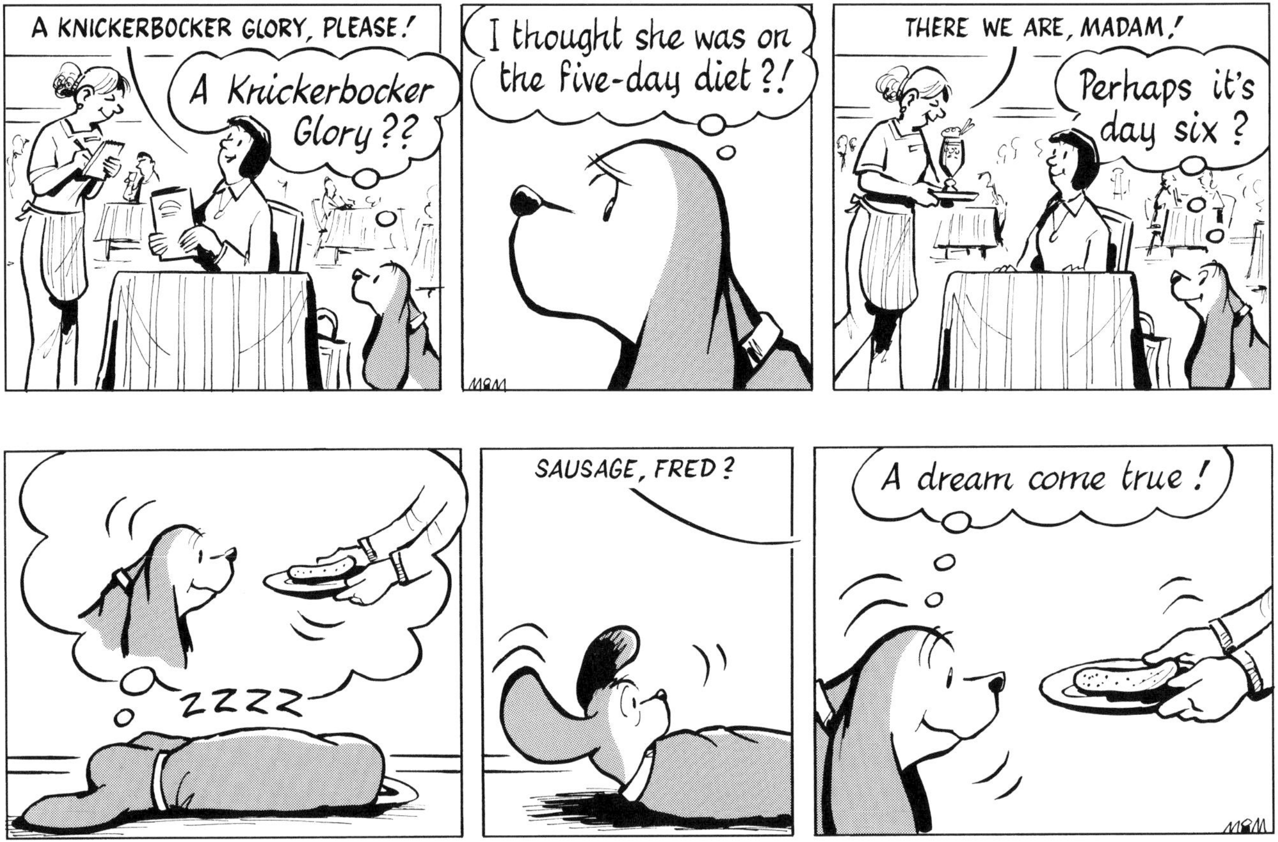
A KNICKERBOCKER GLORY, PLEASE!
A Knickerbocker Glory??
I thought she was on the five-day diet?!
THERE WE ARE, MADAM!
Perhaps it's day six?
ZZZZ
SAUSAGE, FRED?
A dream come true!

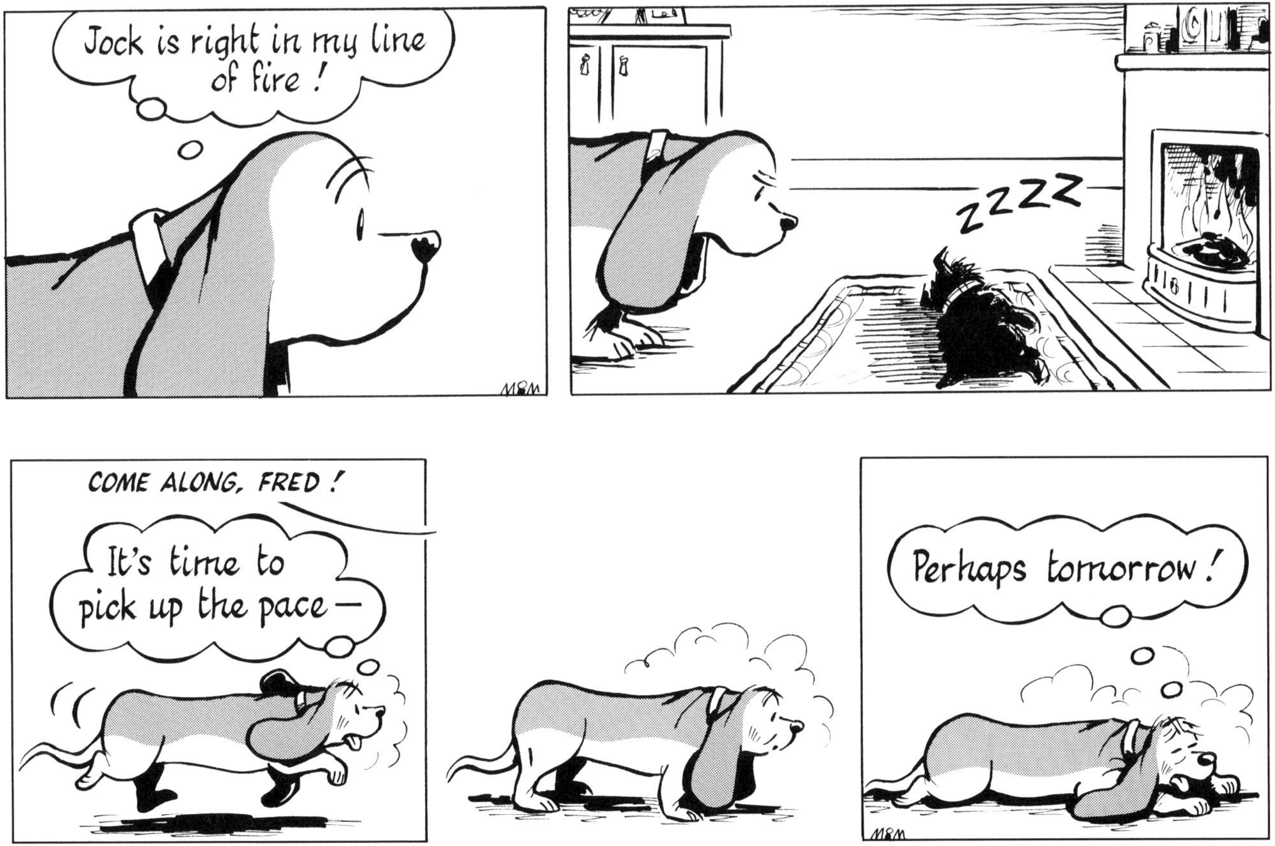
Jock is right in my line of fire!
ZZZZ
COME ALONG, FRED!
It's time to pick up the pace –
Perhaps tomorrow!

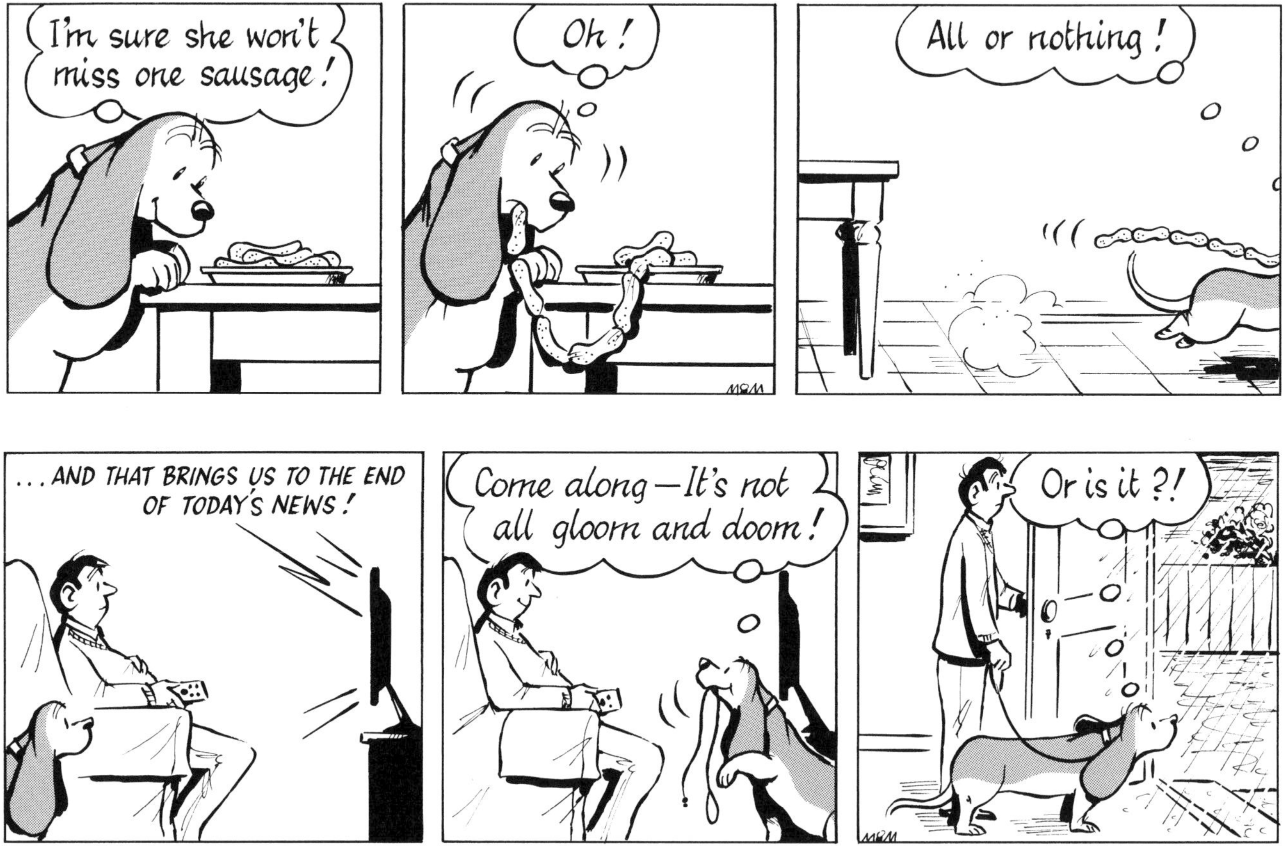
I'm sure she won't miss one sausage!
Oh!
All or nothing!
...AND THAT BRINGS US TO THE END OF TODAY'S NEWS!
Come along—It's not all gloom and doom!
Or is it?!

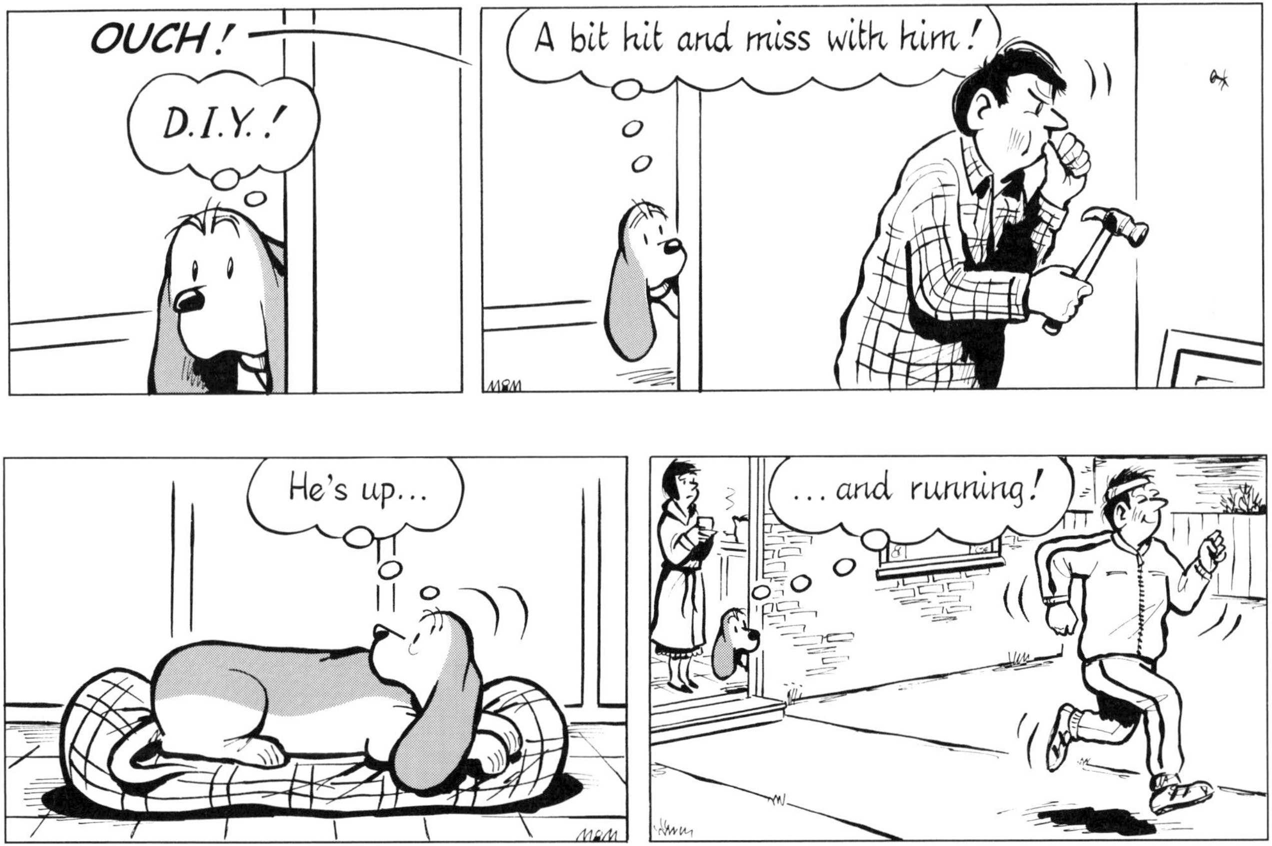
OUCH!
D.I.Y.!
A bit hit and miss with him!
He's up...
...and running!

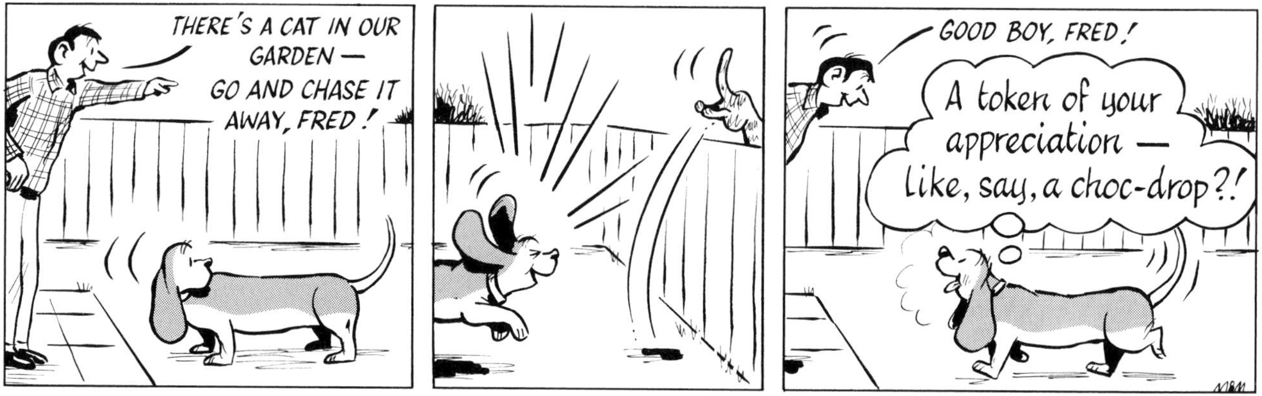
THERE'S A CAT IN OUR GARDEN — GO AND CHASE IT AWAY, FRED!
GOOD BOY, FRED!
A token of your appreciation — like, say, a choc-drop?!
M&M

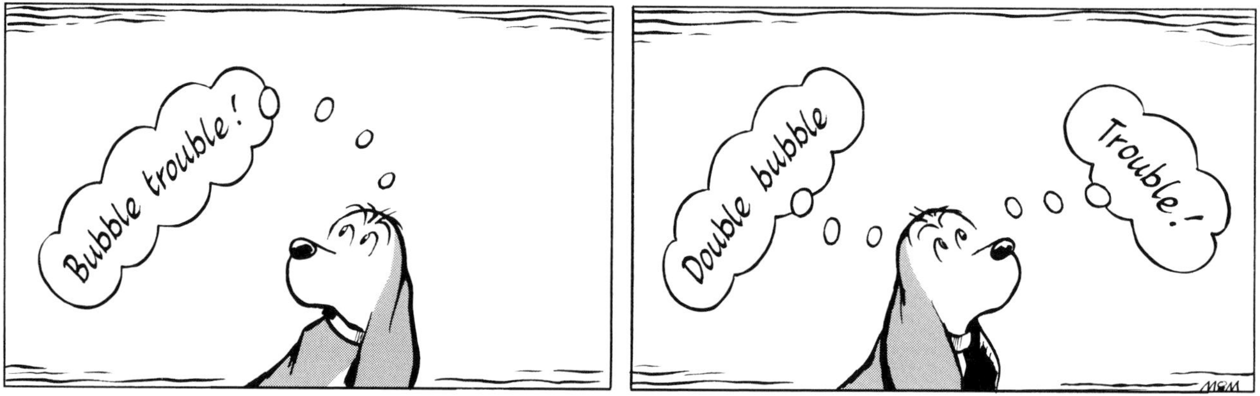
Bubble trouble!
Double bubble
Trouble!
M&M

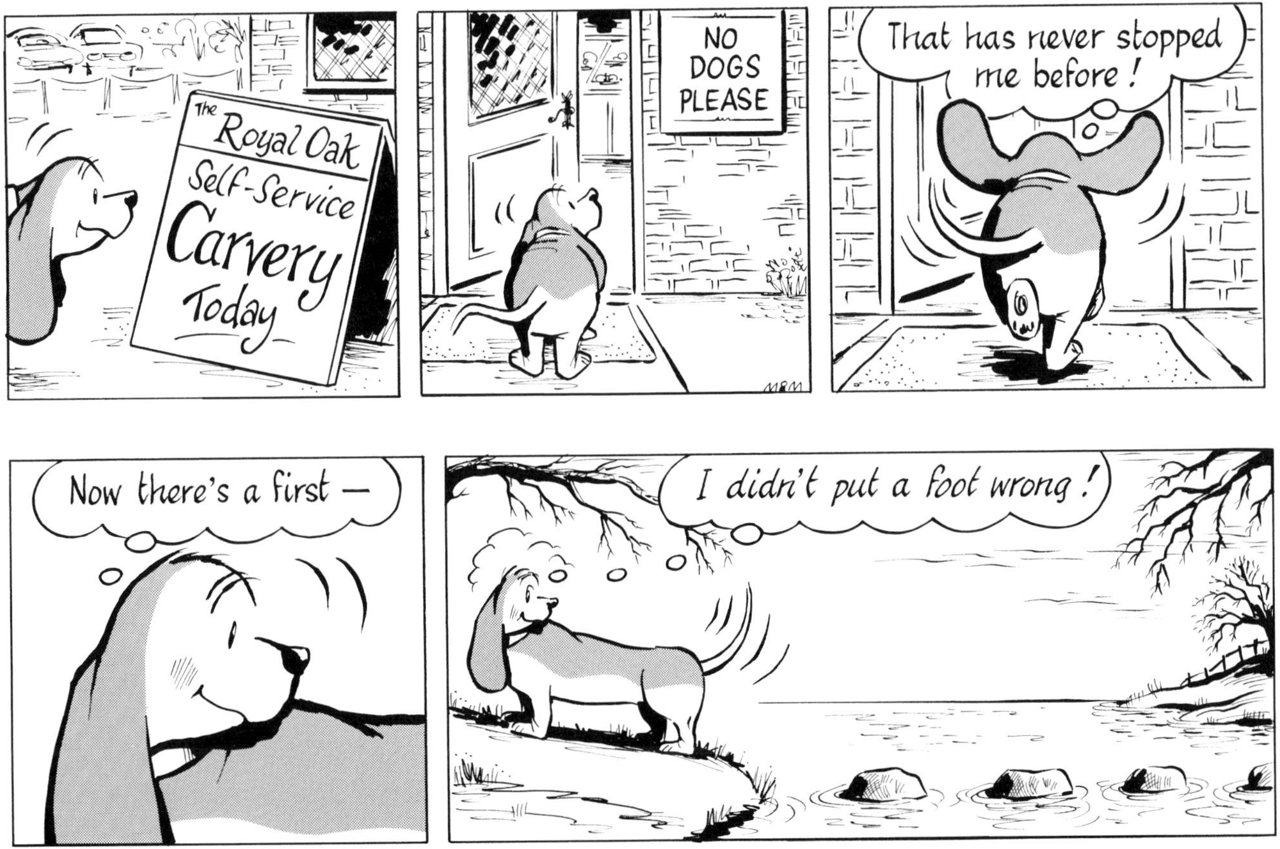
The Royal Oak
Self-Service
Carvery
Today
NO
DOGS
PLEASE
That has never stopped me before !
Now there's a first —
I didn't put a foot wrong !

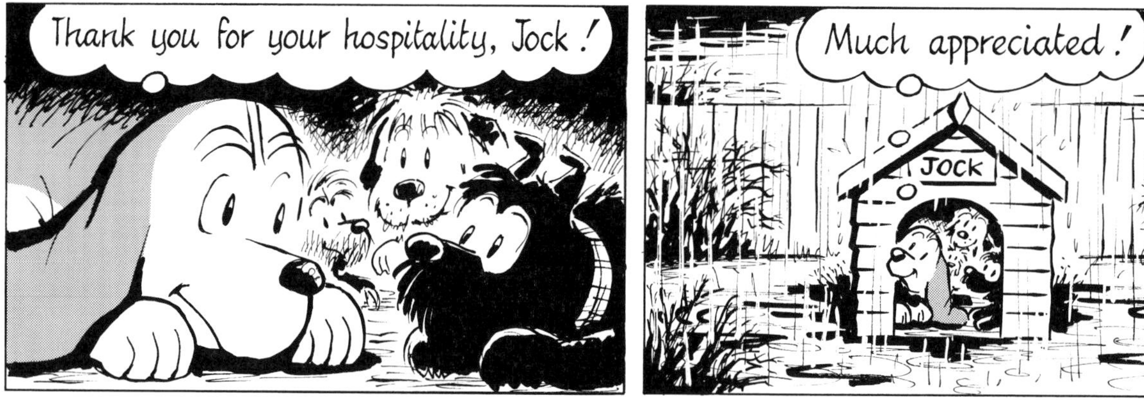
Thank you for your hospitality, Jock !
Much appreciated !
JOCK

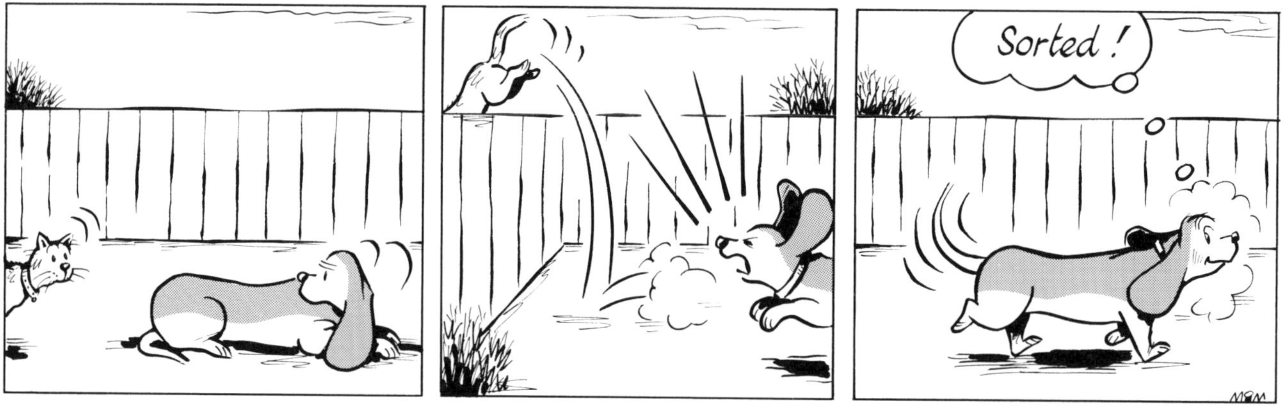
Sorted !

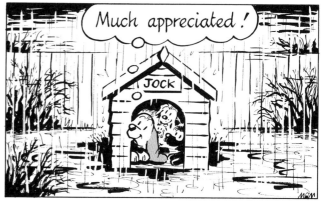

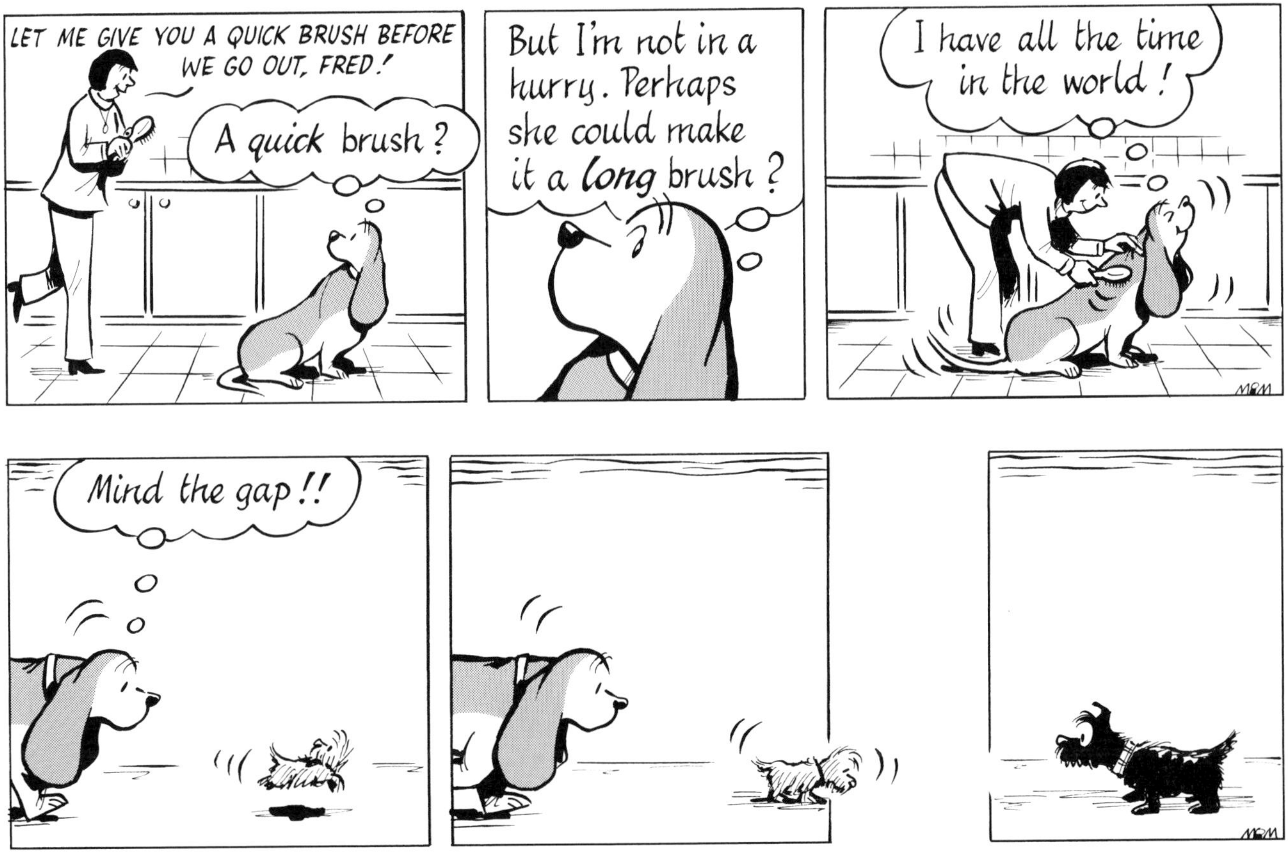
LET ME GIVE YOU A QUICK BRUSH BEFORE WE GO OUT, FRED.!
A quick brush ?
But I'm not in a hurry. Perhaps she could make it a long brush ?
I have all the time in the world !
MGM
Mind the gap!!
MGM

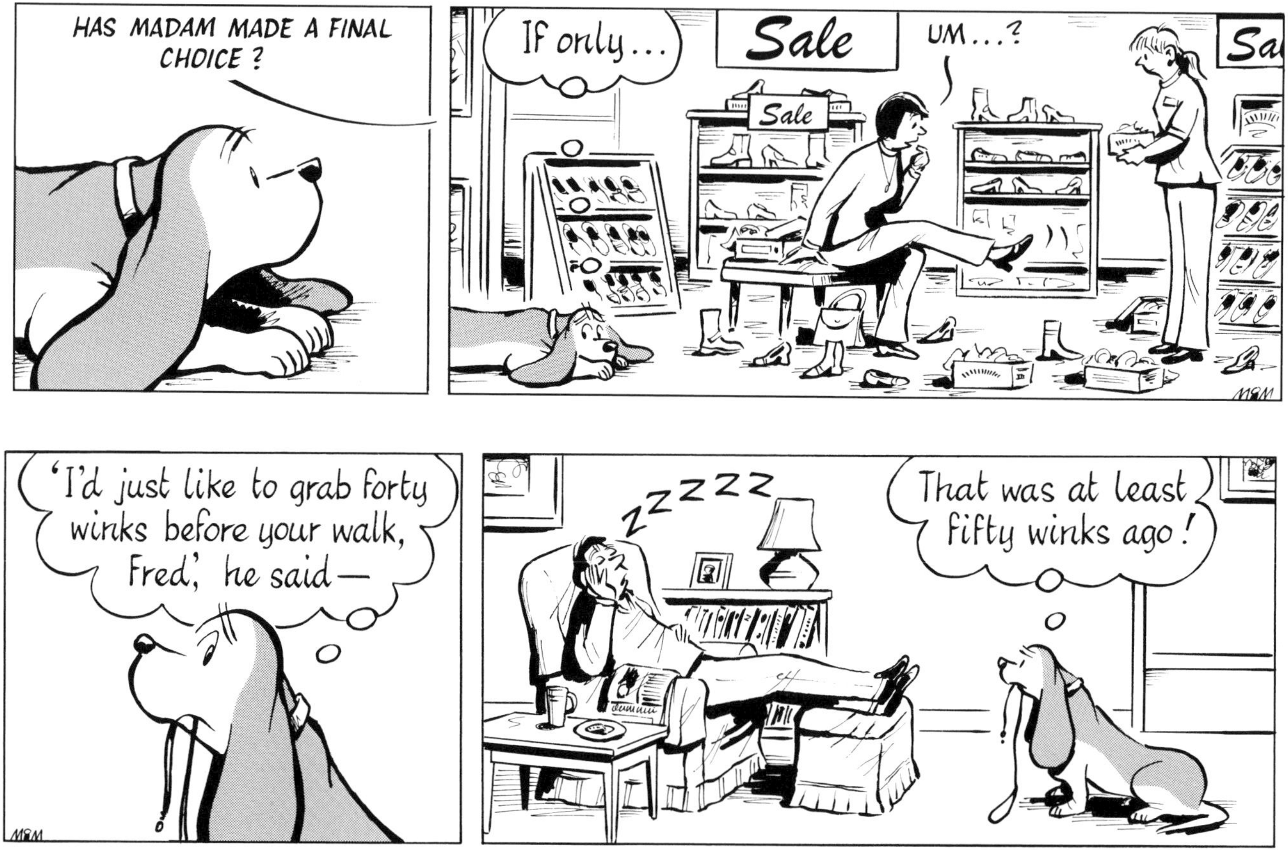
HAS MADAM MADE A FINAL CHOICE ?
If only . . .
Sale
Sale
UM . . . ?
'I'd just like to grab forty winks before your walk, Fred,' he said —
ZZZZZZ
That was at least fifty winks ago!

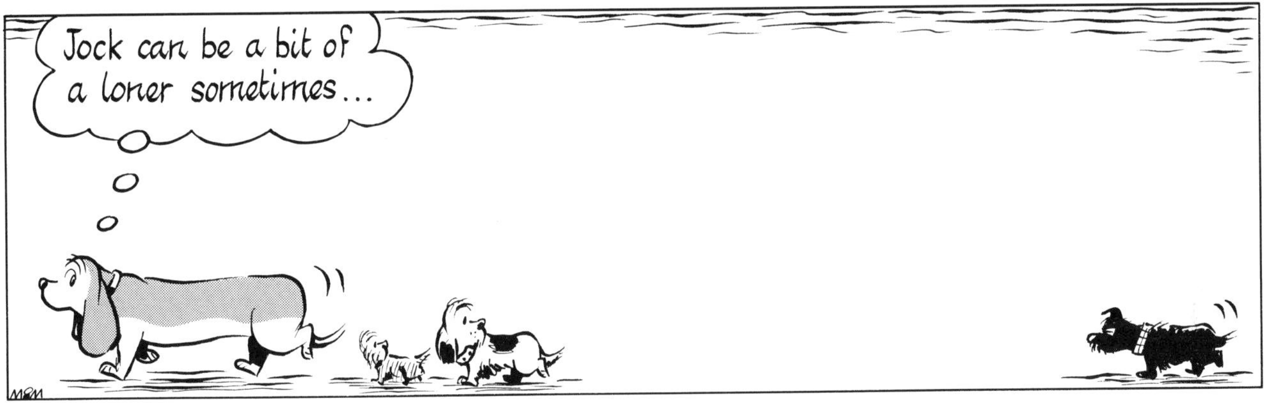
Jock can be a bit of a loner sometimes...
MGM

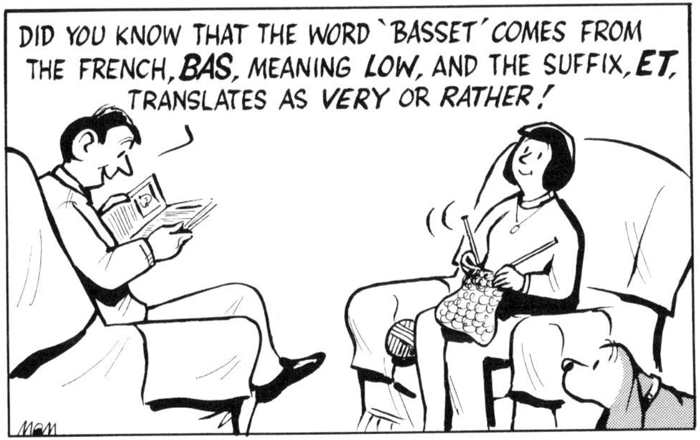
DID YOU KNOW THAT THE WORD 'BASSET' COMES FROM THE FRENCH, BAS, MEANING LOW, AND THE SUFFIX, ET, TRANSLATES AS VERY OR RATHER!
MGM

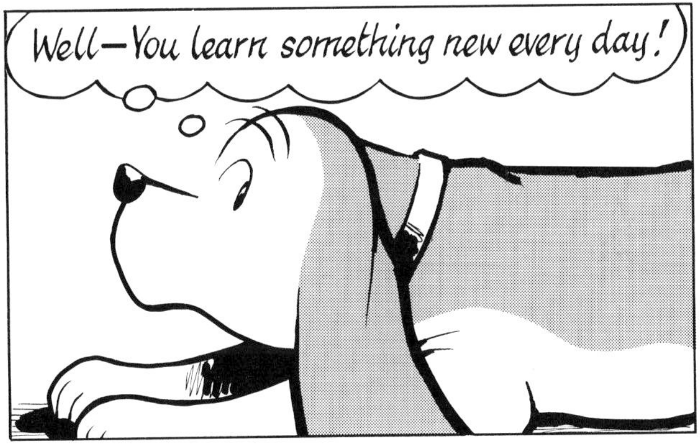
Well—You learn something new every day!

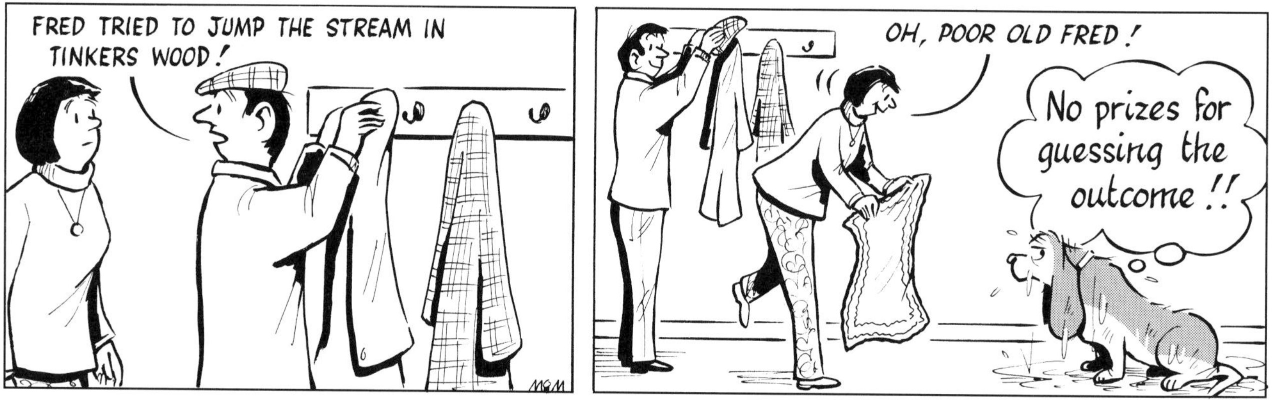
FRED TRIED TO JUMP THE STREAM IN TINKERS WOOD!
OH, POOR OLD FRED!
No prizes for guessing the outcome!!
M&M

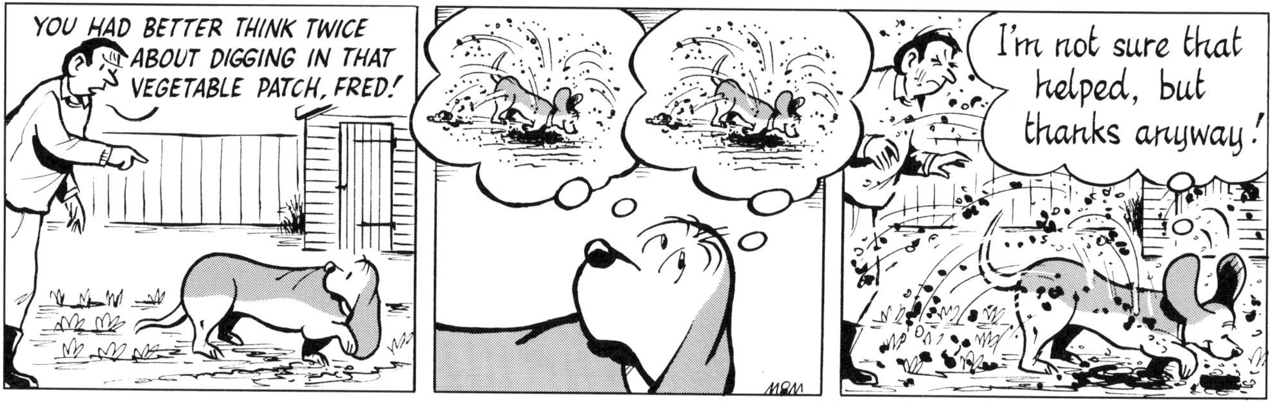
YOU HAD BETTER THINK TWICE ABOUT DIGGING IN THAT VEGETABLE PATCH, FRED!
M&M
I'm not sure that helped, but thanks anyway!

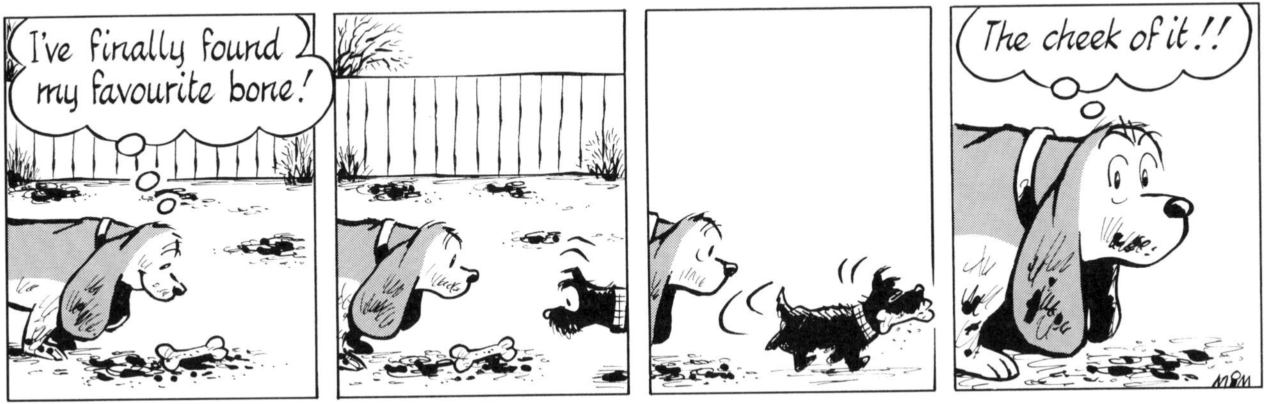
I've finally found my favourite bone!
The cheek of it!!
MGM

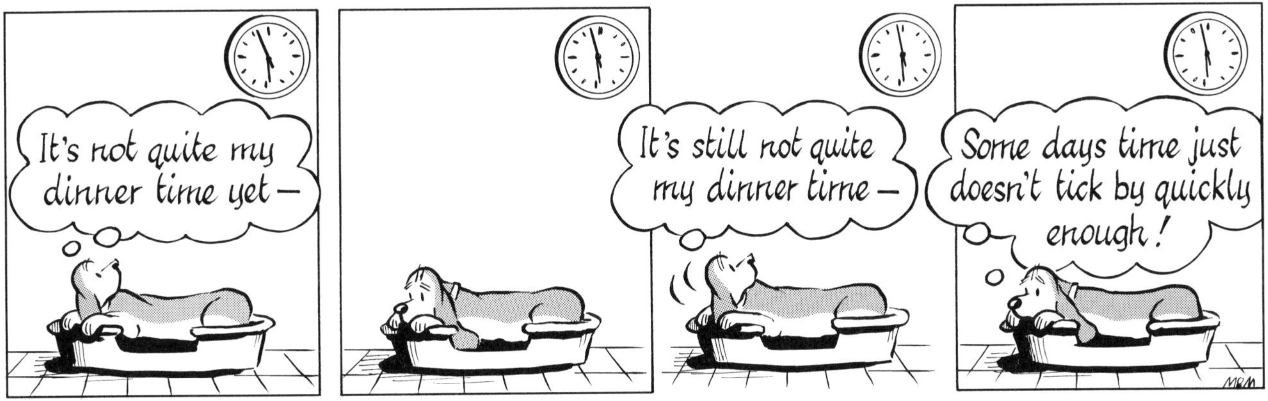
It's not quite my dinner time yet –
It's still not quite my dinner time –
Some days time just doesn't tick by quickly enough!
MGM

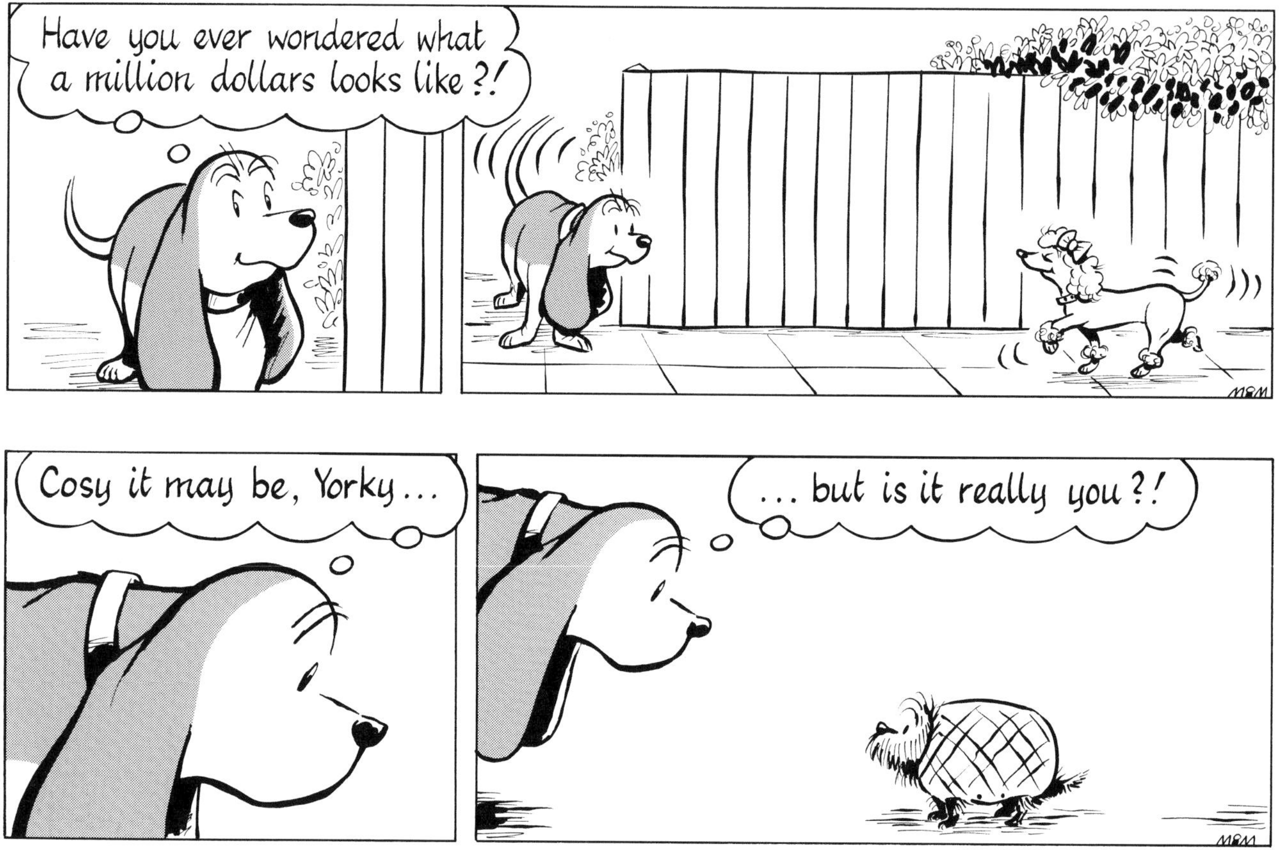
Have you ever wondered what a million dollars looks like?!
MSM
Cosy it may be, Yorky...
... but is it really you?!
MSM

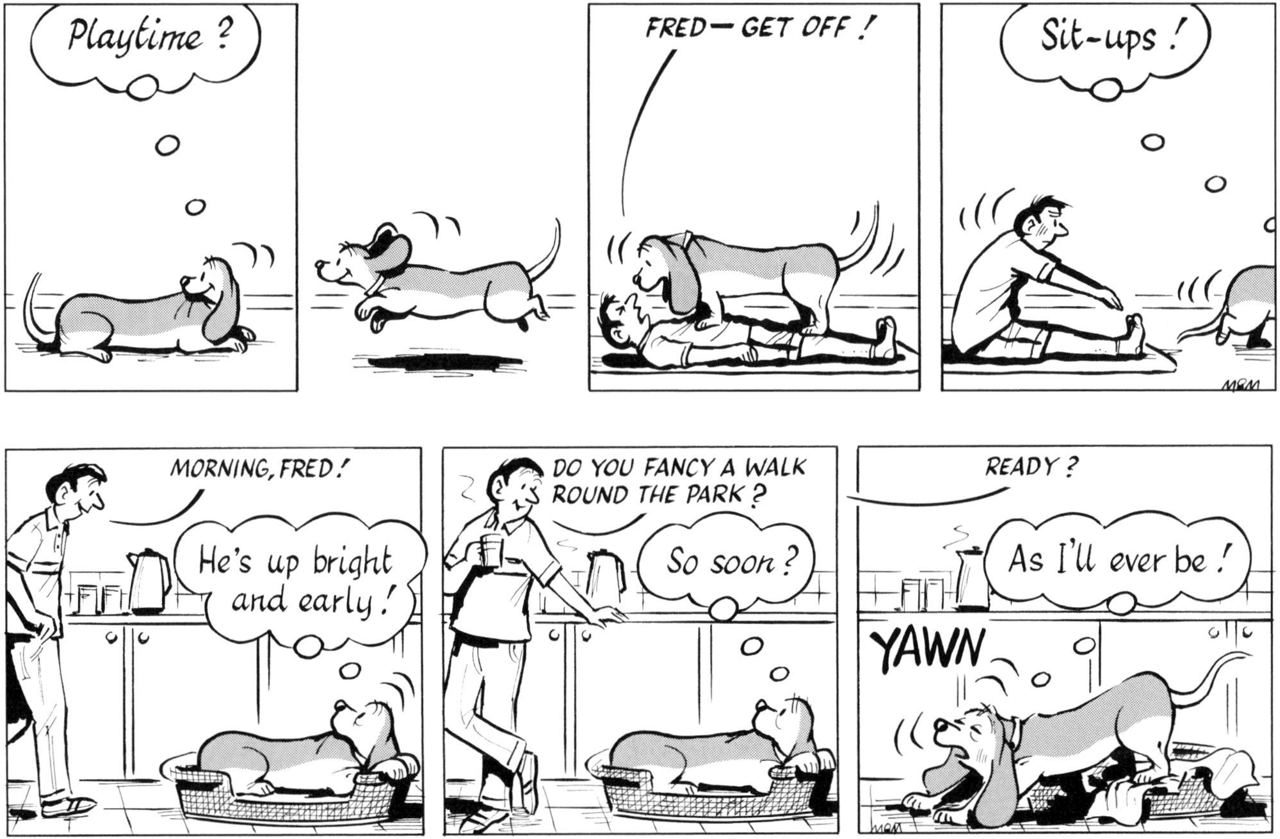
Playtime ?
FRED — GET OFF !
Sit-ups !
MGM
MORNING, FRED !
He's up bright and early !
DO YOU FANCY A WALK ROUND THE PARK ?
So soon ?
READY ?
As I'll ever be !
YAWN
MGM

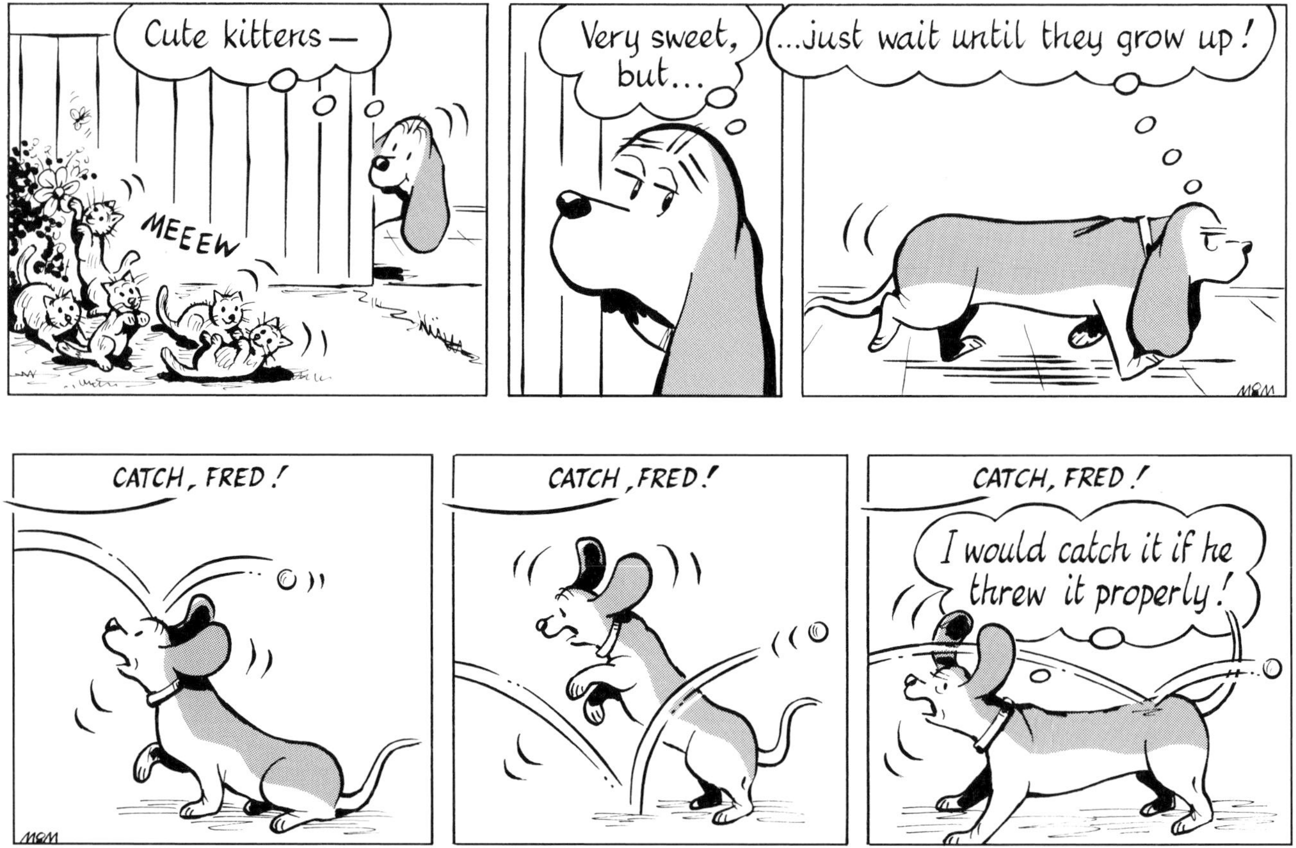
Cute kittens —
MEEEW
Very sweet, but...
...just wait until they grow up!
MGM
CATCH, FRED!
CATCH, FRED!
CATCH, FRED!
I would catch it if he threw it properly!
MGM

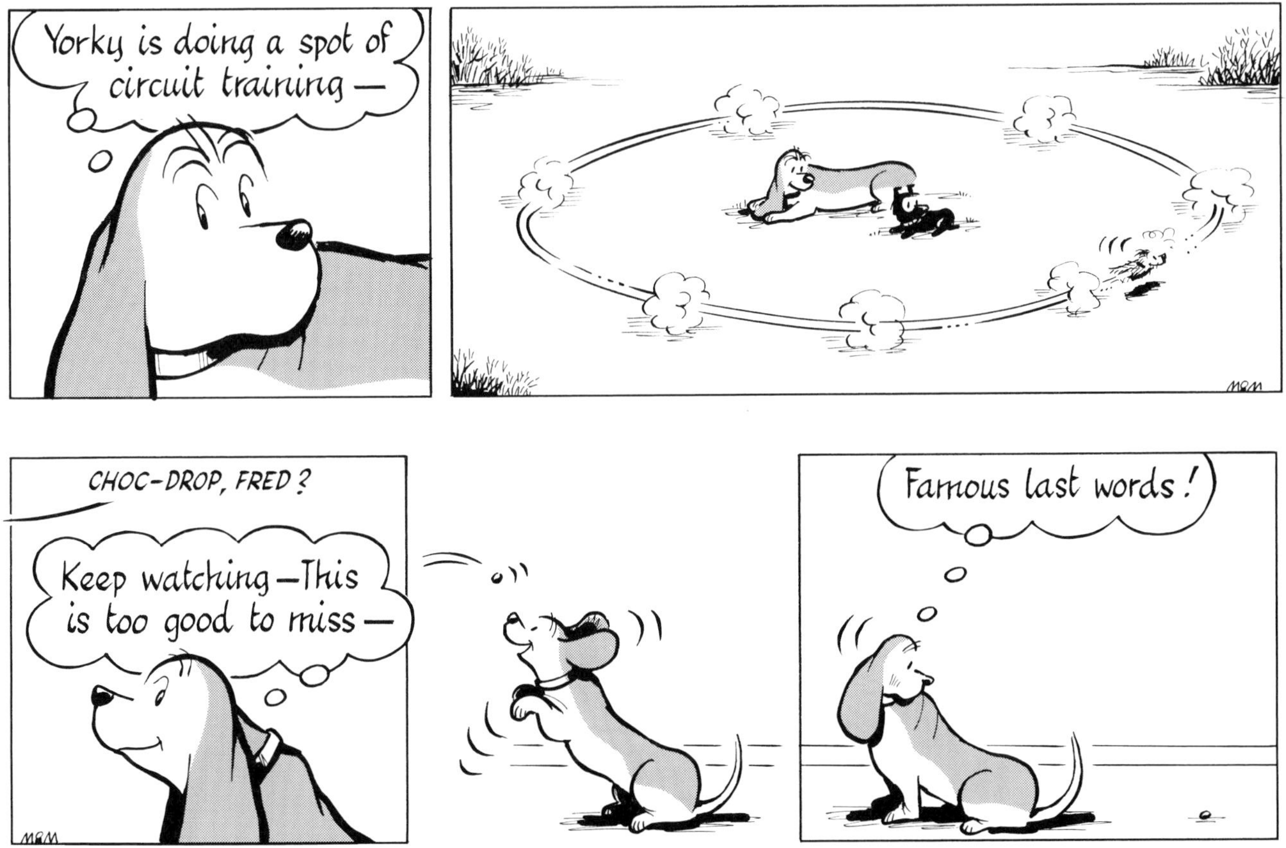

Yorky is doing a spot of circuit training —
MGM
CHOC-DROP, FRED ?
Keep watching — This is too good to miss —
MGM
Famous last words !

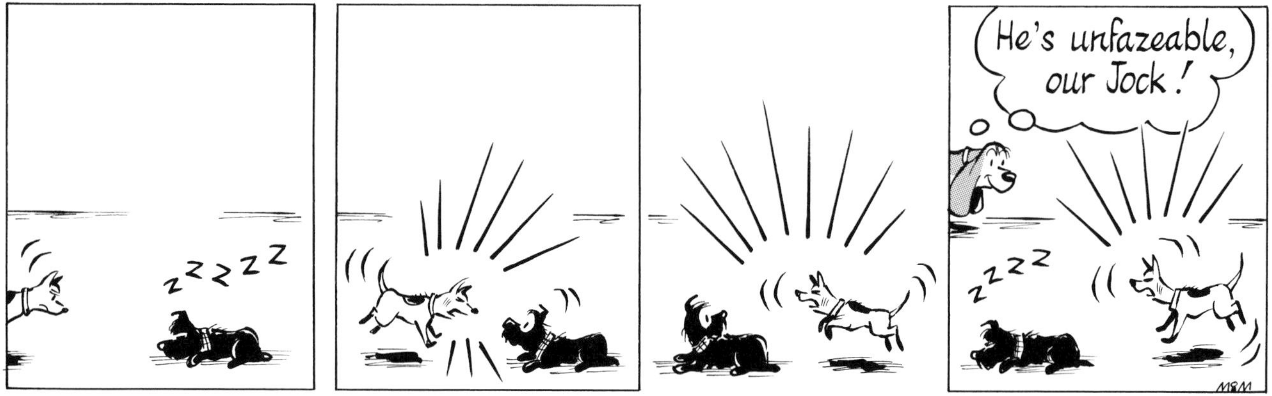
He's unfazeable, our Jock!

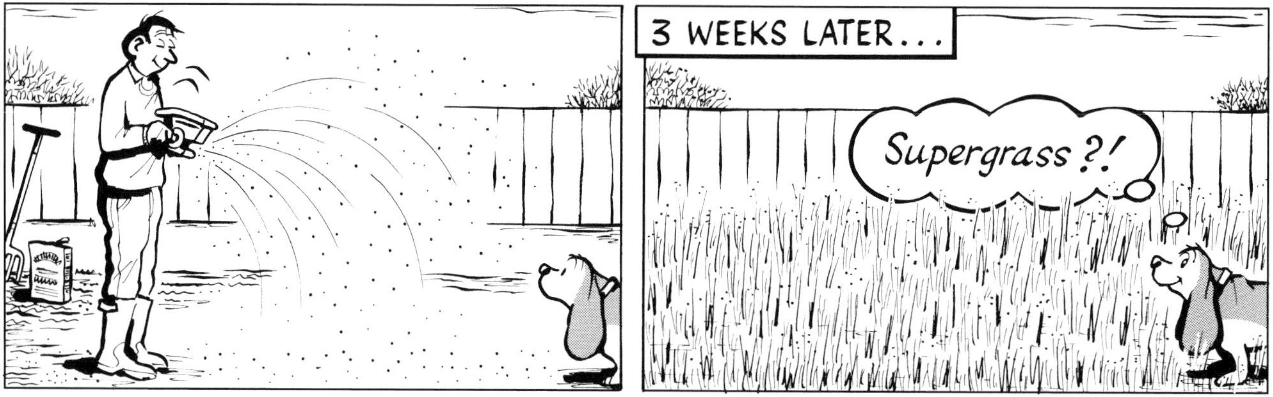
3 WEEKS LATER...
Supergrass?!

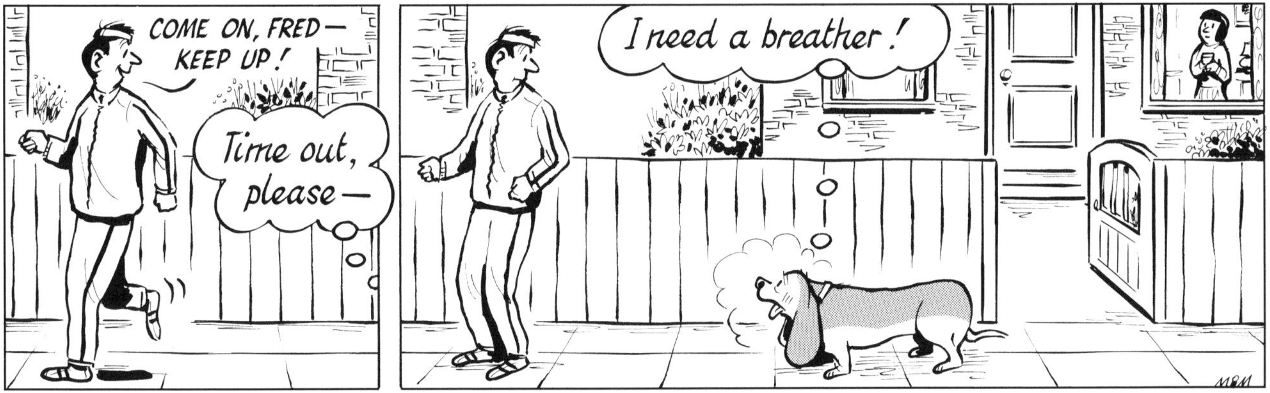
COME ON, FRED— KEEP UP!
Time out, please—
I need a breather!

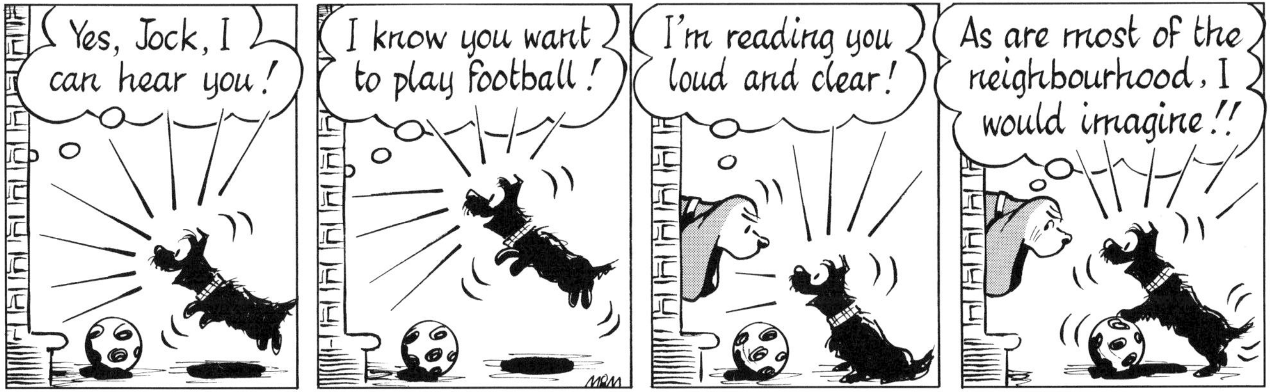
Yes, Jock, I can hear you!
I know you want to play football!
I'm reading you loud and clear!
As are most of the neighbourhood, I would imagine!!

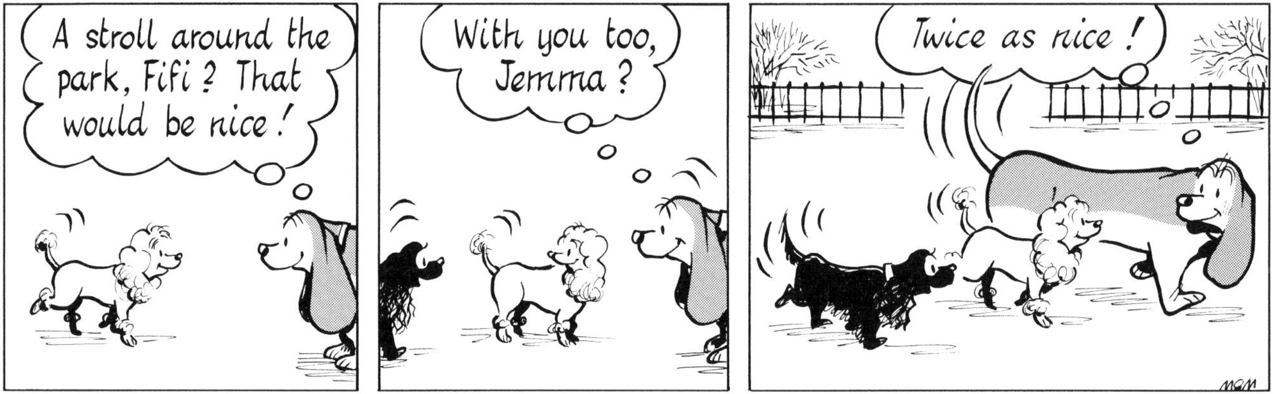
A stroll around the park, Fifi ? That would be nice !
With you too, Jemma ?
Twice as nice !
MGM

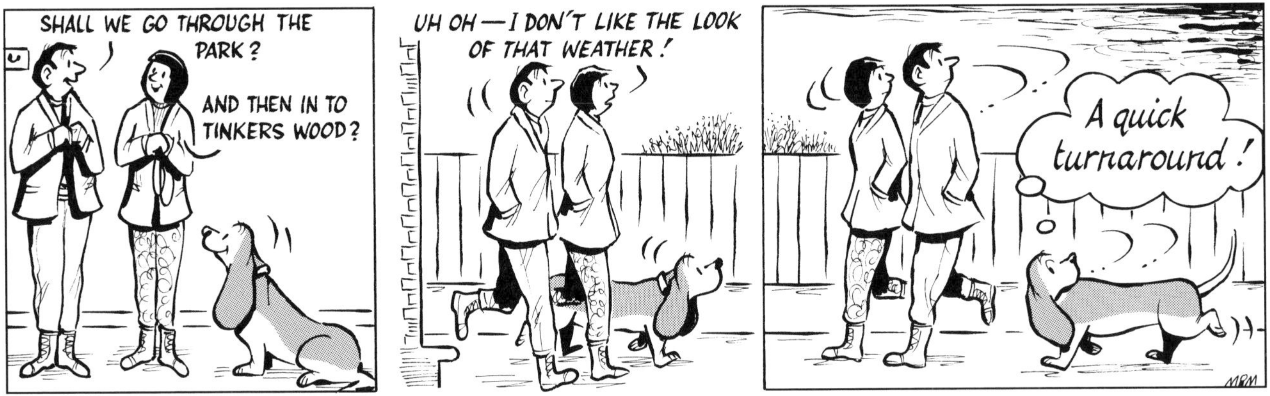
SHALL WE GO THROUGH THE PARK ?
AND THEN IN TO TINKERS WOOD ?
UH OH — I DON'T LIKE THE LOOK OF THAT WEATHER !
A quick turnaround !
MGM

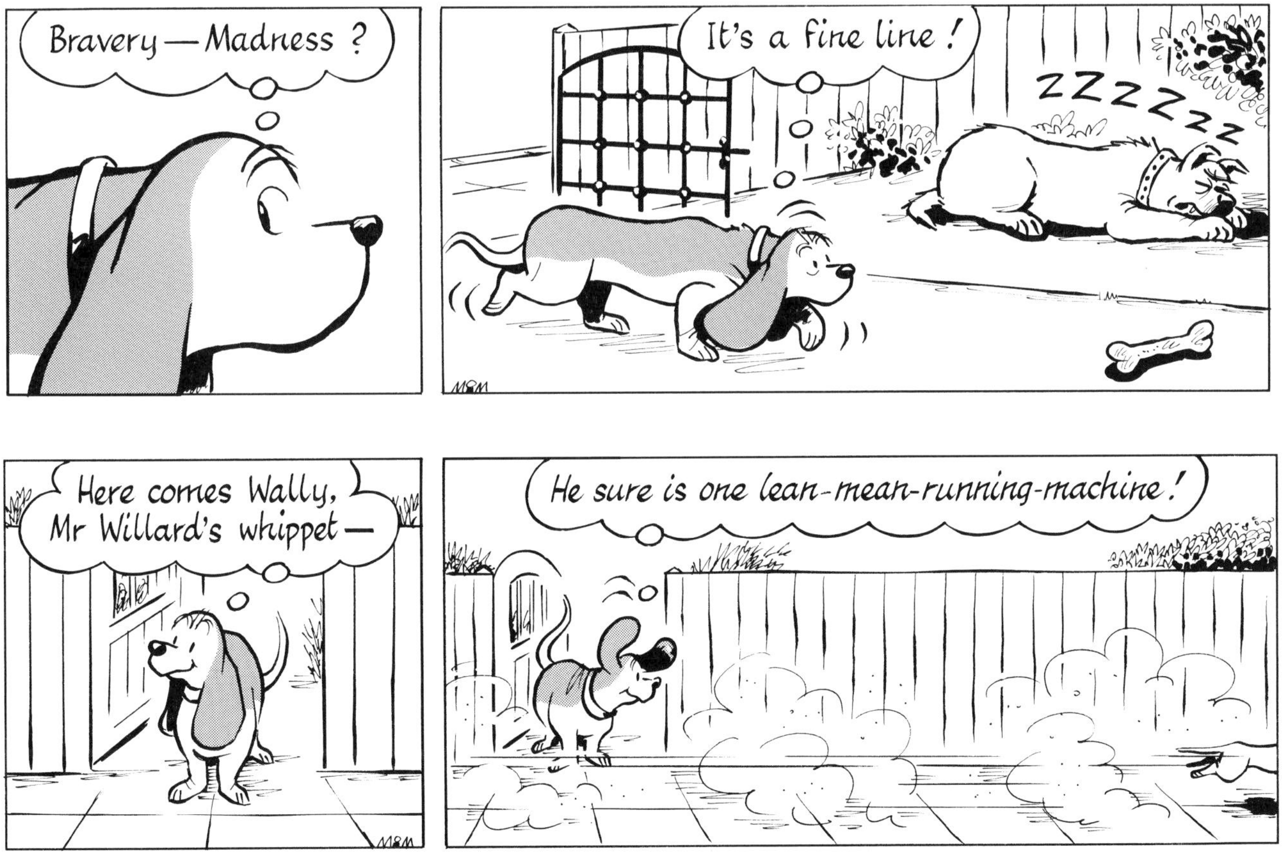
Bravery — Madness ?
It's a fine line !
ZZZZZZZ
M&M
Here comes Wally, Mr Willard's whippet —
M&M
He sure is one lean-mean-running-machine !

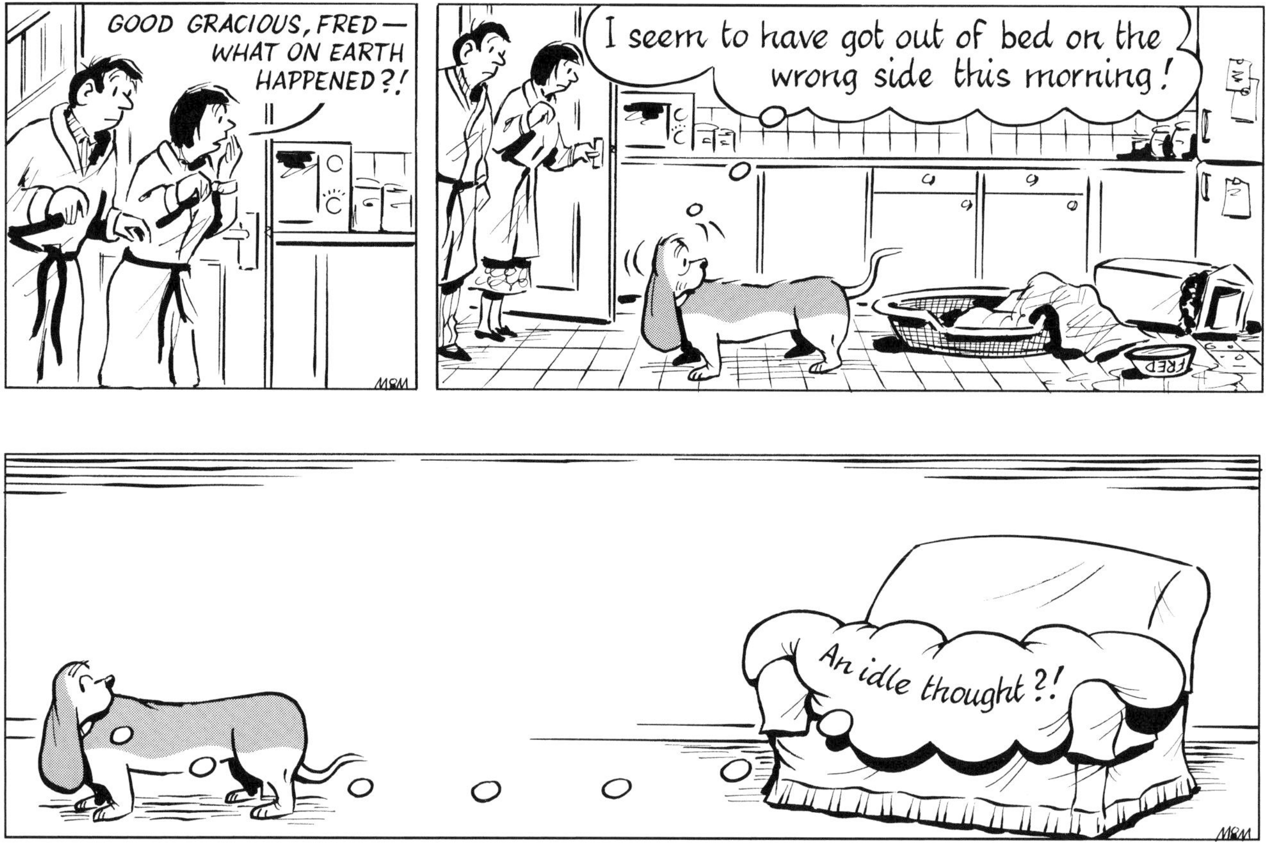
GOOD GRACIOUS, FRED — WHAT ON EARTH HAPPENED ?!
I seem to have got out of bed on the wrong side this morning !
FRED
An idle thought ?!

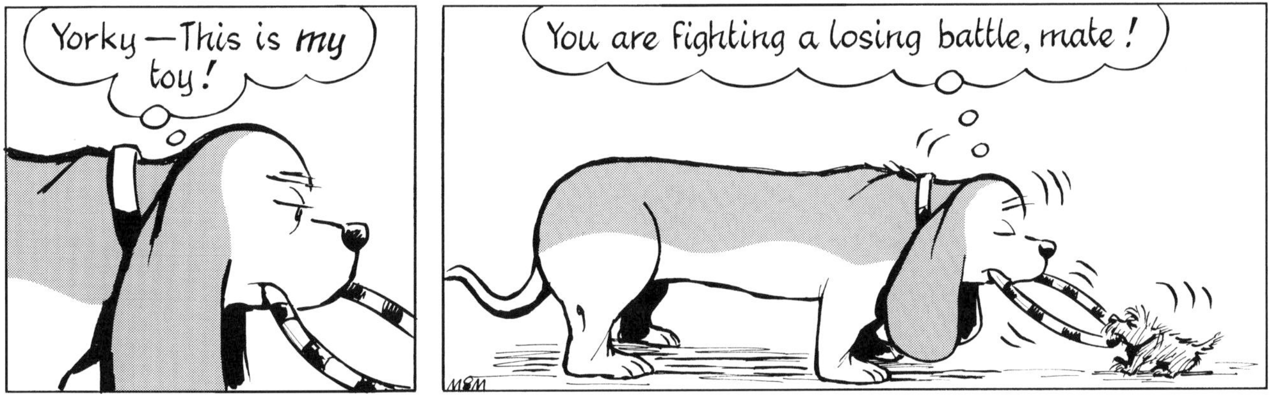
Yorky—This is *my* toy!
You are fighting a losing battle, mate!
M&M

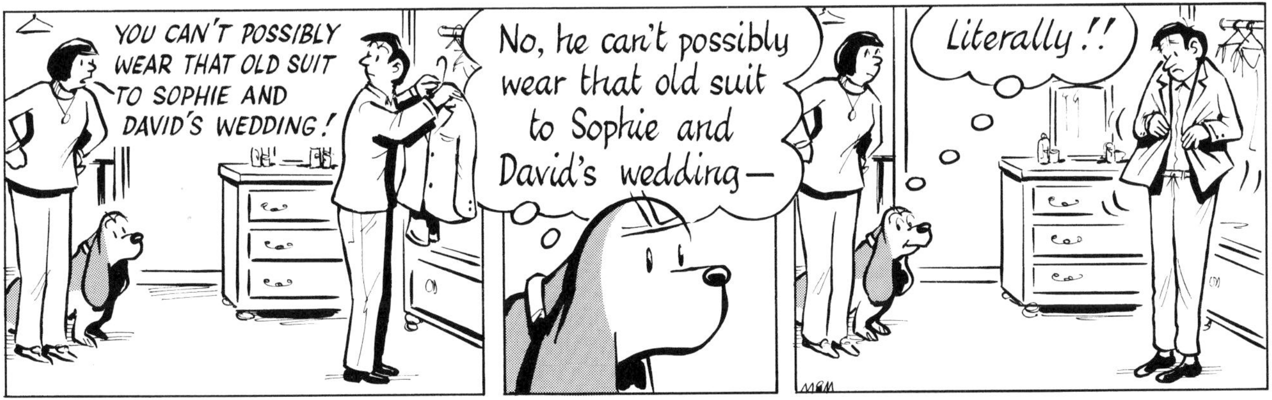
YOU CAN'T POSSIBLY WEAR THAT OLD SUIT TO SOPHIE AND DAVID'S WEDDING!
No, he can't possibly wear that old suit to Sophie and David's wedding—
Literally!!
M&M

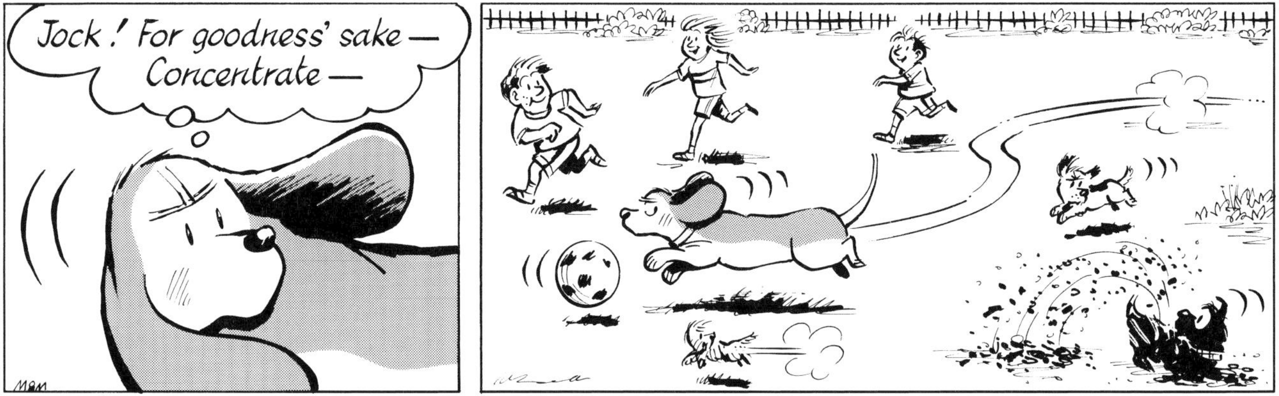
Jock! For goodness' sake — Concentrate —

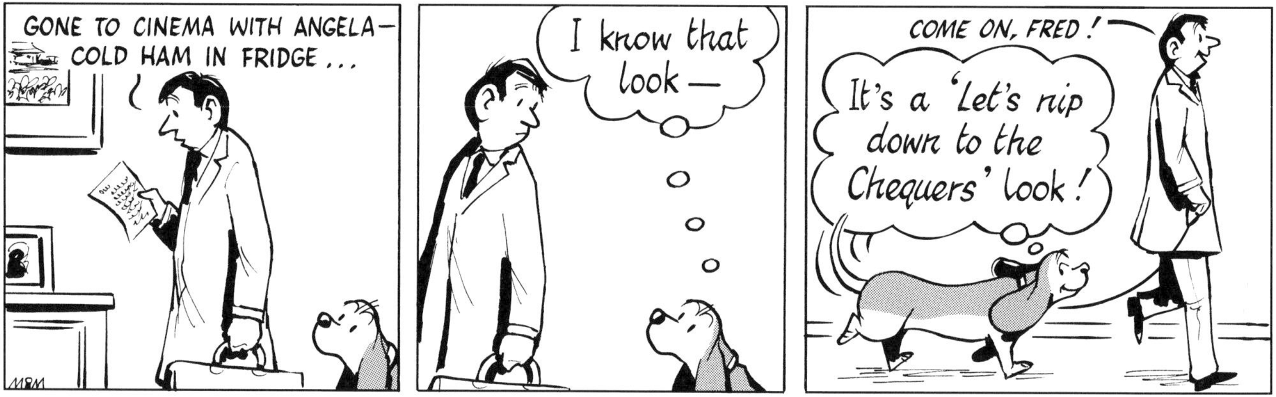
GONE TO CINEMA WITH ANGELA — COLD HAM IN FRIDGE...
I know that look —
COME ON, FRED!
It's a 'Let's nip down to the Chequers' look!

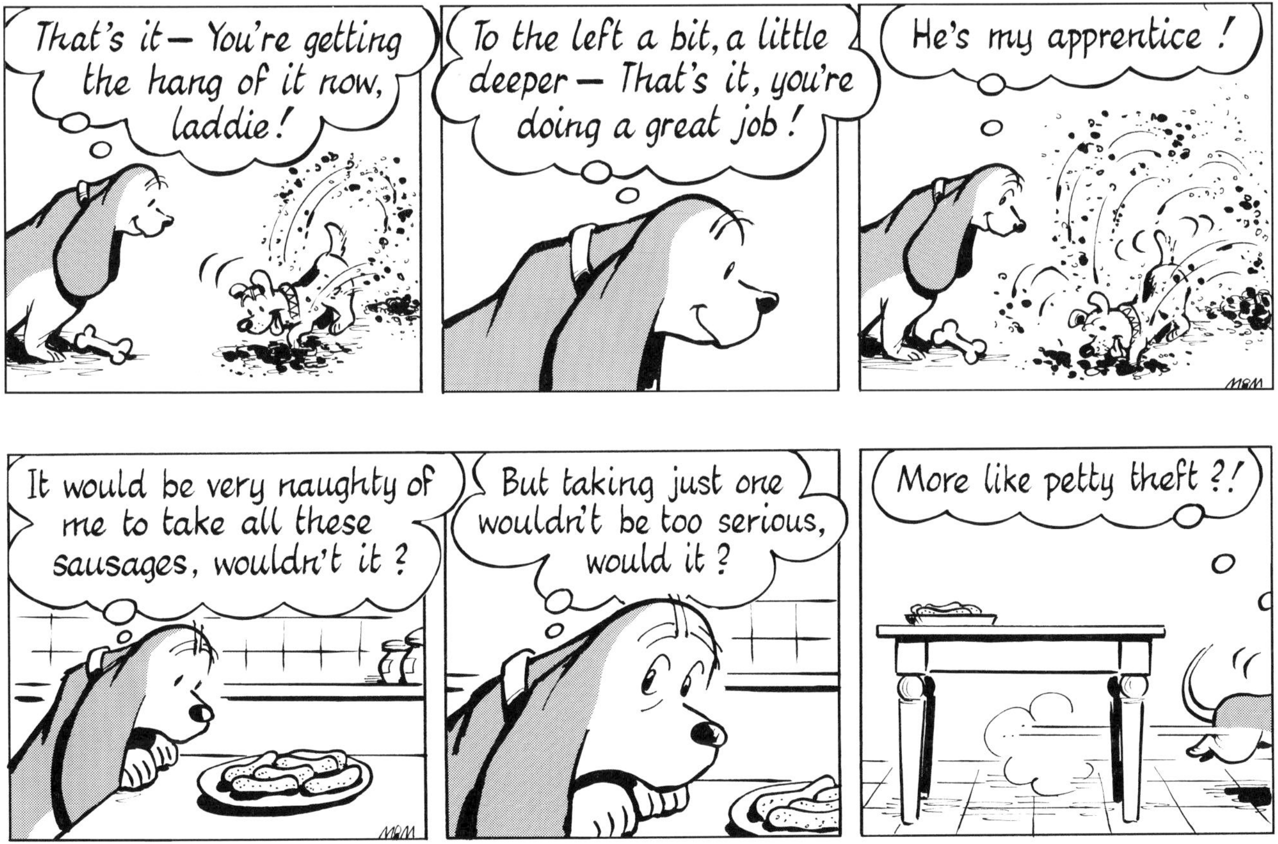
That's it— You're getting the hang of it now, laddie!
To the left a bit, a little deeper— That's it, you're doing a great job!
He's my apprentice!
MBM
It would be very naughty of me to take all these sausages, wouldn't it?
But taking just one wouldn't be too serious, would it?
More like petty theft ?!
MBM

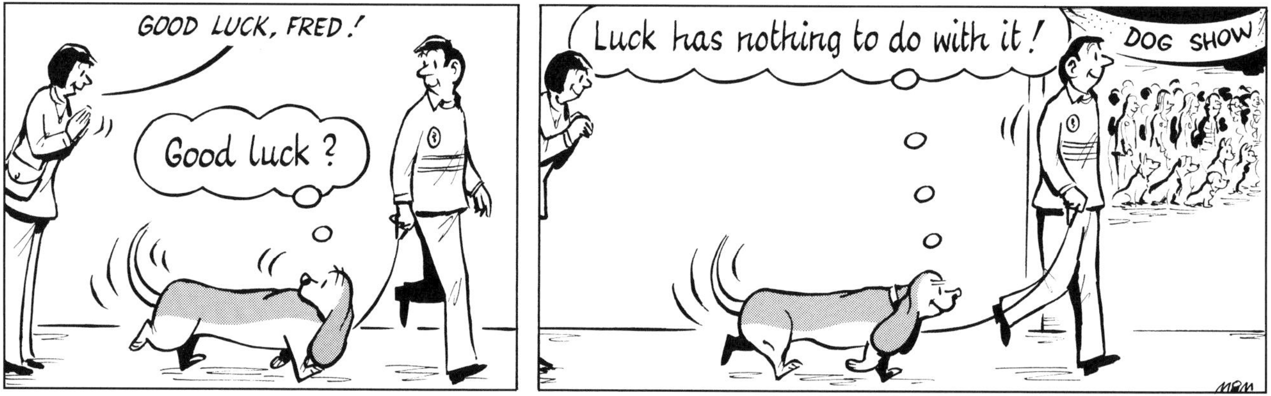
GOOD LUCK, FRED!
Good luck?
Luck has nothing to do with it!
DOG SHOW

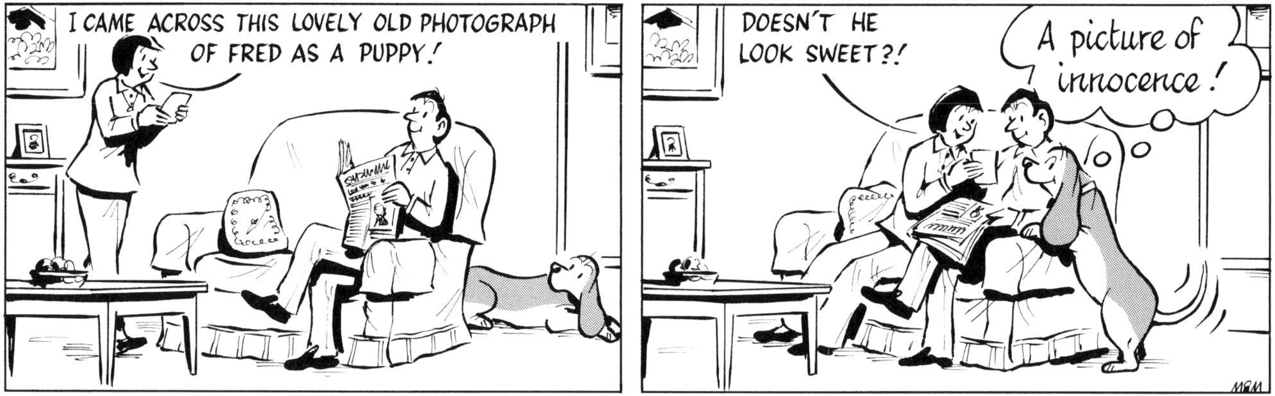
I CAME ACROSS THIS LOVELY OLD PHOTOGRAPH OF FRED AS A PUPPY!
DOESN'T HE LOOK SWEET?!
A picture of innocence!

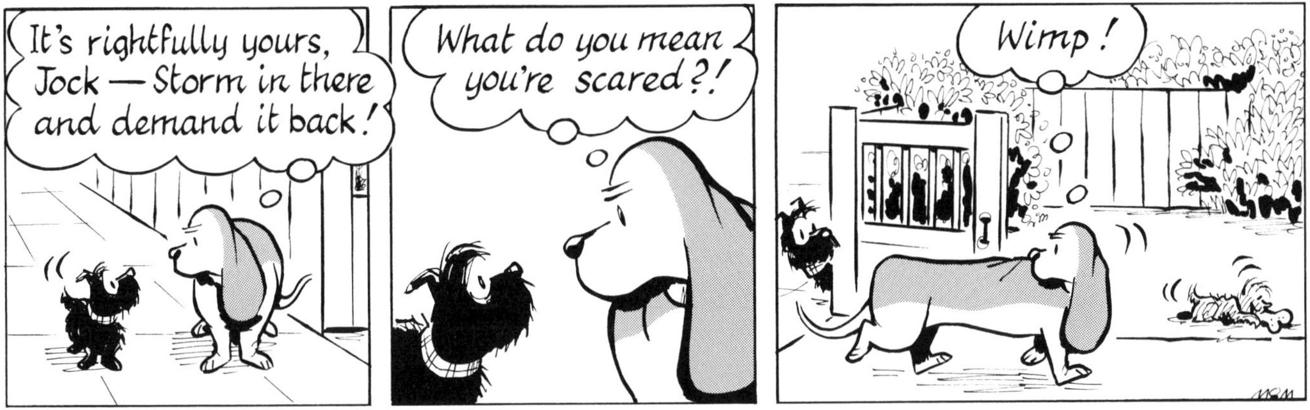
It's rightfully yours, Jock — Storm in there and demand it back!
What do you mean you're scared?!
Wimp!

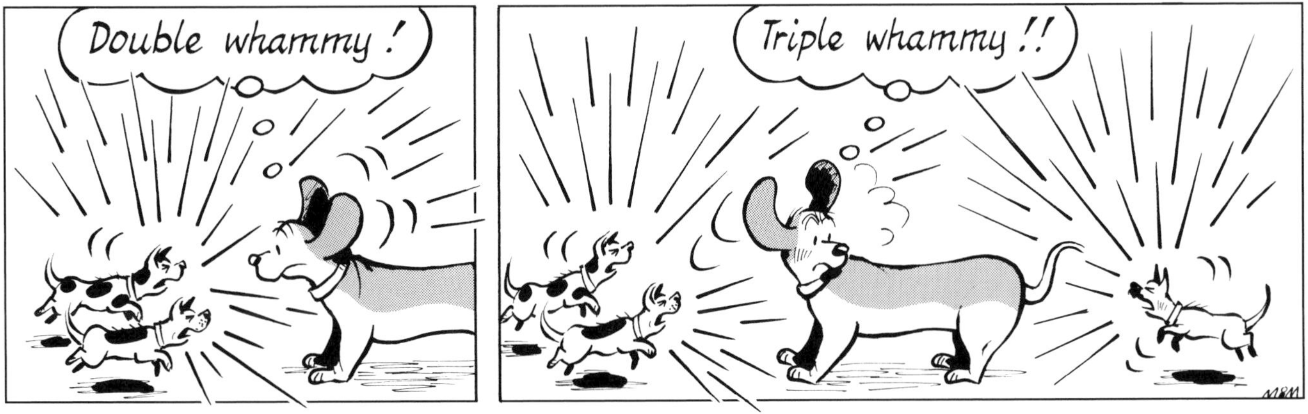
Double whammy!
Triple whammy!!

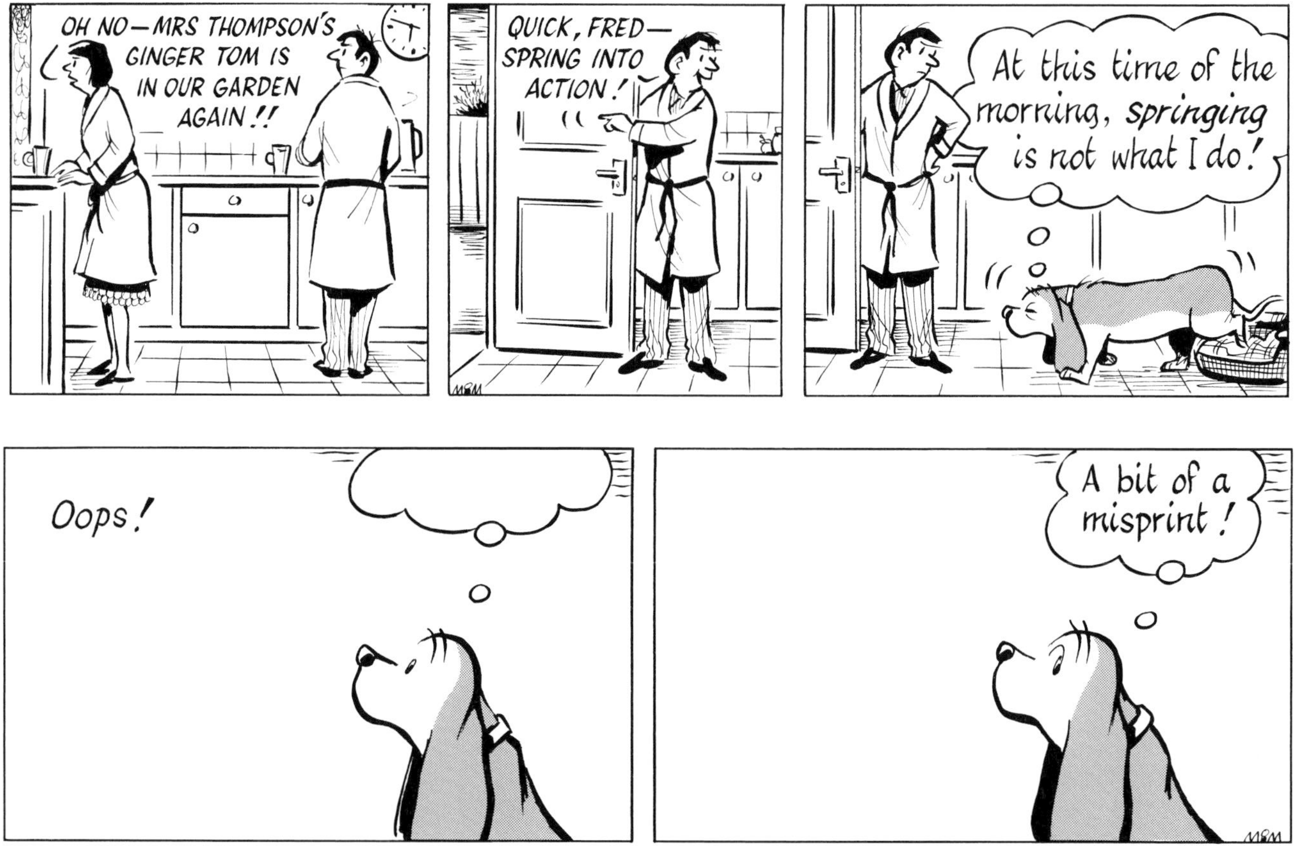
OH NO—MRS THOMPSON'S GINGER TOM IS IN OUR GARDEN AGAIN!!
QUICK, FRED—SPRING INTO ACTION!
At this time of the morning, *springing* is not what I do!
Oops!
A bit of a misprint!
MBM

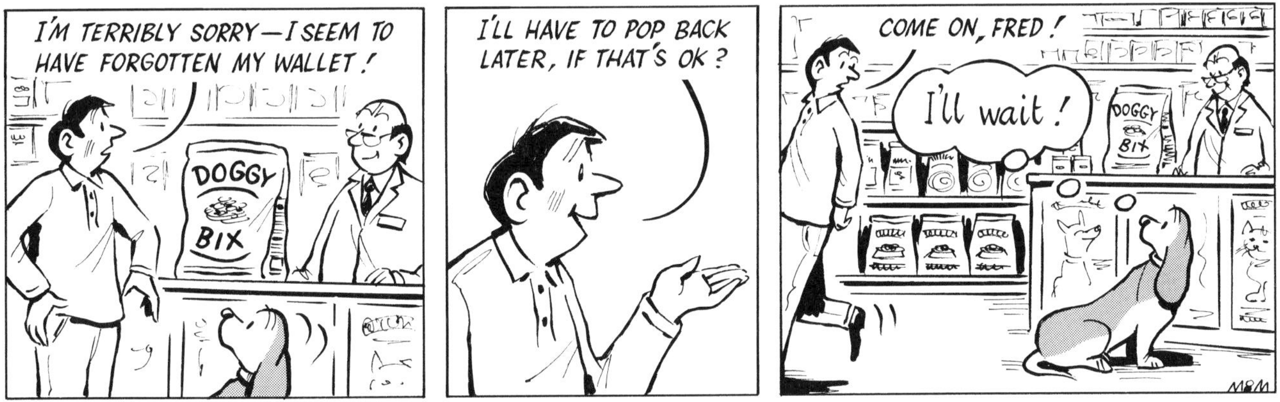
I'M TERRIBLY SORRY—I SEEM TO HAVE FORGOTTEN MY WALLET!
DOGGY BIX
I'LL HAVE TO POP BACK LATER, IF THAT'S OK?
COME ON, FRED!
I'll wait!
DOGGY BIX

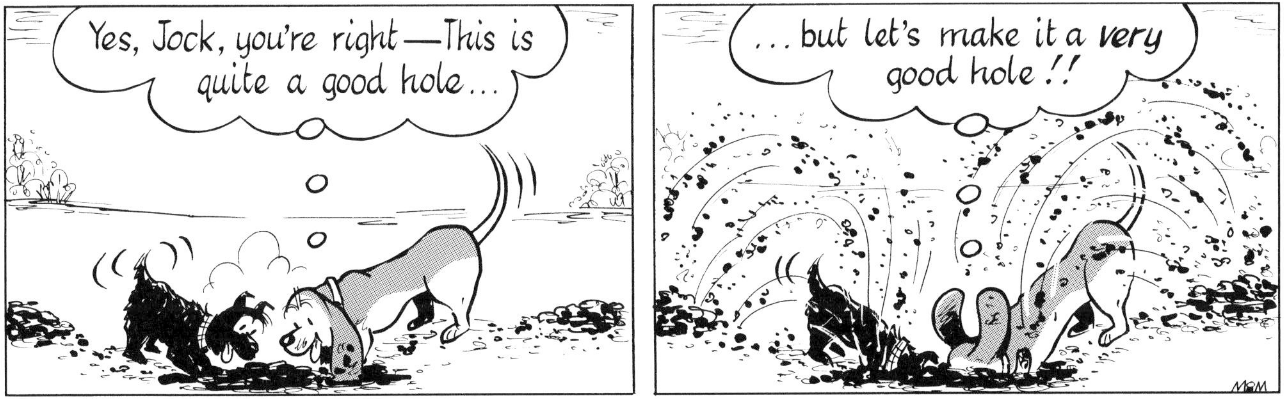
Yes, Jock, you're right—This is quite a good hole...
...but let's make it a *very* good hole!!

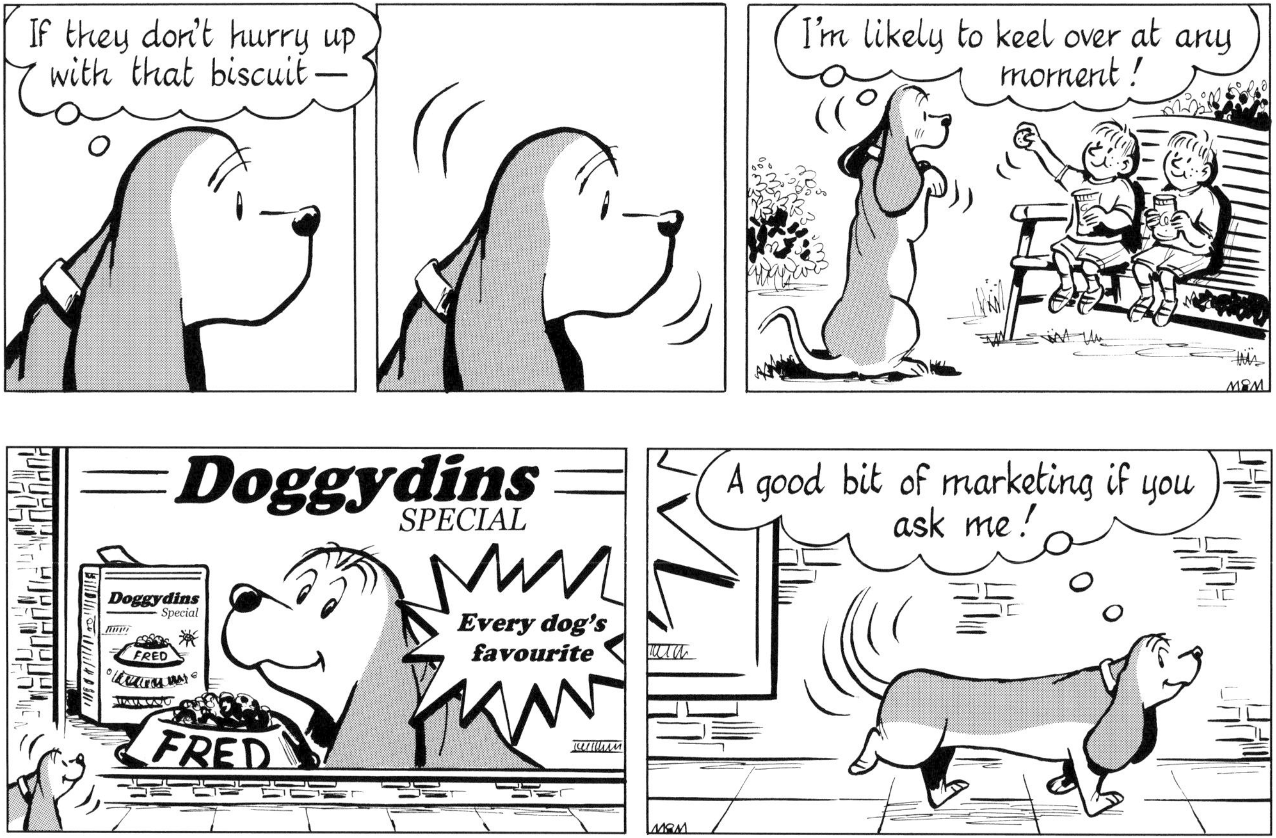

If they don't hurry up with that biscuit—
I'm likely to keel over at any moment!
Doggydins
SPECIAL
Doggydins
Special
FRED
FRED
Every dog's favourite
A good bit of marketing if you ask me!

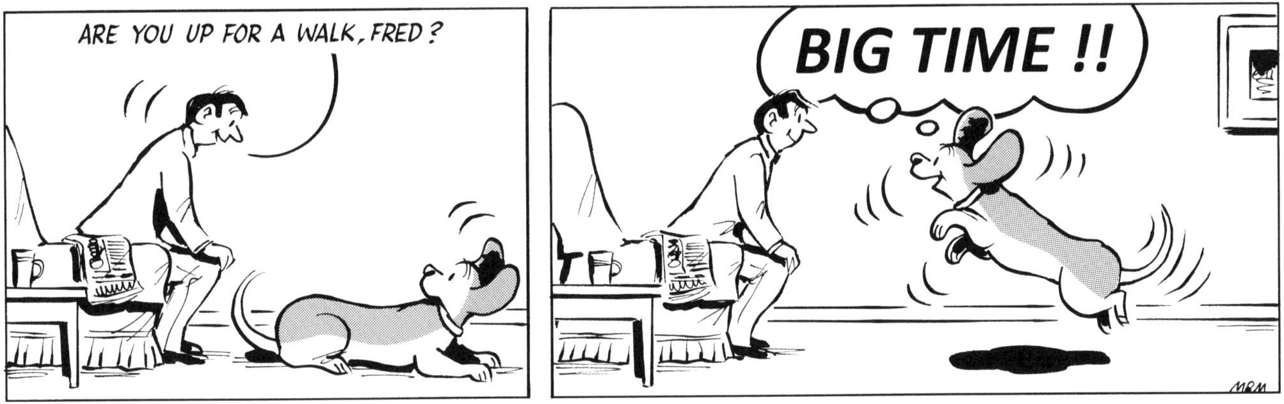
ARE YOU UP FOR A WALK, FRED?
BIG TIME !!
MRM

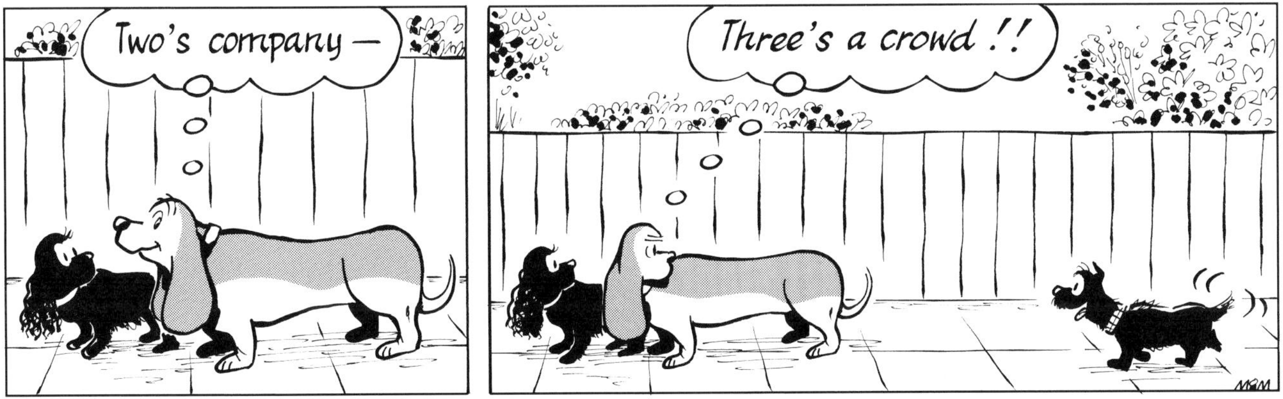
Two's company –
Three's a crowd !!
MRM

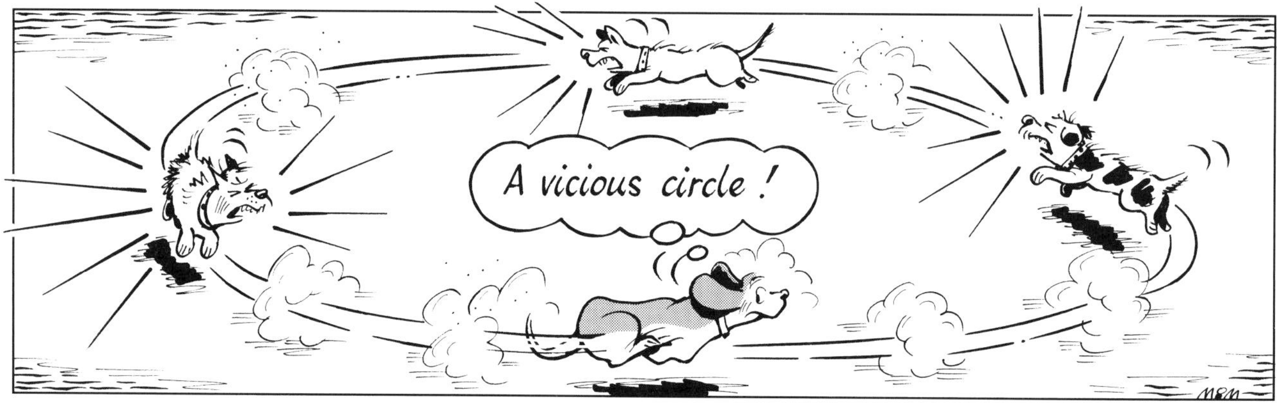
A vicious circle !
MSM

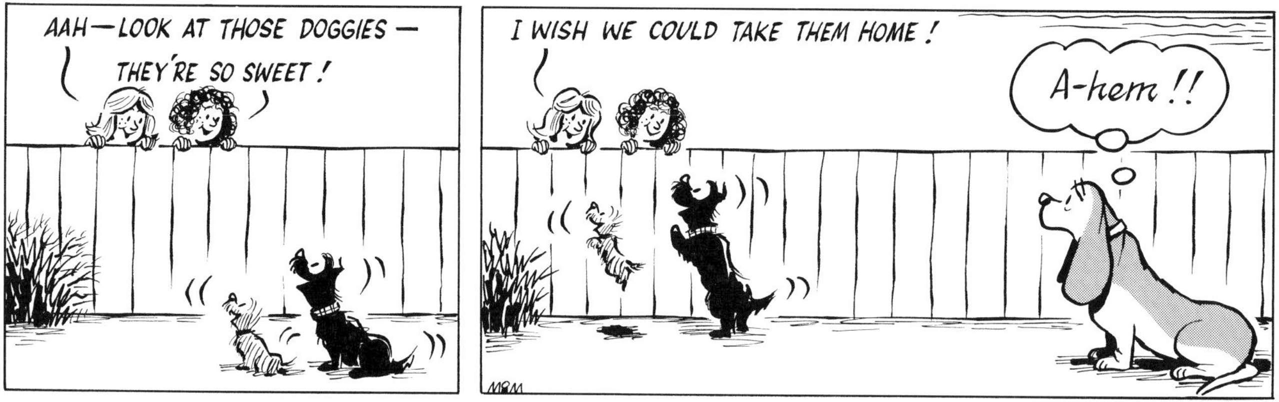
AAH—LOOK AT THOSE DOGGIES — THEY'RE SO SWEET !
I WISH WE COULD TAKE THEM HOME !
A-hem !!
MSM

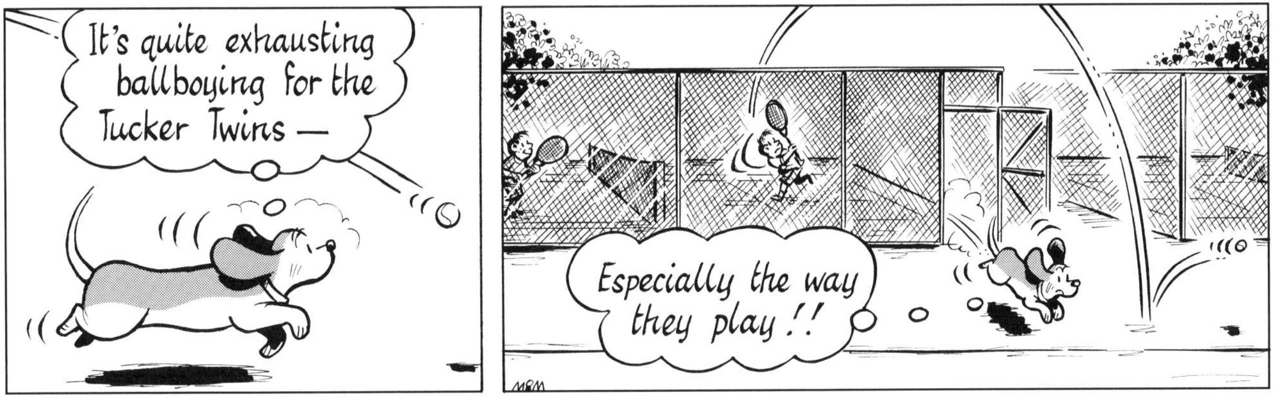
It's quite exhausting ballboying for the Tucker Twins —
Especially the way they play !!

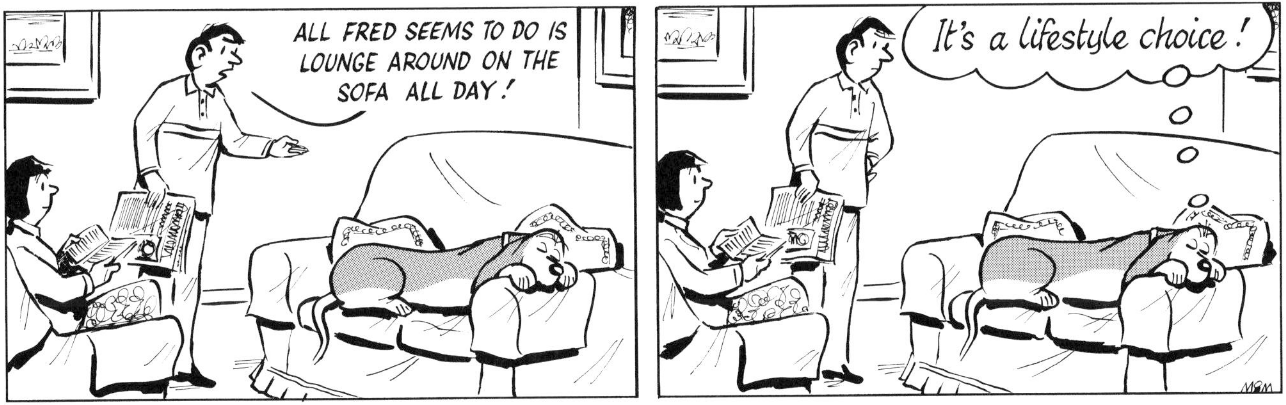
ALL FRED SEEMS TO DO IS LOUNGE AROUND ON THE SOFA ALL DAY !
It's a lifestyle choice !

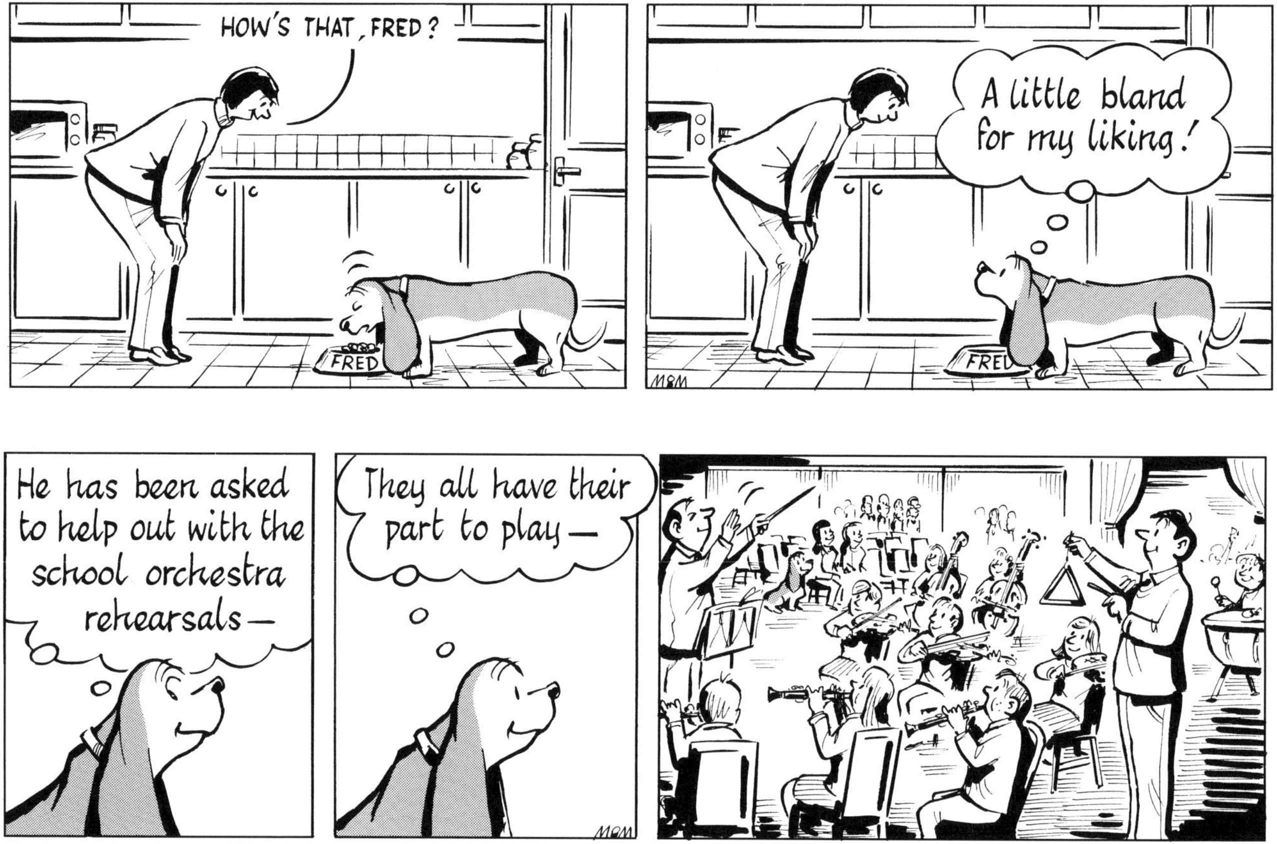
HOW'S THAT, FRED?
FRED
A little bland for my liking!
FRED
He has been asked to help out with the school orchestra rehearsals—
They all have their part to play—

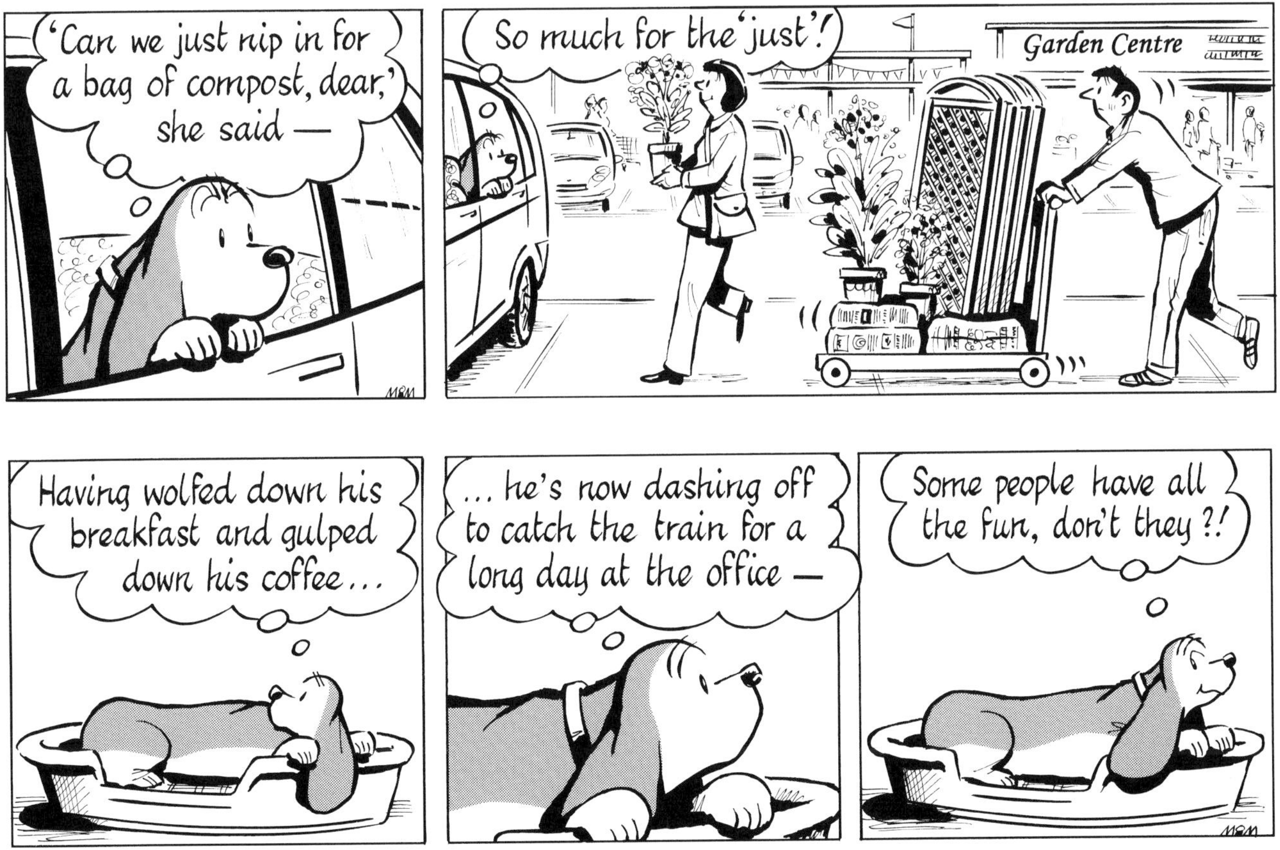

'Can we just nip in for a bag of compost, dear,' she said —
MBM
So much for the 'just'!
Garden Centre
Having wolfed down his breakfast and gulped down his coffee...
... he's now dashing off to catch the train for a long day at the office —
Some people have all the fun, don't they?!
MBM

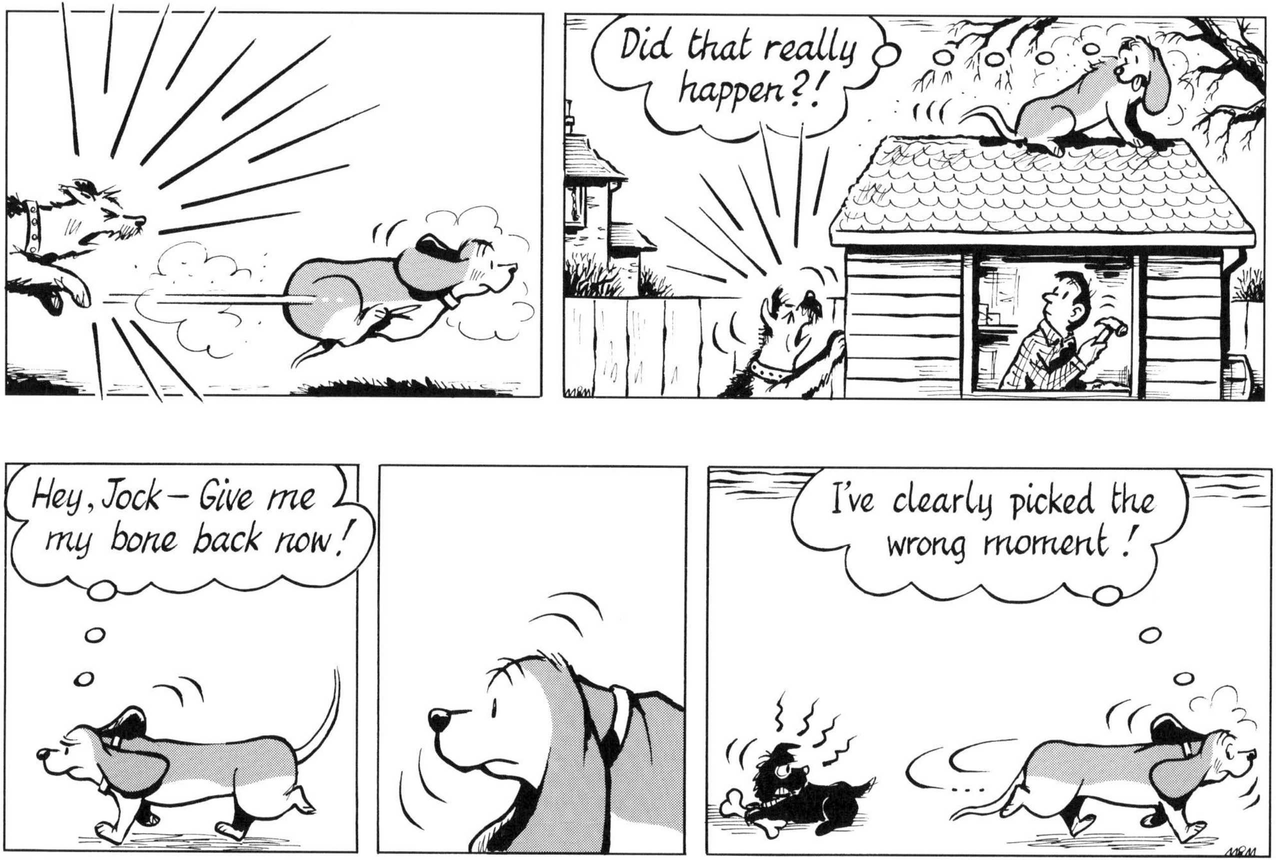
Did that really happen?!
Hey, Jock – Give me my bone back now!
I've clearly picked the wrong moment!

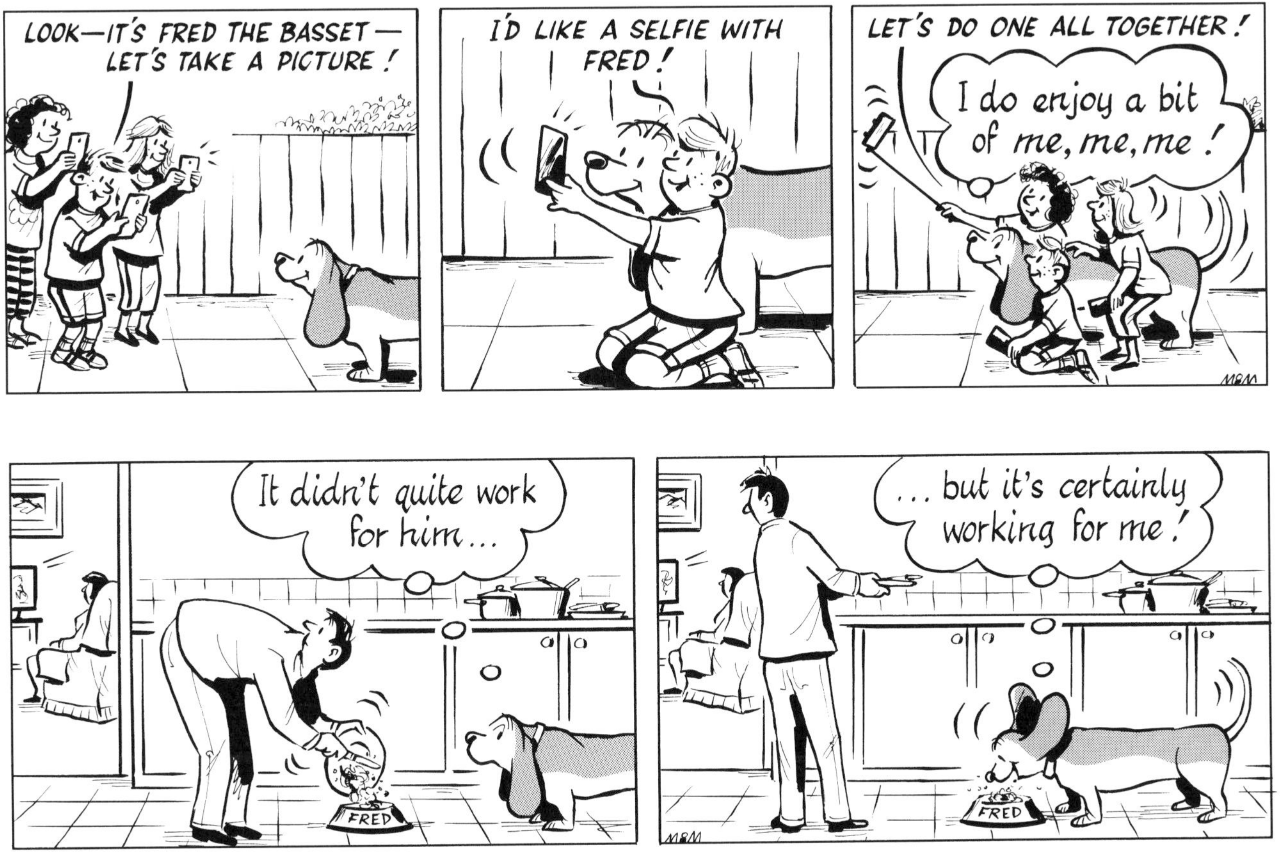
LOOK—IT'S FRED THE BASSET—
LET'S TAKE A PICTURE!
I'D LIKE A SELFIE WITH FRED!
LET'S DO ONE ALL TOGETHER!
I do enjoy a bit of me, me, me!
M&M
It didn't quite work for him...
FRED
M&M
... but it's certainly working for me!
FRED

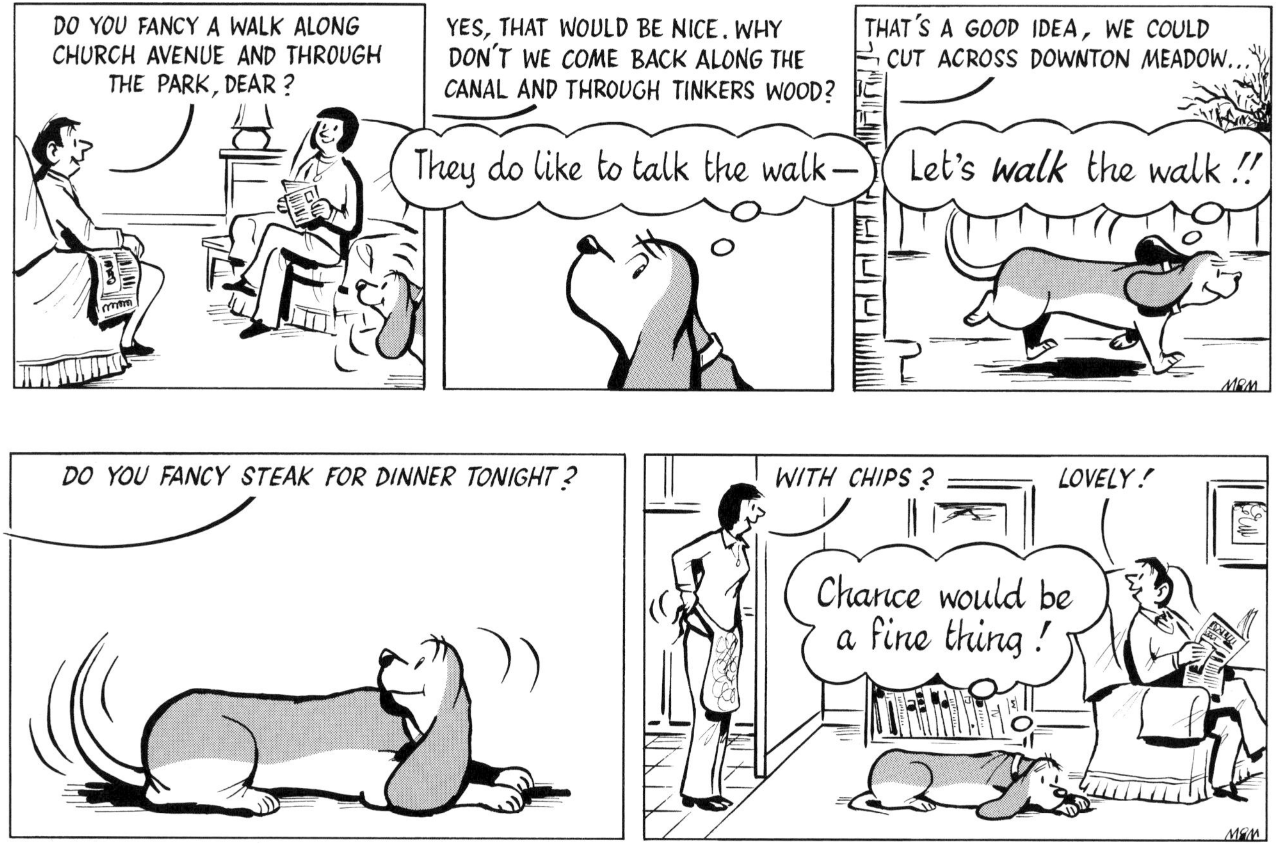

DO YOU FANCY A WALK ALONG CHURCH AVENUE AND THROUGH THE PARK, DEAR?
YES, THAT WOULD BE NICE. WHY DON'T WE COME BACK ALONG THE CANAL AND THROUGH TINKERS WOOD?
They do like to talk the walk—
THAT'S A GOOD IDEA, WE COULD CUT ACROSS DOWNTON MEADOW...
Let's **walk** the walk!!
MSM
DO YOU FANCY STEAK FOR DINNER TONIGHT?
WITH CHIPS?
LOVELY!
Chance would be a fine thing!
MSM

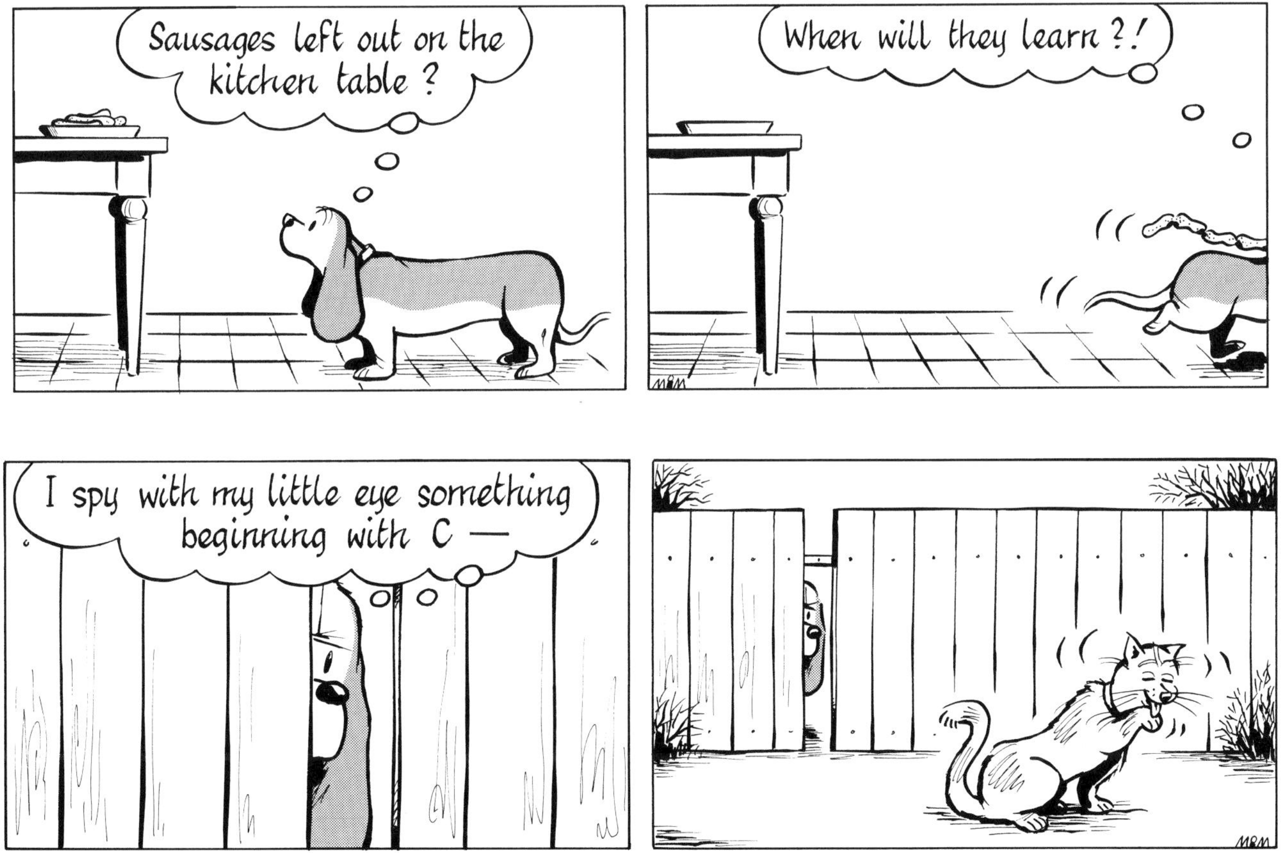
Sausages left out on the kitchen table ?
When will they learn ?!
I spy with my little eye something beginning with C —

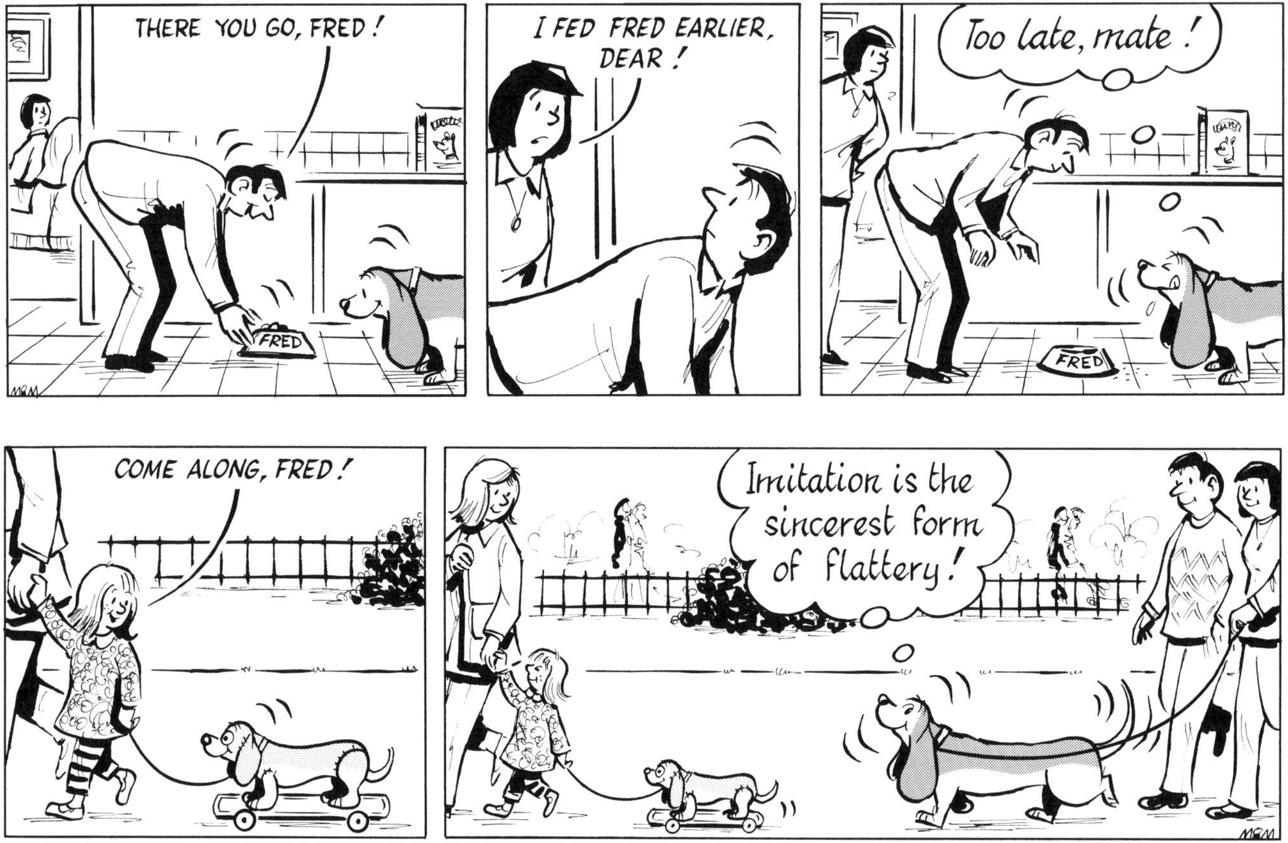
THERE YOU GO, FRED!
FRED
I FED FRED EARLIER, DEAR!
Too late, mate!
FRED
COME ALONG, FRED!
Imitation is the sincerest form of flattery!

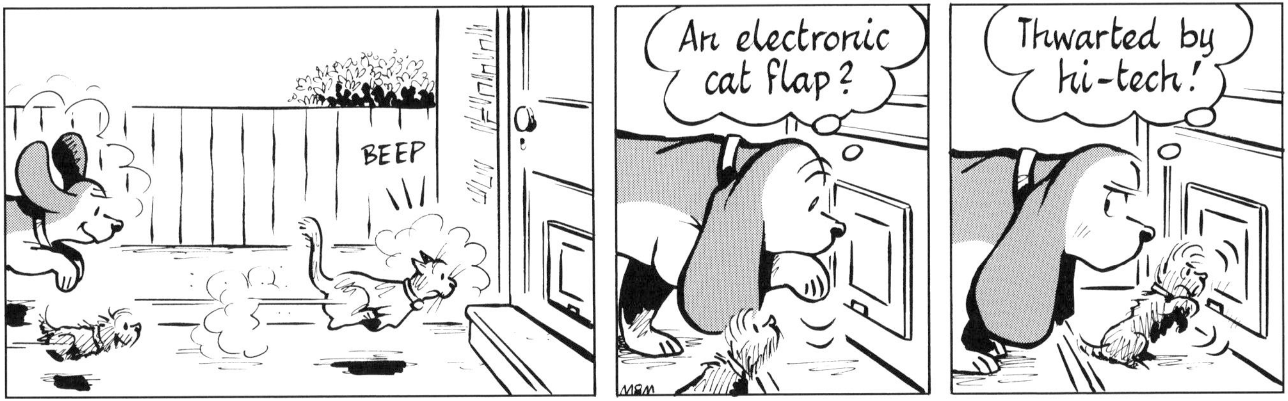
BEEP
An electronic cat flap?
Thwarted by hi-tech!

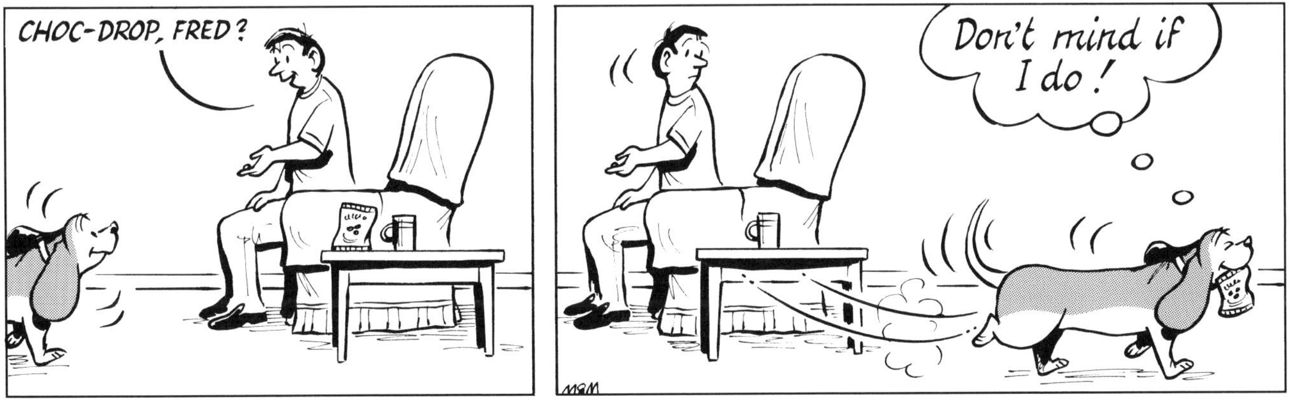
CHOC-DROP, FRED?
Don't mind if I do!

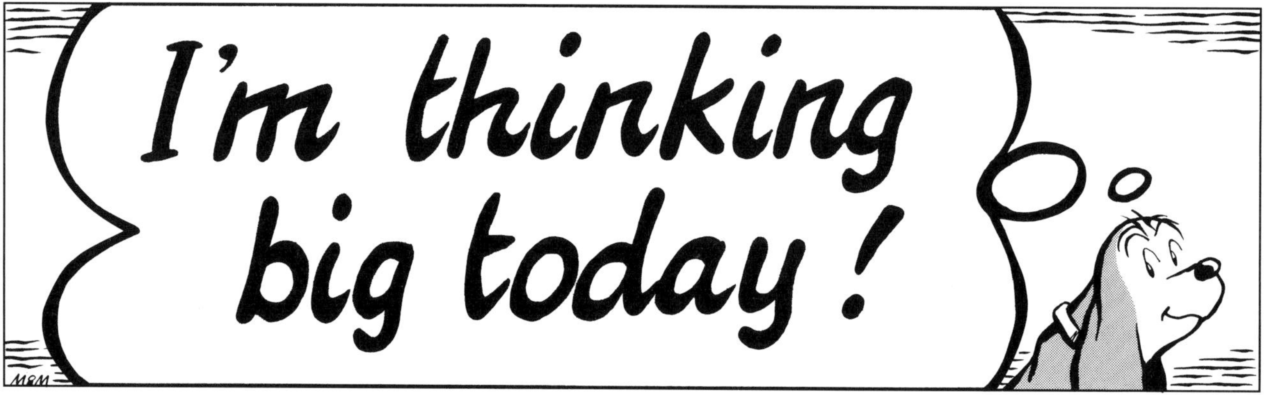
I'm thinking big today!
M&M

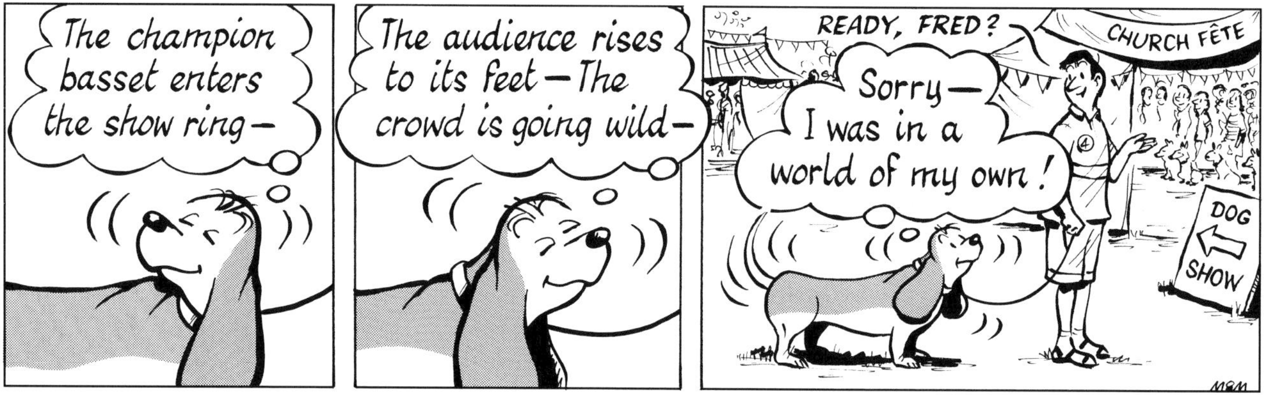
The champion basset enters the show ring–
The audience rises to its feet–The crowd is going wild–
READY, FRED?
CHURCH FÊTE
Sorry– I was in a world of my own!
DOG SHOW
M&M

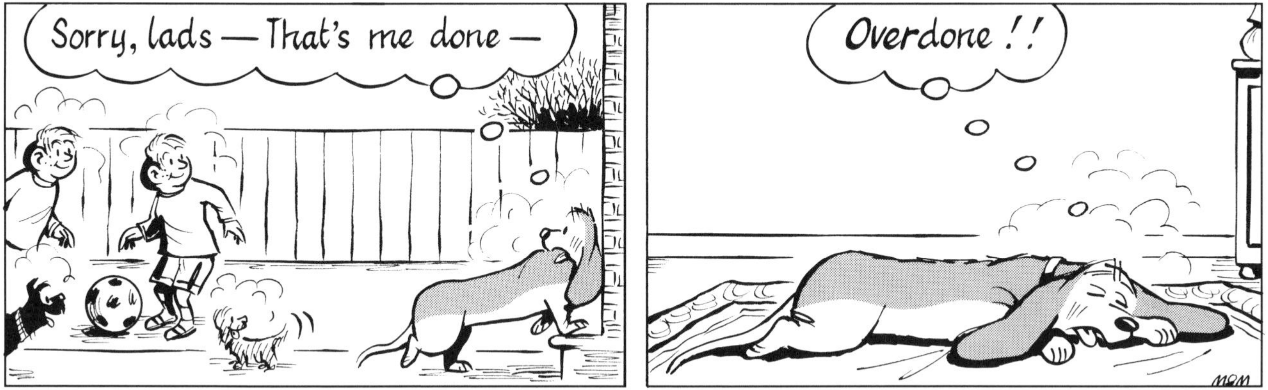
Sorry, lads — That's me done —
Overdone !!
MGM

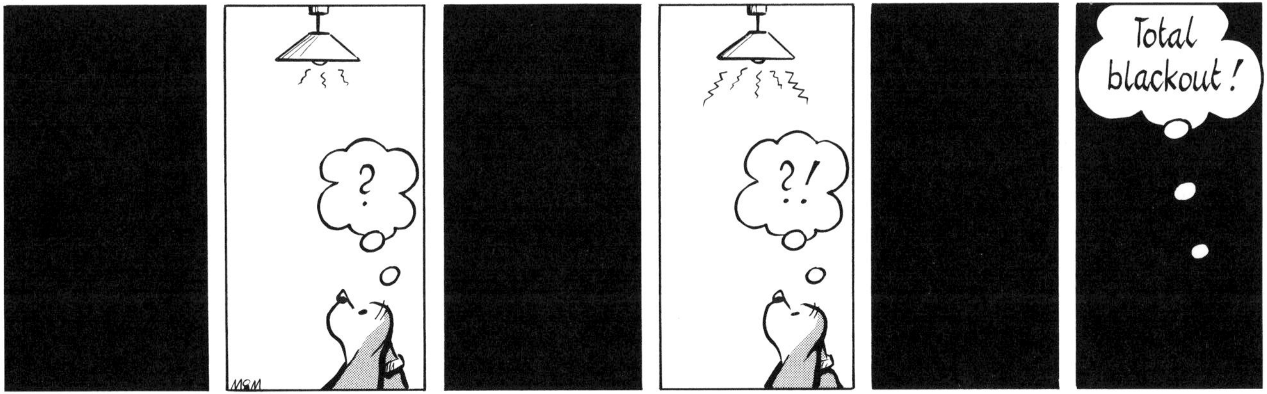
?
MGM
?!
Total blackout!

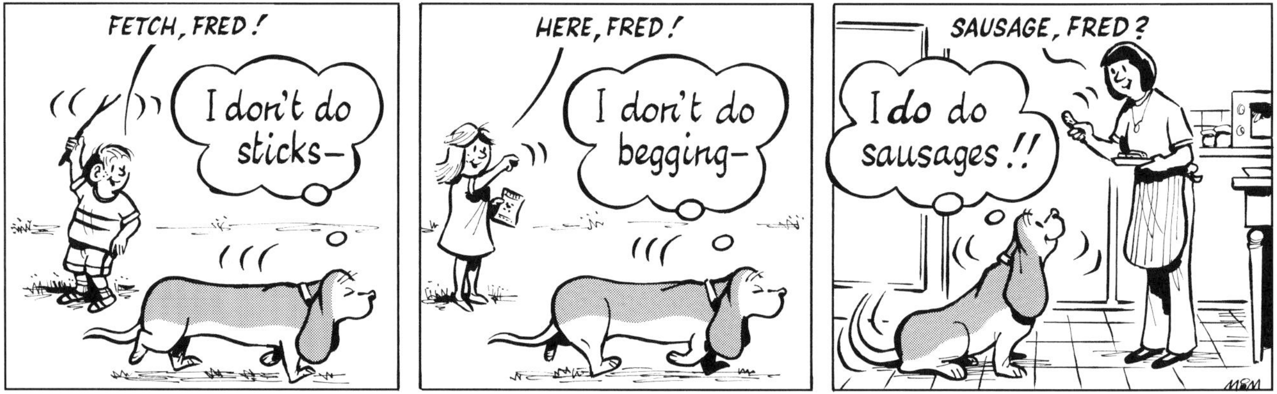
FETCH, FRED!
I don't do sticks–
HERE, FRED!
I don't do begging–
SAUSAGE, FRED?
I do do sausages!!
MBM

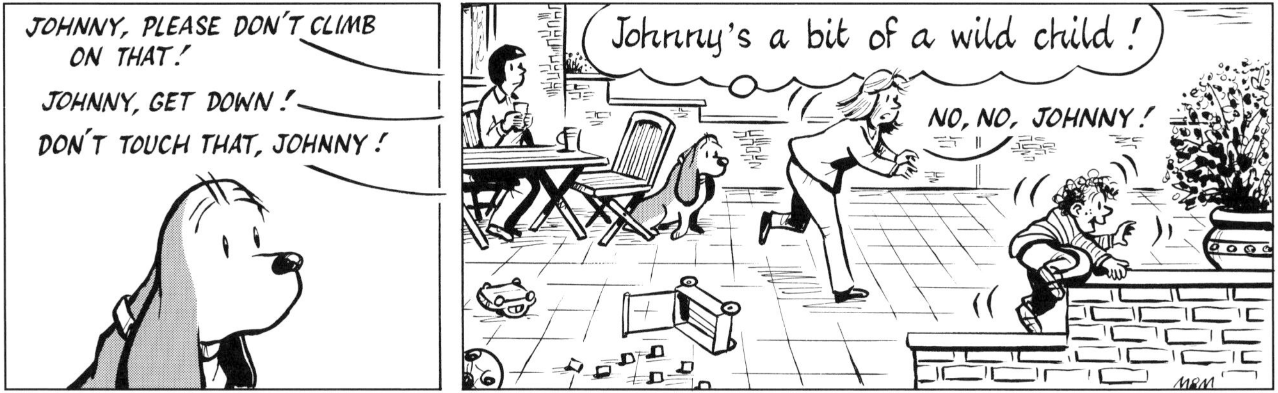
JOHNNY, PLEASE DON'T CLIMB ON THAT!
JOHNNY, GET DOWN!
DON'T TOUCH THAT, JOHNNY!
Johnny's a bit of a wild child!
NO, NO, JOHNNY!
MBM

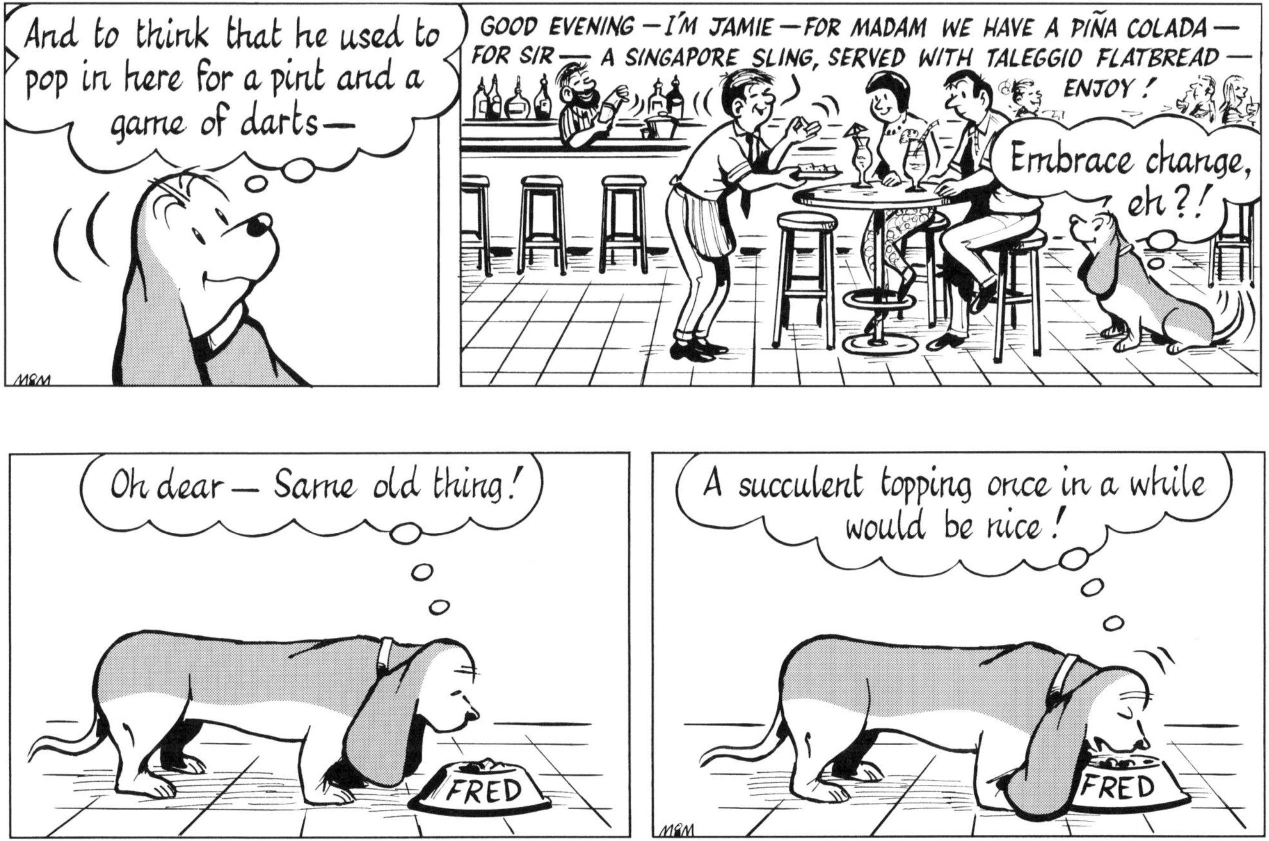
And to think that he used to pop in here for a pint and a game of darts—
GOOD EVENING —I'M JAMIE —FOR MADAM WE HAVE A PIÑA COLADA — FOR SIR — A SINGAPORE SLING, SERVED WITH TALEGGIO FLATBREAD — ENJOY!
Embrace change, eh?!
M&M
Oh dear — Same old thing!
FRED
A succulent topping once in a while would be nice!
FRED
M&M

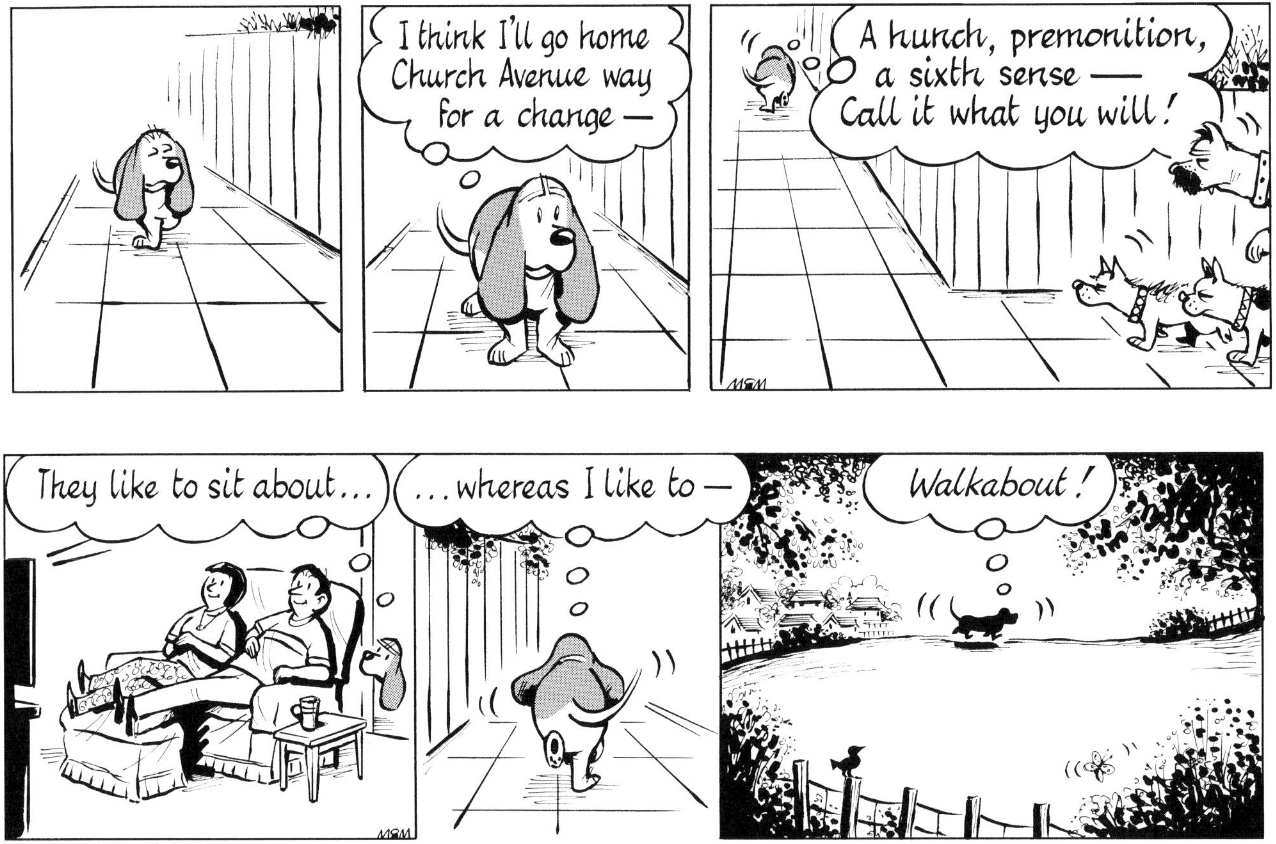
I think I'll go home Church Avenue way for a change —
A hunch, premonition, a sixth sense — Call it what you will!
They like to sit about...
...whereas I like to —
Walkabout!

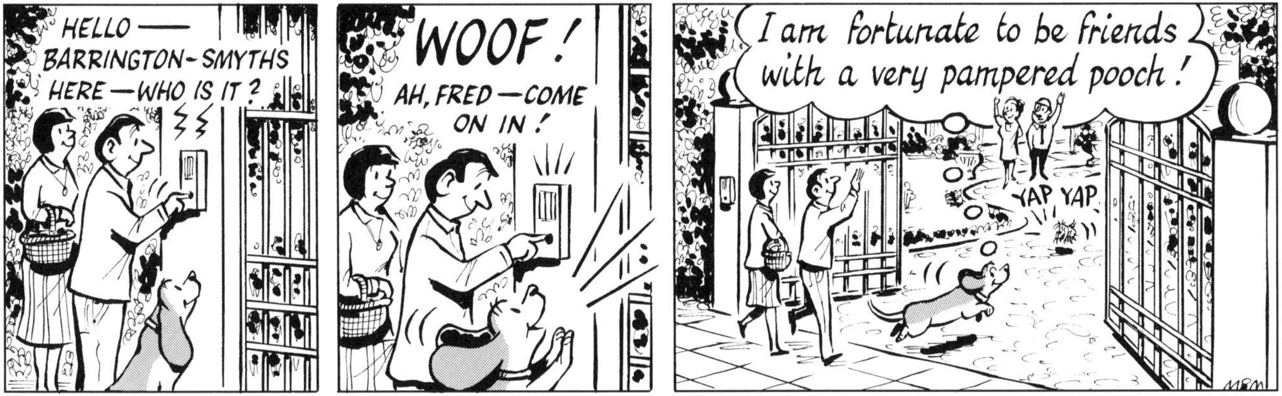
HELLO — BARRINGTON-SMYTHS HERE — WHO IS IT?
WOOF!
AH, FRED — COME ON IN!
I am fortunate to be friends with a very pampered pooch!
YAP YAP

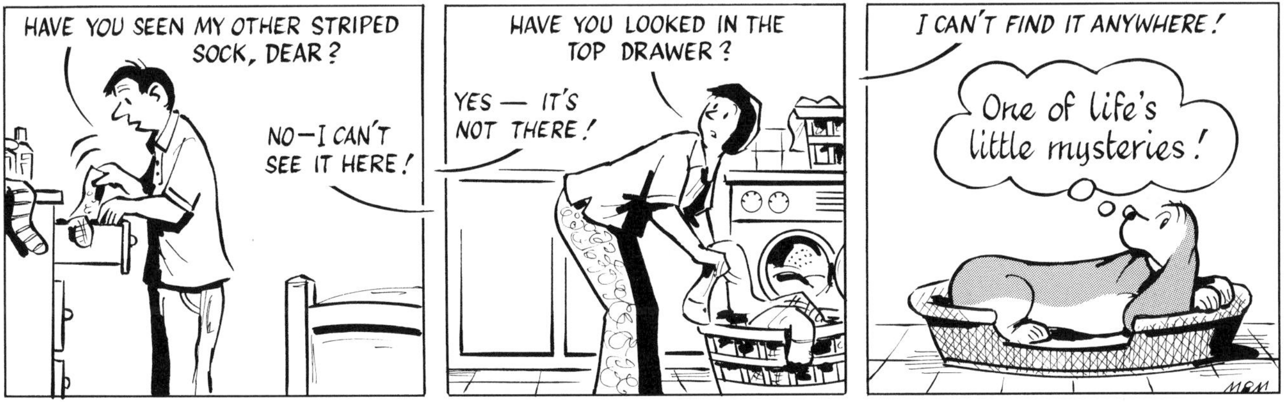
HAVE YOU SEEN MY OTHER STRIPED SOCK, DEAR?
NO — I CAN'T SEE IT HERE!
HAVE YOU LOOKED IN THE TOP DRAWER?
YES — IT'S NOT THERE!
I CAN'T FIND IT ANYWHERE!
One of life's little mysteries!

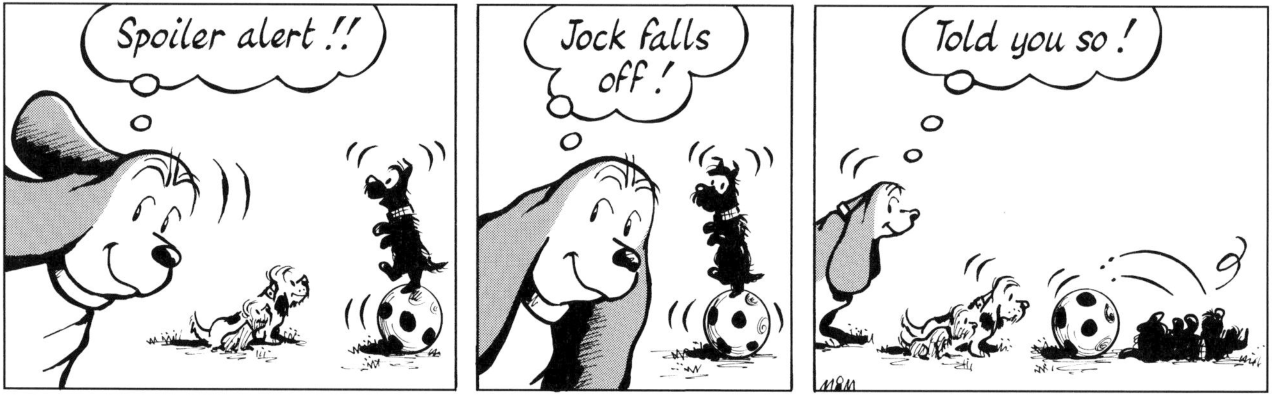
Spoiler alert !!
Jock falls off !
Told you so !
MSM

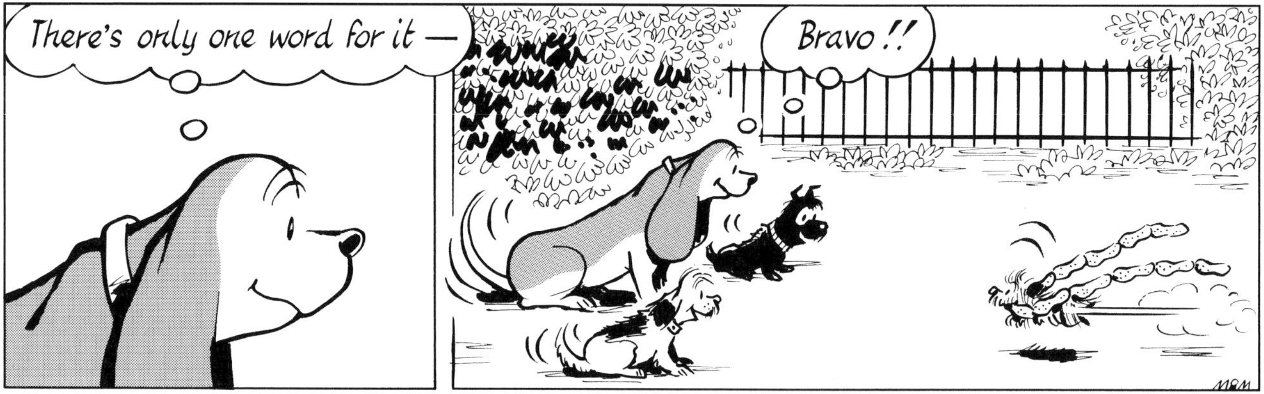
There's only one word for it —
Bravo !!
MSM

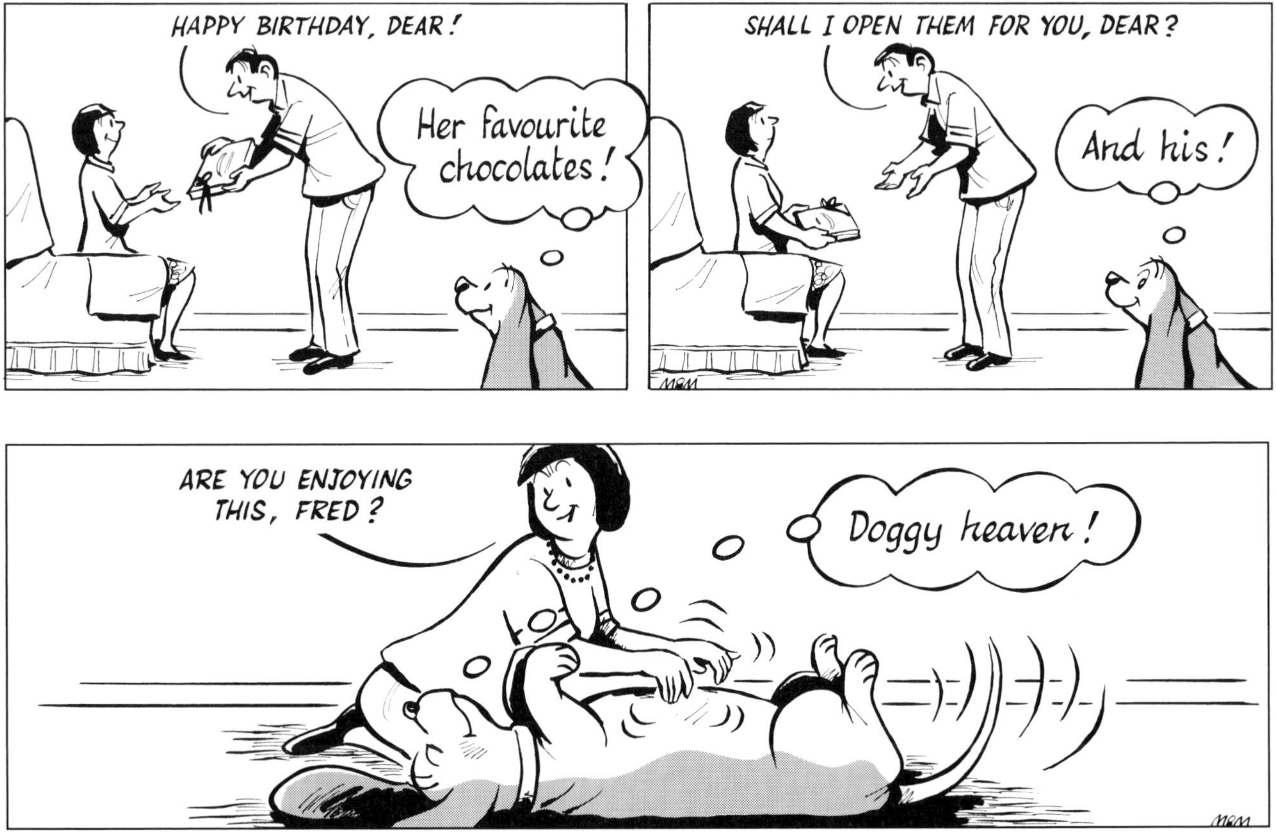
HAPPY BIRTHDAY, DEAR!
Her favourite chocolates!
SHALL I OPEN THEM FOR YOU, DEAR?
And his!
ARE YOU ENJOYING THIS, FRED?
Doggy heaven!

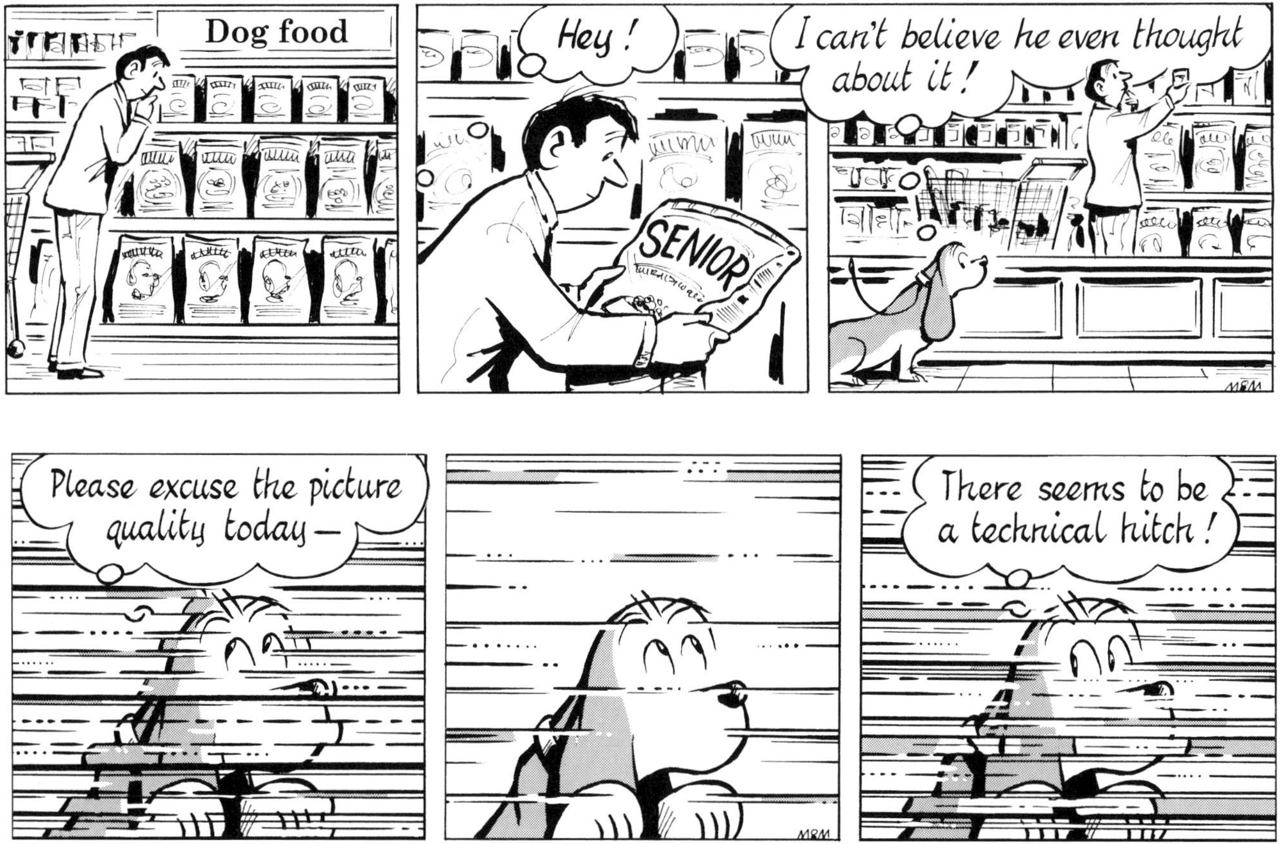
Dog food
Hey!
SENIOR
I can't believe he even thought about it!
M&M
Please excuse the picture quality today –
M&M
There seems to be a technical hitch!

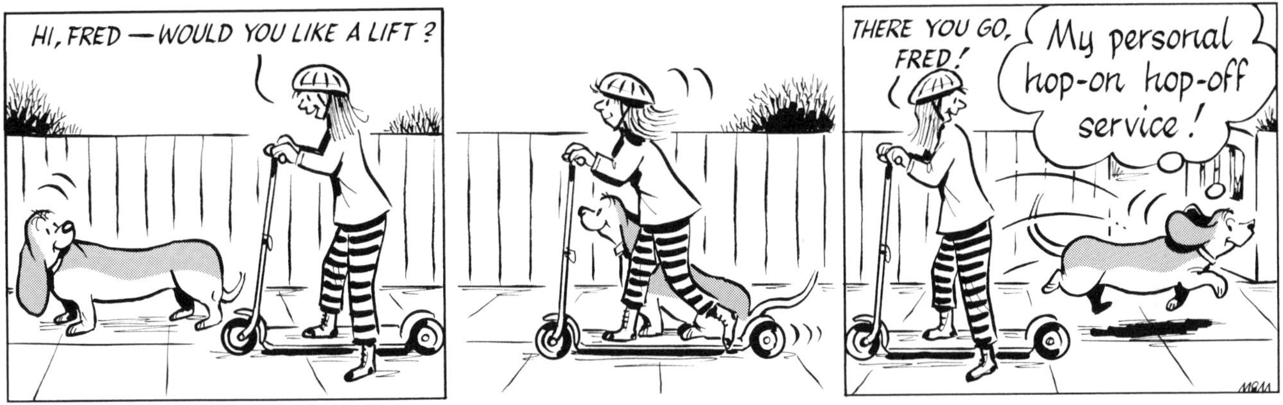
HI, FRED — WOULD YOU LIKE A LIFT ?
THERE YOU GO, FRED !
My personal hop-on hop-off service !

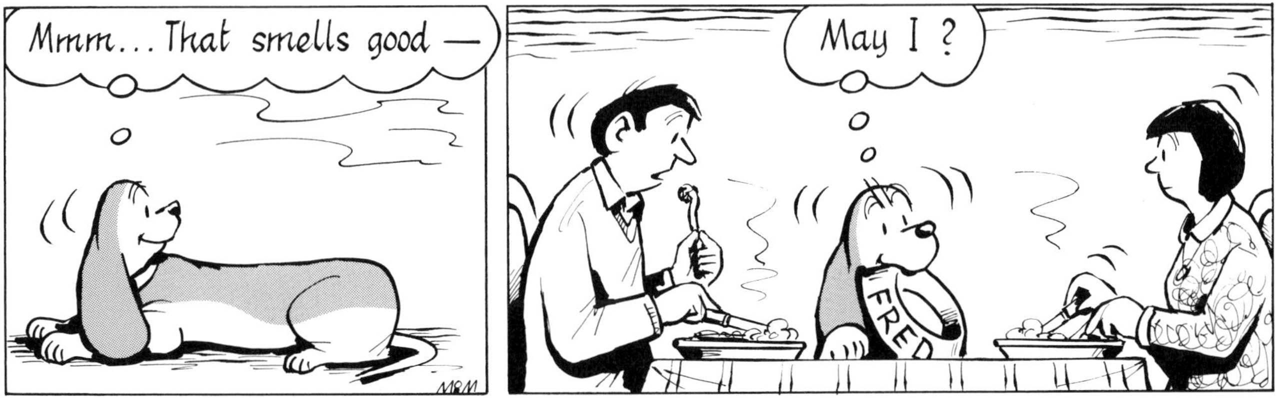
Mmm... That smells good —
May I ?
FRED

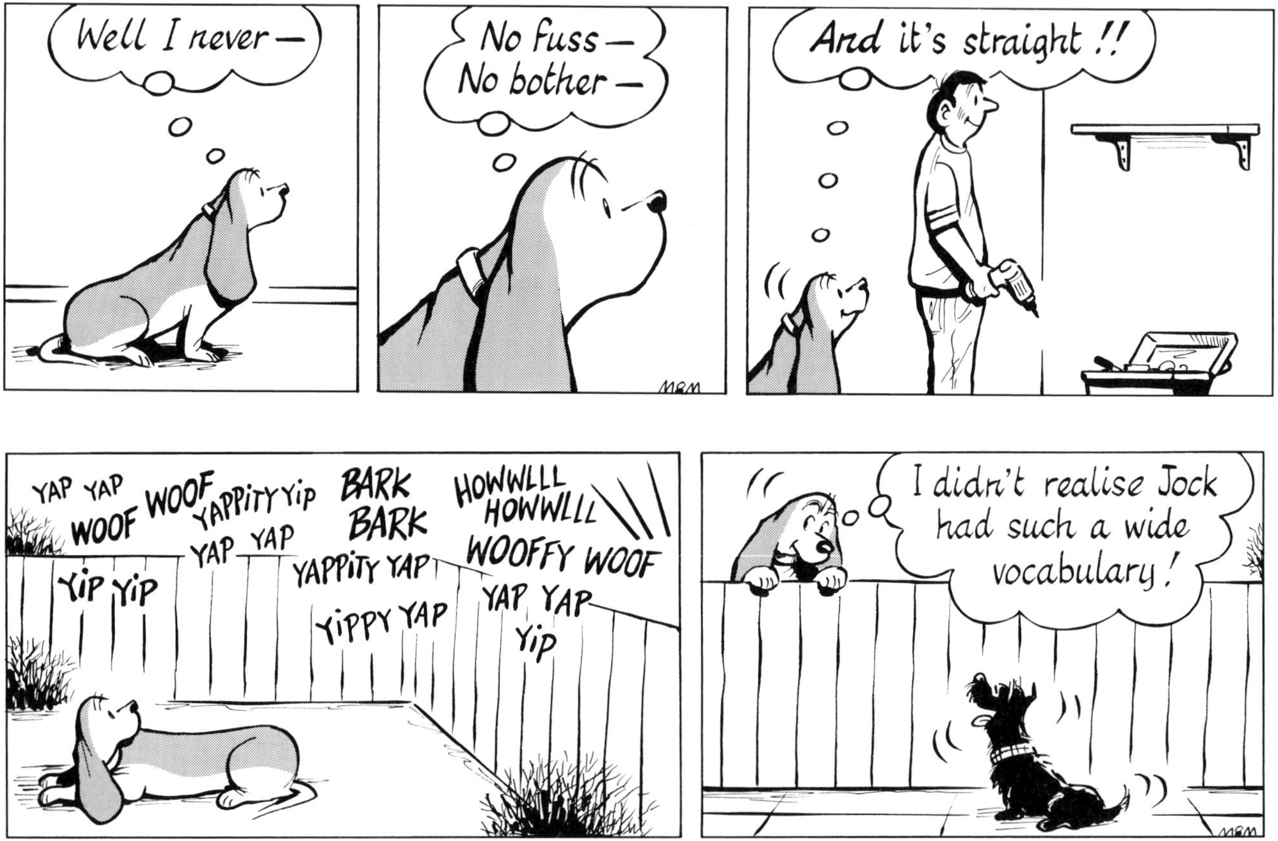
Well I never –
No fuss –
No bother –
MSM
And it's straight !!
YAP YAP
WOOF WOOF
YAPPITY YIP
BARK
BARK
HOWWLLL
HOWWLLL
YAP YAP
YIP YIP
YAPPITY YAP
WOOFFY WOOF
YIPPY YAP
YAP YAP
YIP
I didn't realise Jock had such a wide vocabulary!
MSM

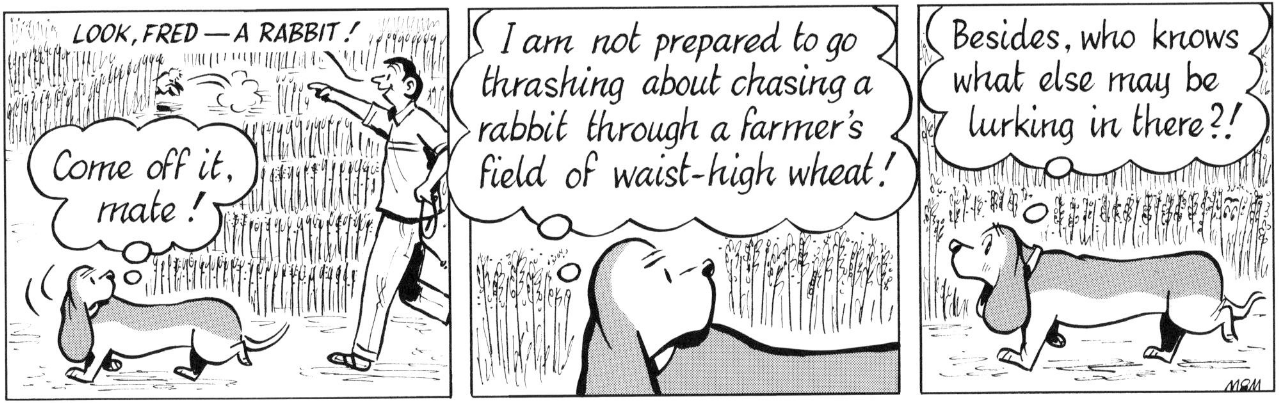
LOOK, FRED — A RABBIT!
Come off it, mate!
I am not prepared to go thrashing about chasing a rabbit through a farmer's field of waist-high wheat!
Besides, who knows what else may be lurking in there?!

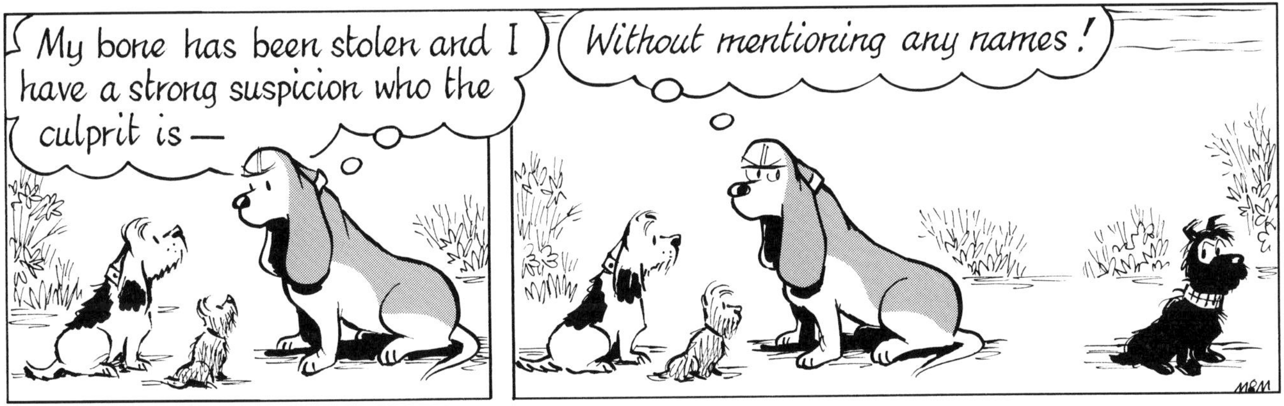
My bone has been stolen and I have a strong suspicion who the culprit is —
Without mentioning any names!

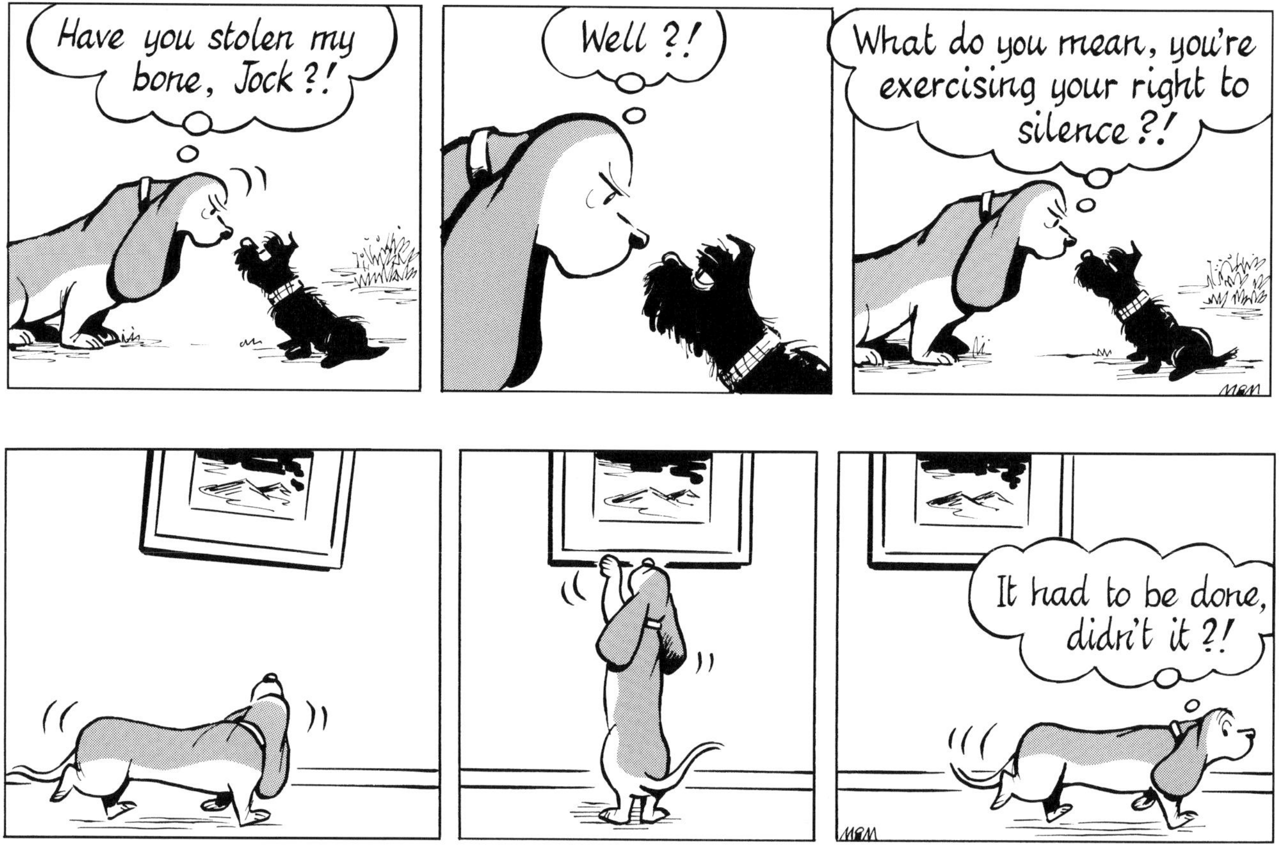
Have you stolen my bone, Jock ?!
Well ?!
What do you mean, you're exercising your right to silence ?!
MGM
MGM
It had to be done, didn't it ?!

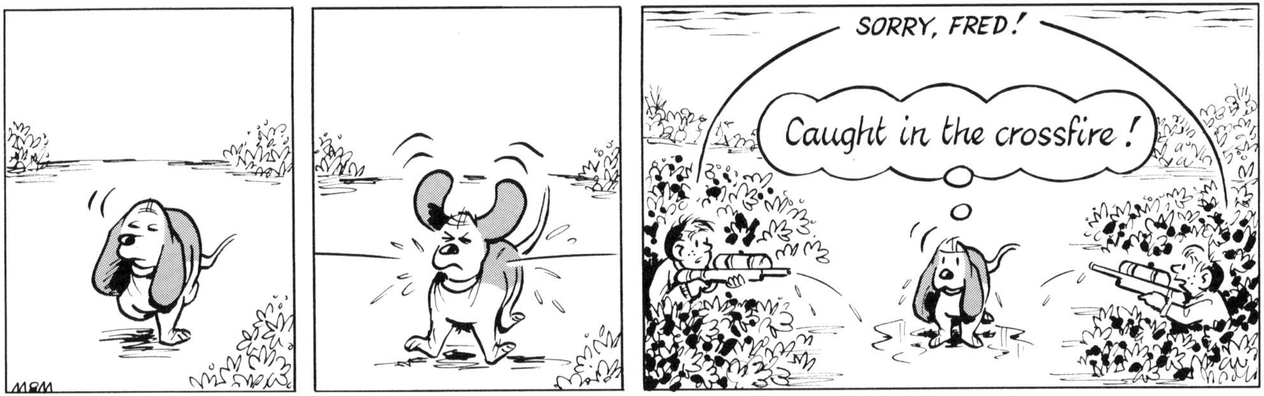
SORRY, FRED!
Caught in the crossfire!

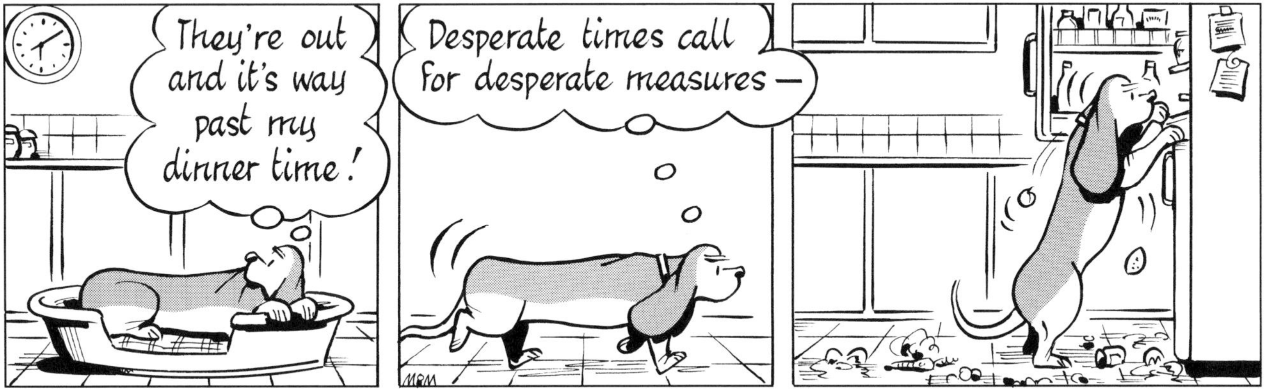
They're out and it's way past my dinner time!
Desperate times call for desperate measures —

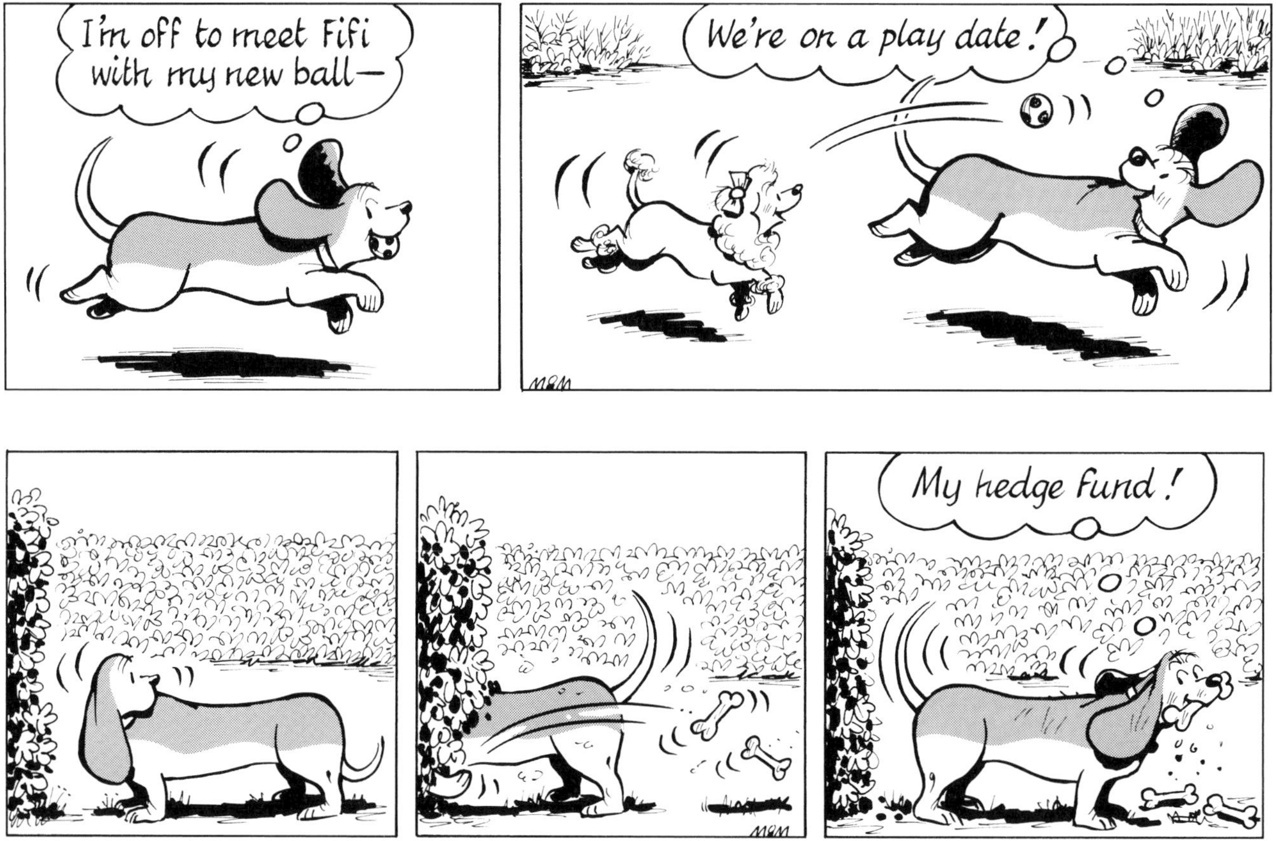
I'm off to meet Fifi with my new ball—
We're on a play date!
MGM
MGM
My hedge fund!

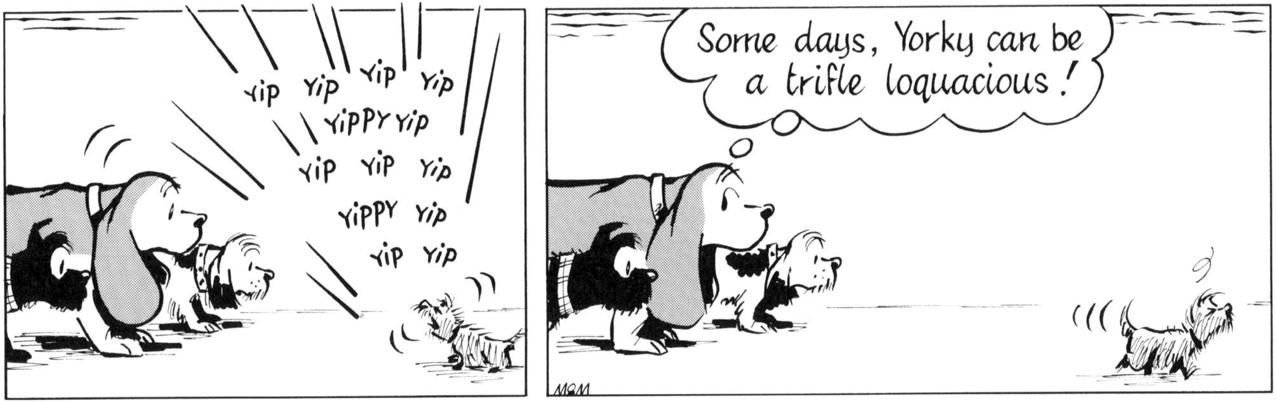
Yip Yip Yip Yip
YIPPY YIP
YIP YIP YIP
YIPPY YIP
YIP YIP
Some days, Yorky can be a trifle loquacious!

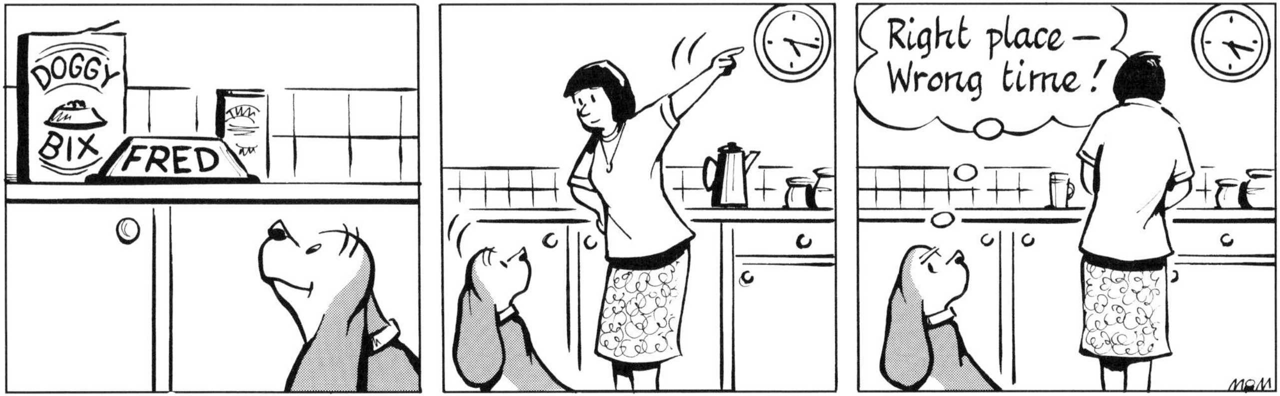
DOGGY BIX
FRED
Right place — Wrong time!

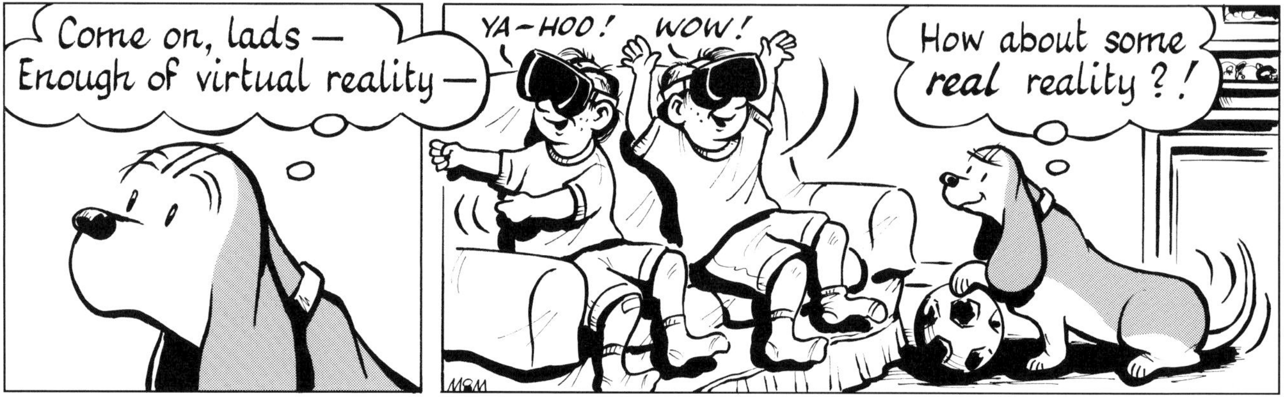
Come on, lads —
Enough of virtual reality —
YA-HOO!
WOW!
How about some **real** reality?!

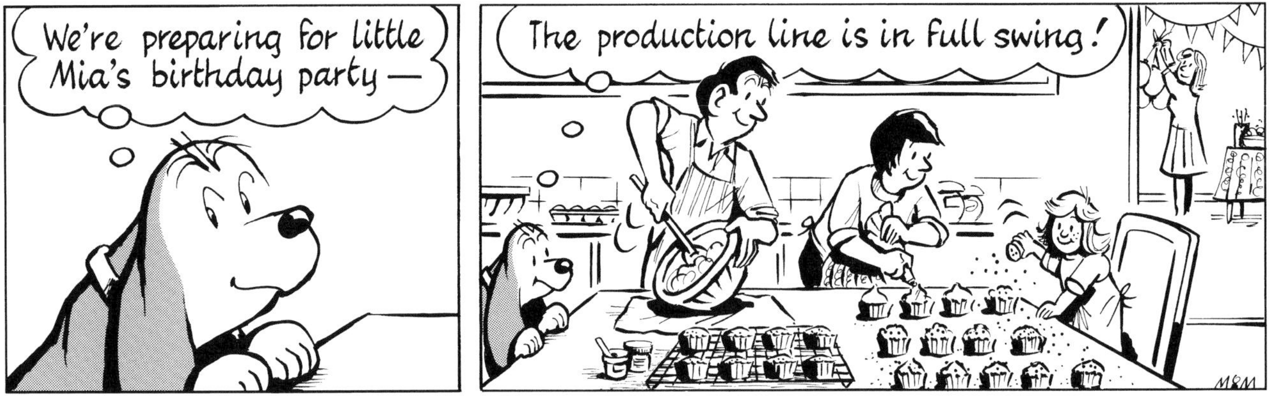
We're preparing for little Mia's birthday party —
The production line is in full swing!

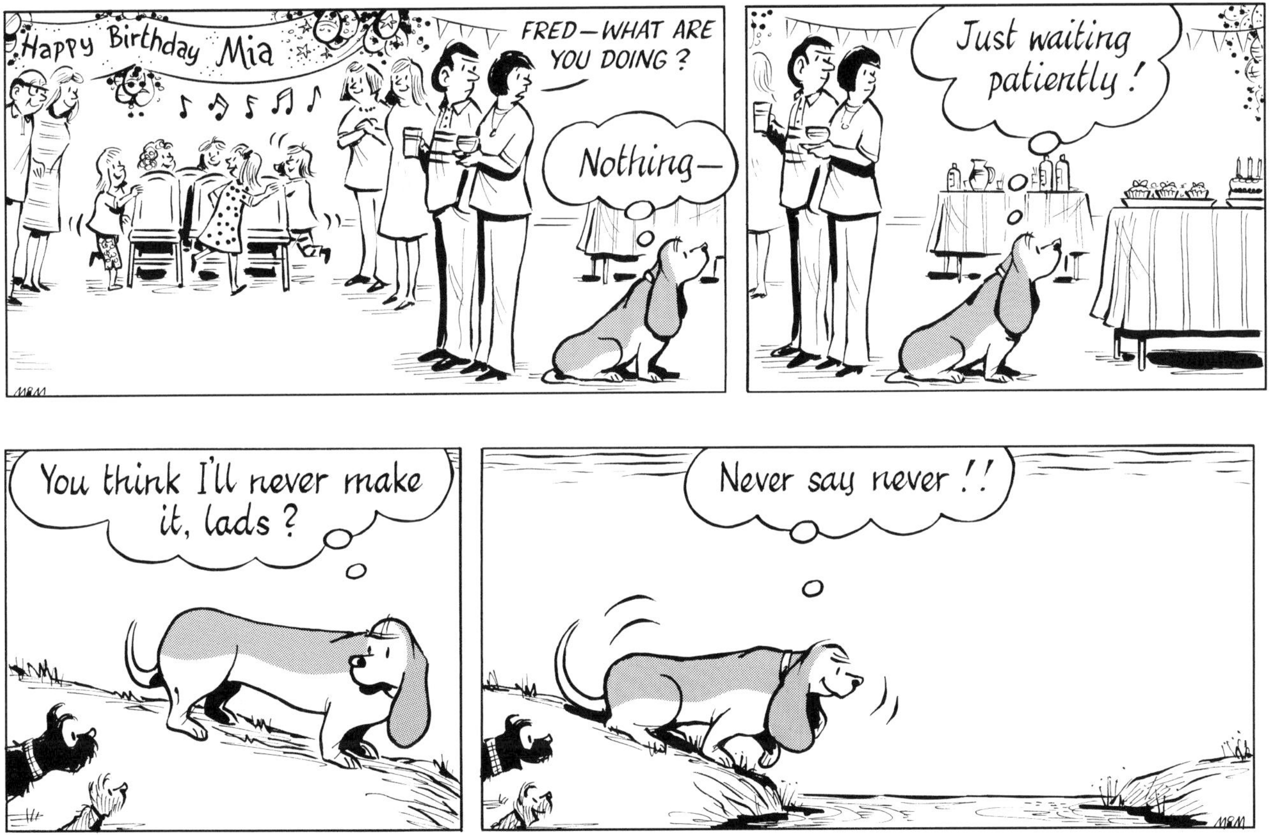
Happy Birthday Mia
FRED—WHAT ARE YOU DOING ?
Nothing—
Just waiting patiently !
You think I'll never make it, lads ?
Never say never !!

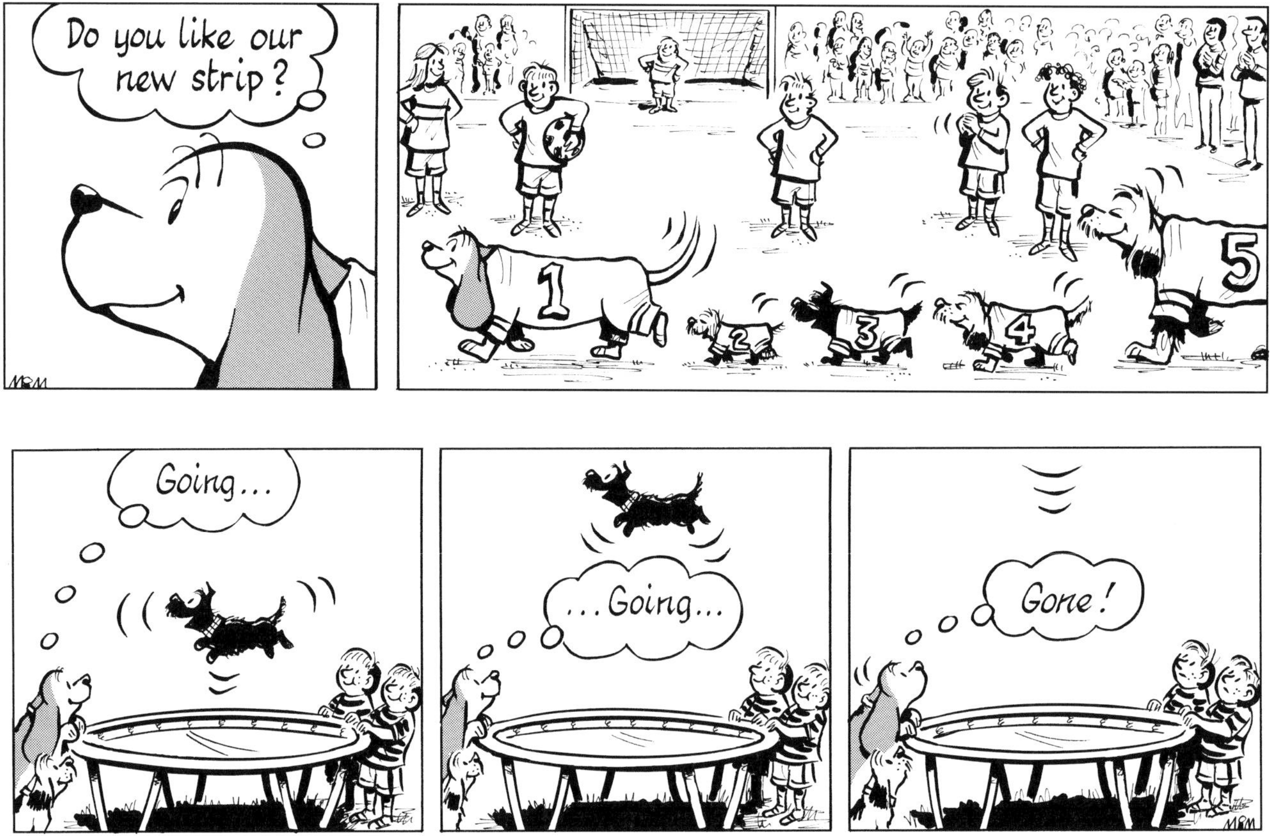
Do you like our new strip?
1
2
3
4
5
Going...
...Going...
Gone!

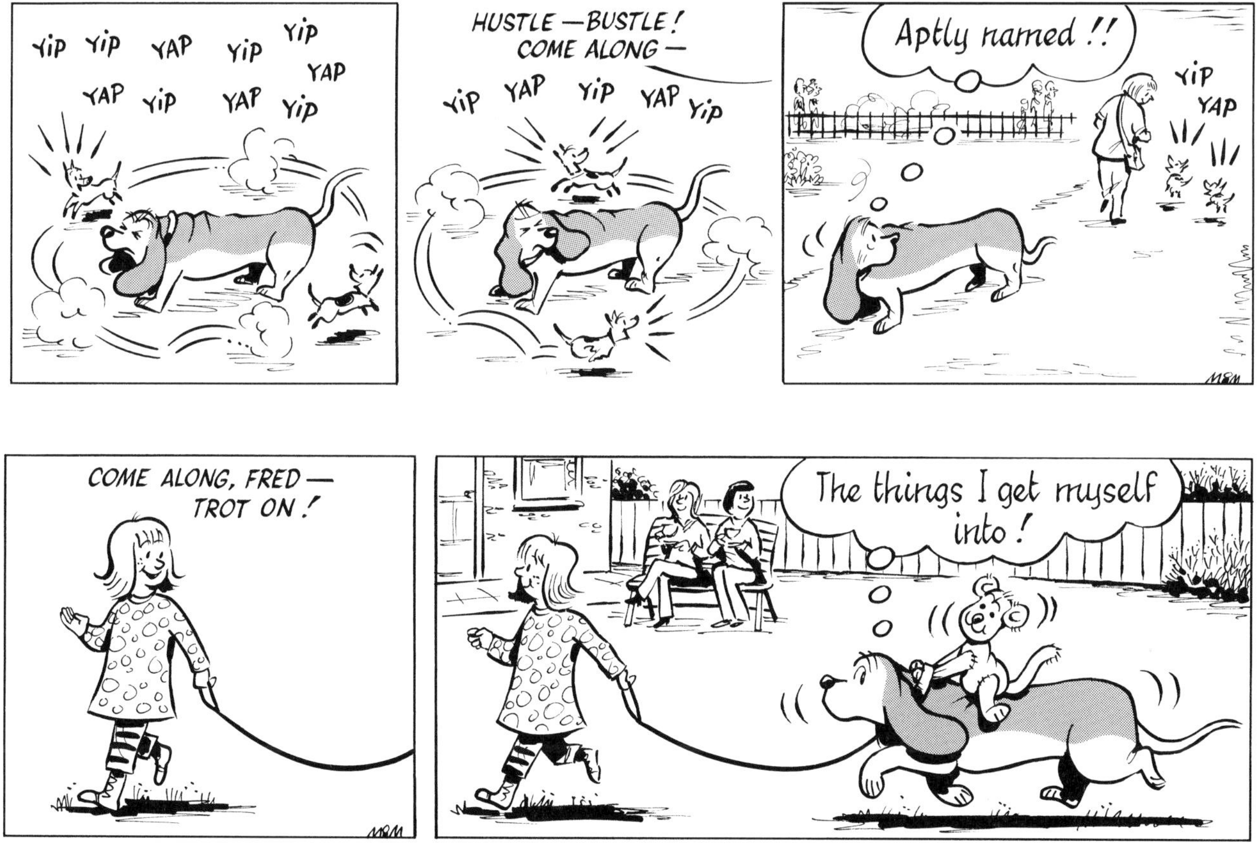
YIP YIP YAP YIP YIP YAP
YAP YIP YAP YIP
HUSTLE — BUSTLE! COME ALONG —
YIP YAP YIP YAP YIP
Aptly named !!
YIP YAP
COME ALONG, FRED — TROT ON!
The things I get myself into!

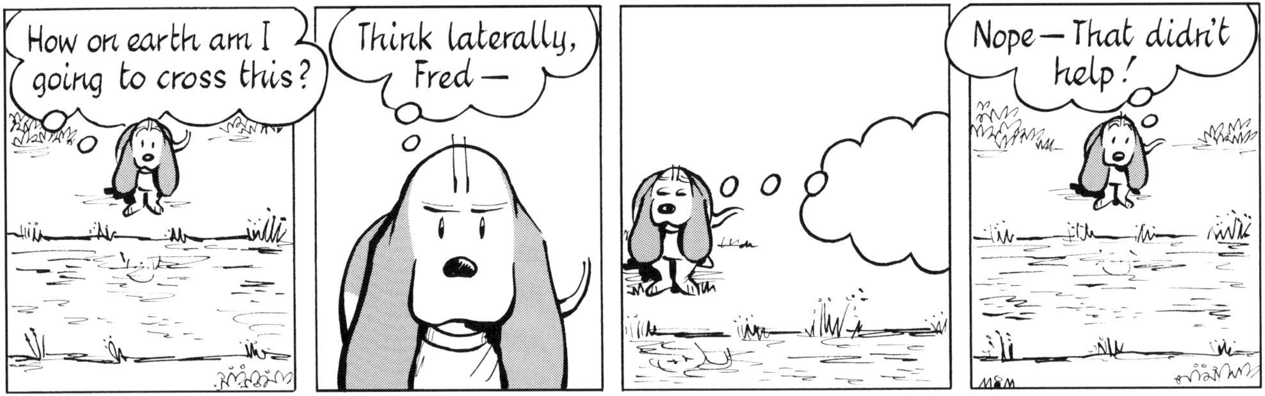
How on earth am I going to cross this?
Think laterally, Fred —
Nope — That didn't help!
M&M

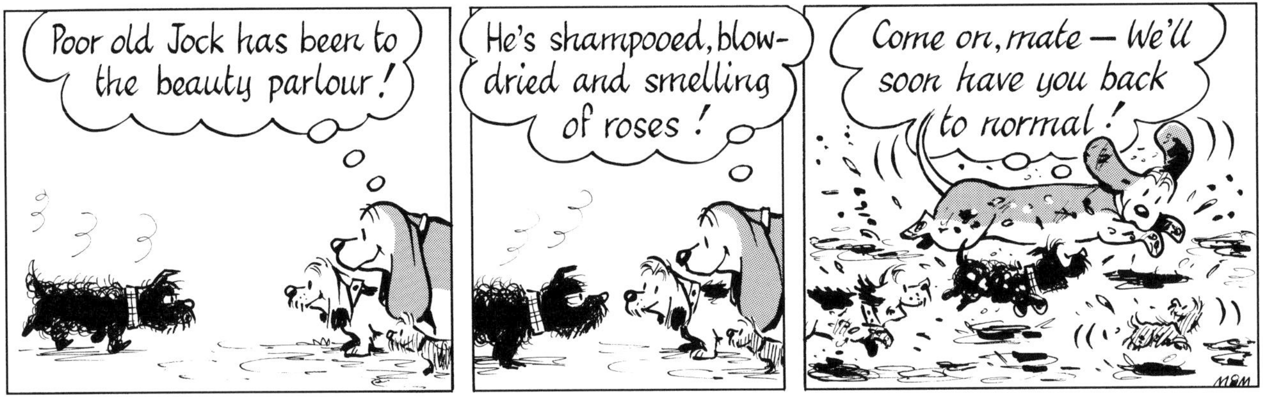
Poor old Jock has been to the beauty parlour!
He's shampooed, blow-dried and smelling of roses!
Come on, mate — We'll soon have you back to normal!
M&M

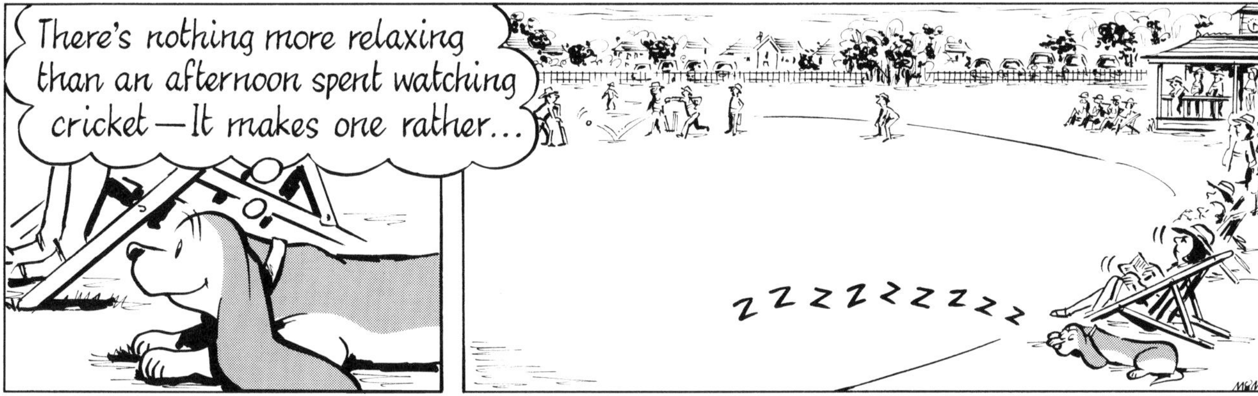
There's nothing more relaxing than an afternoon spent watching cricket—It makes one rather...
ZZZZZZZZZZ

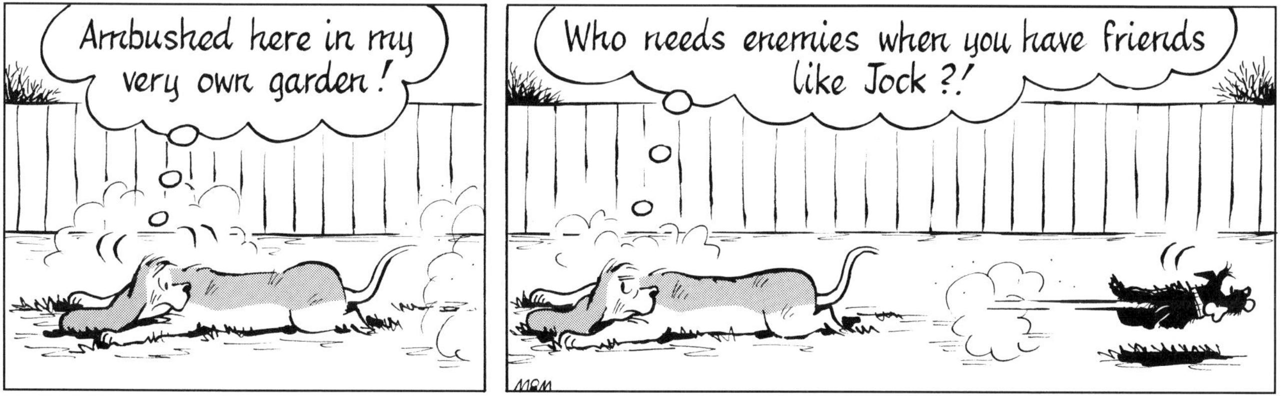
Ambushed here in my very own garden!
Who needs enemies when you have friends like Jock?!

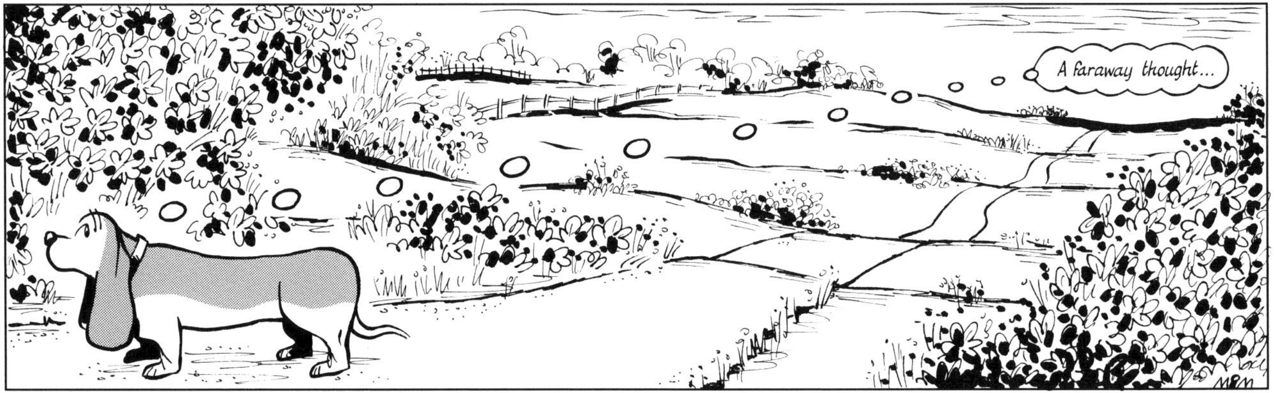
A faraway thought...

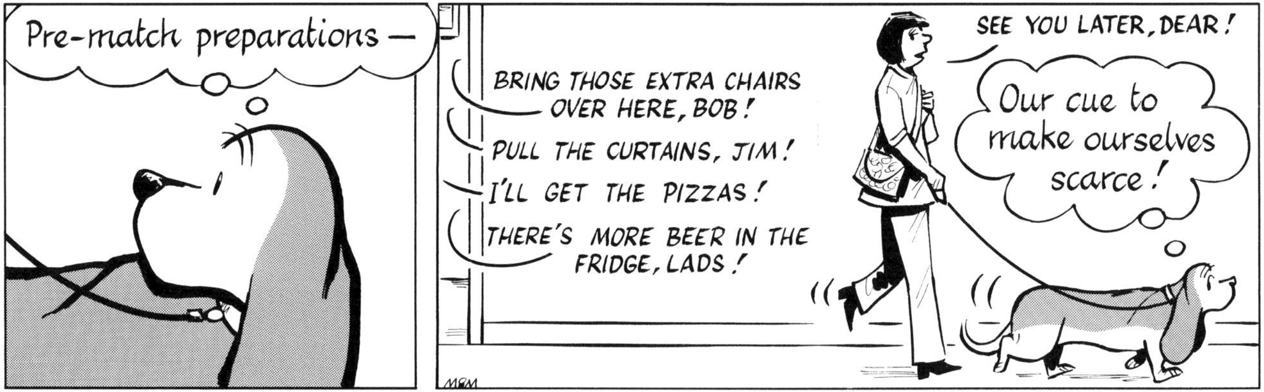
Pre-match preparations –
BRING THOSE EXTRA CHAIRS OVER HERE, BOB!
PULL THE CURTAINS, JIM!
I'LL GET THE PIZZAS!
THERE'S MORE BEER IN THE FRIDGE, LADS!
SEE YOU LATER, DEAR!
Our cue to make ourselves scarce!

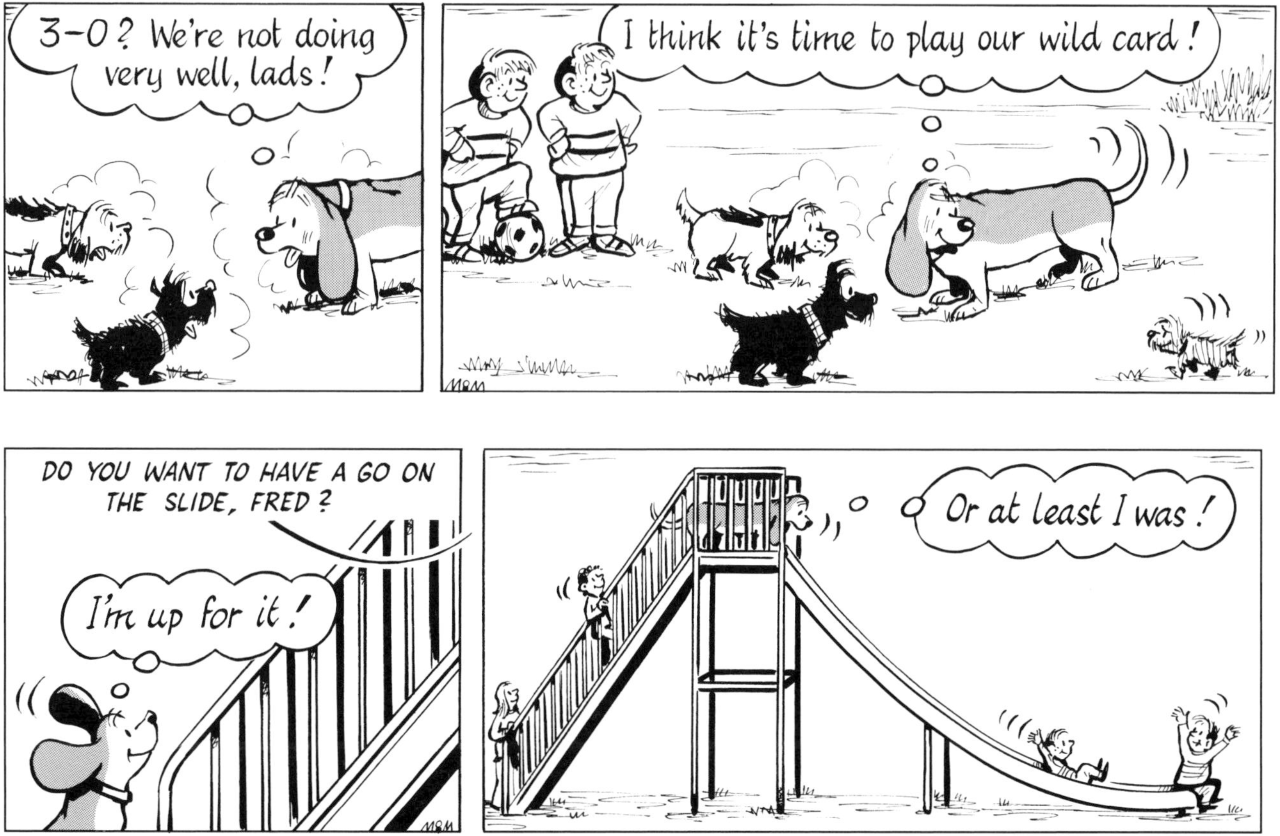
3–0? We're not doing very well, lads!
I think it's time to play our wild card!
DO YOU WANT TO HAVE A GO ON THE SLIDE, FRED?
I'm up for it!
Or at least I was!

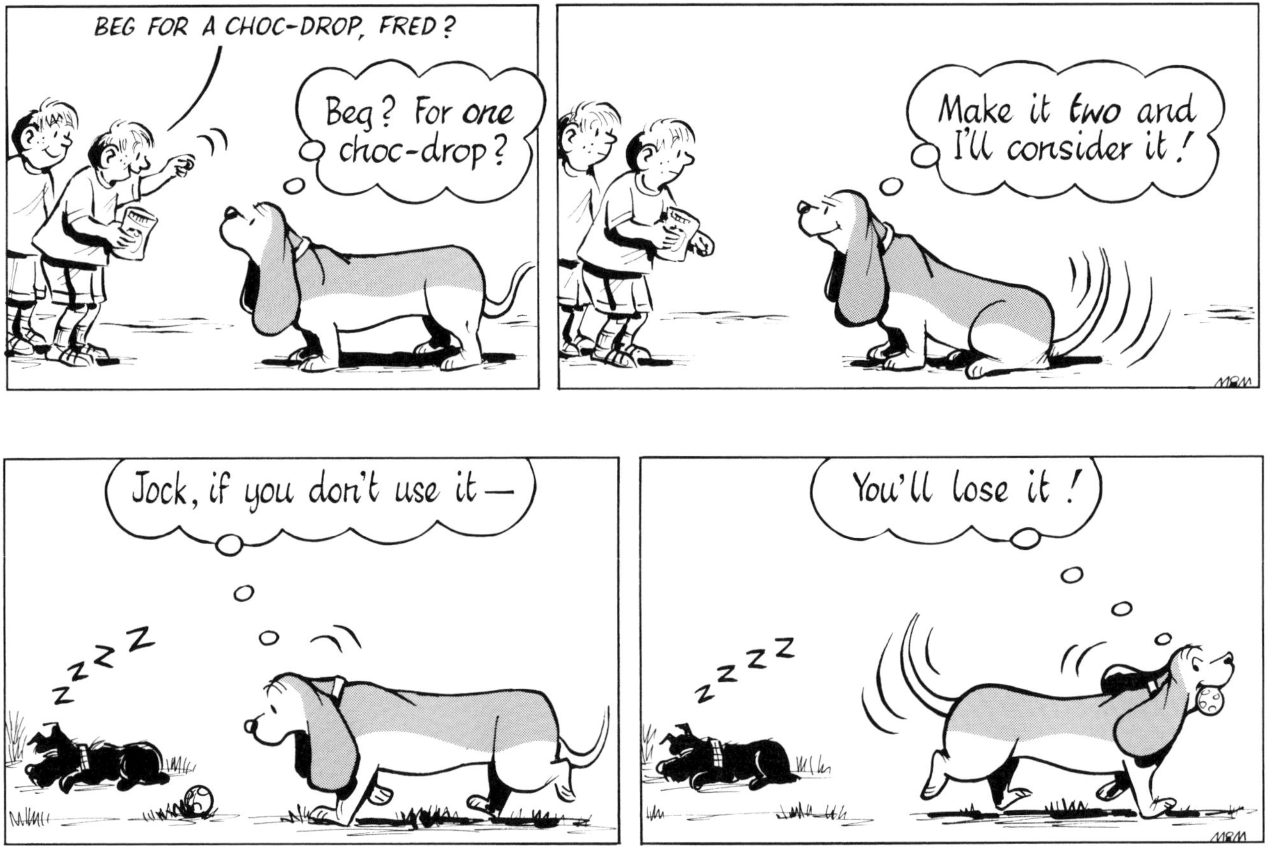
BEG FOR A CHOC-DROP, FRED?
Beg? For one choc-drop?
Make it two and I'll consider it!
MRM
Jock, if you don't use it —
You'll lose it!
MRM

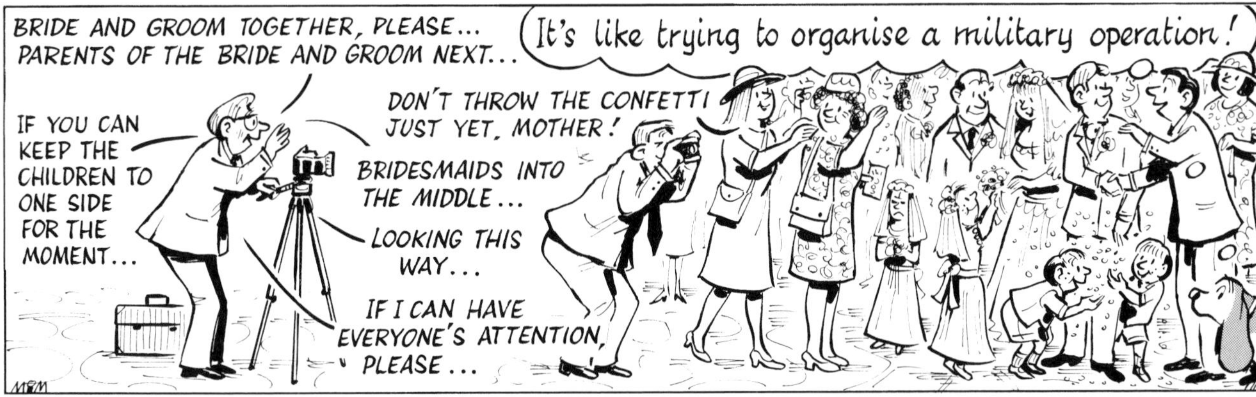
BRIDE AND GROOM TOGETHER, PLEASE...
PARENTS OF THE BRIDE AND GROOM NEXT...
IF YOU CAN KEEP THE CHILDREN TO ONE SIDE FOR THE MOMENT...
BRIDESMAIDS INTO THE MIDDLE...
LOOKING THIS WAY...
IF I CAN HAVE EVERYONE'S ATTENTION, PLEASE...
DON'T THROW THE CONFETTI JUST YET, MOTHER!
It's like trying to organise a military operation!
MBM

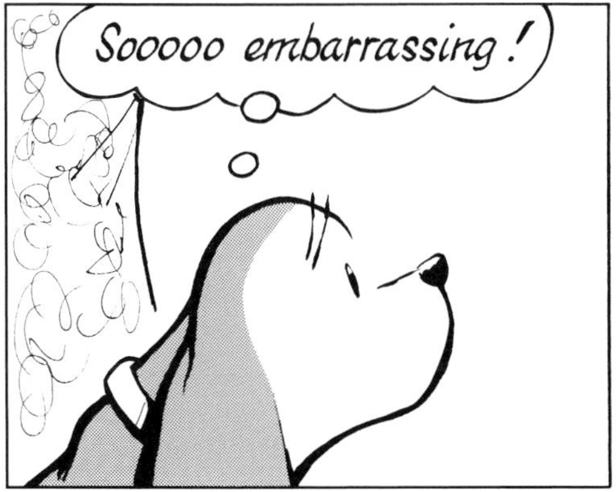
Sooooo embarrassing!

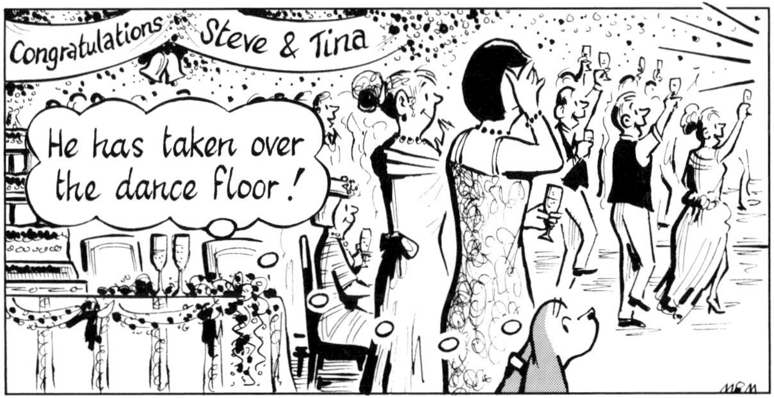
Congratulations Steve & Tina
He has taken over the dance floor!
MBM

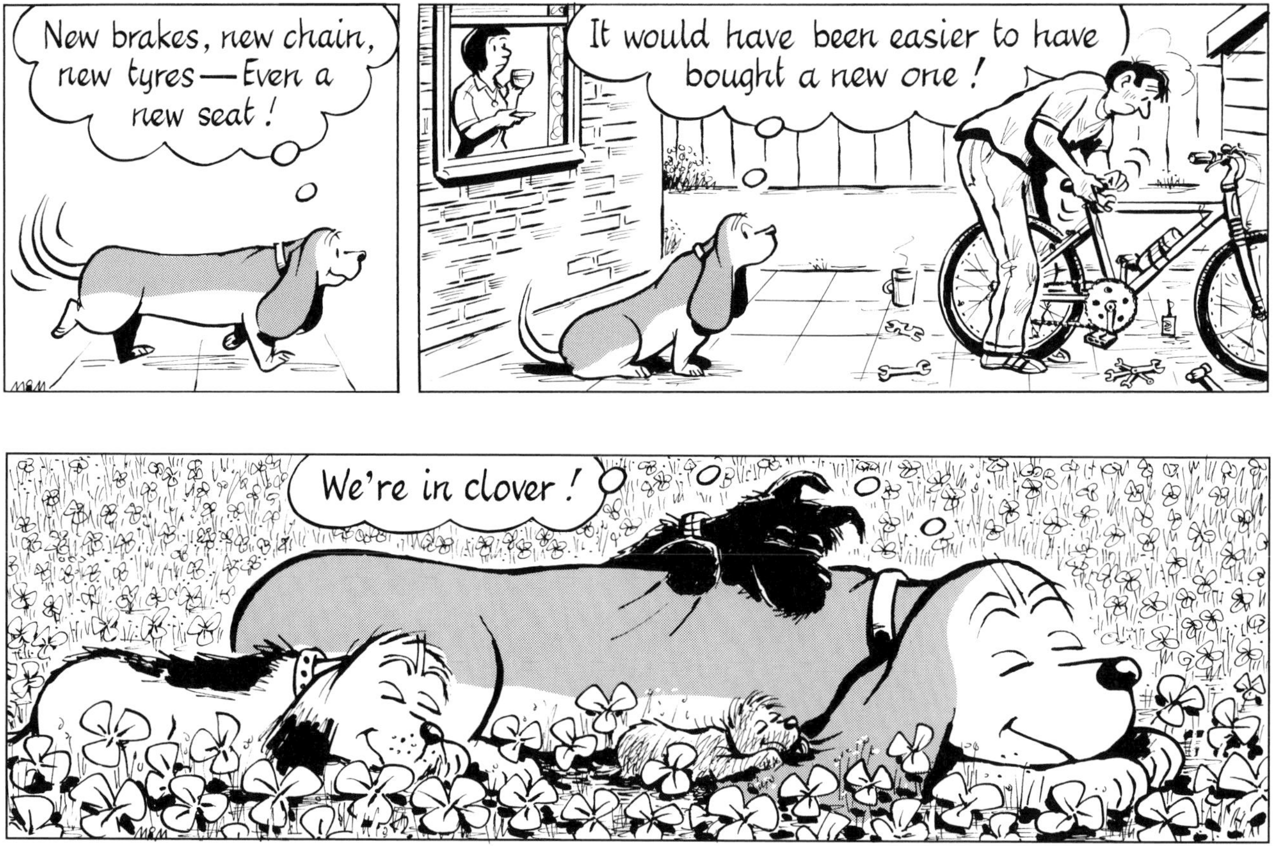
New brakes, new chain, new tyres—Even a new seat!
It would have been easier to have bought a new one!
We're in clover!

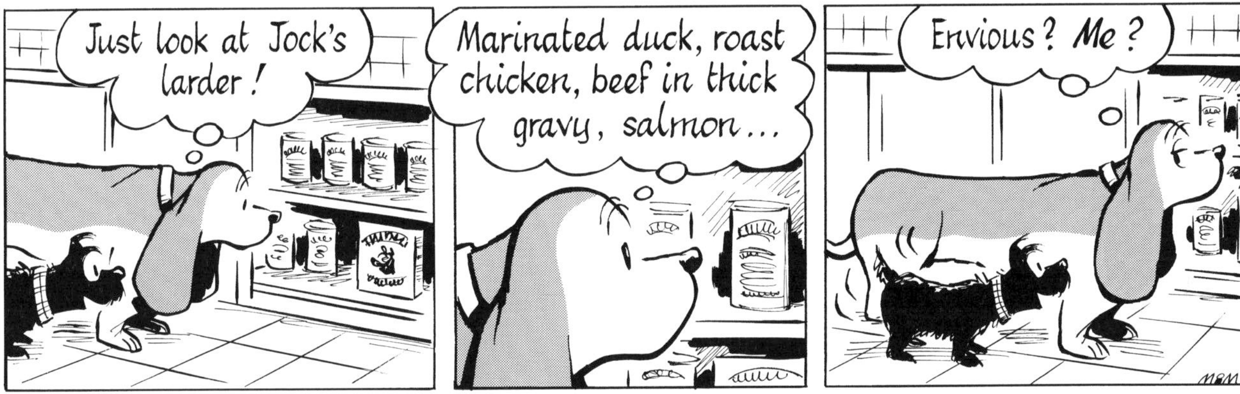

Just look at Jock's larder!
Marinated duck, roast chicken, beef in thick gravy, salmon...
Envious? Me?

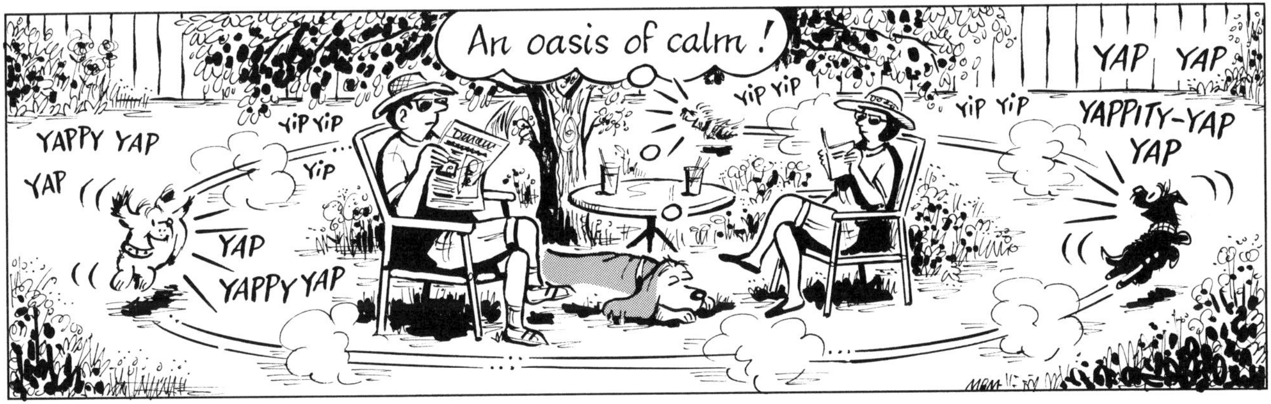

An oasis of calm!
YAPPY YAP
YAP
YAP
YAPPY YAP
YIP YIP
YIP
YIP YIP
YIP YIP
YAP YAP
YAPPITY-YAP
YAP

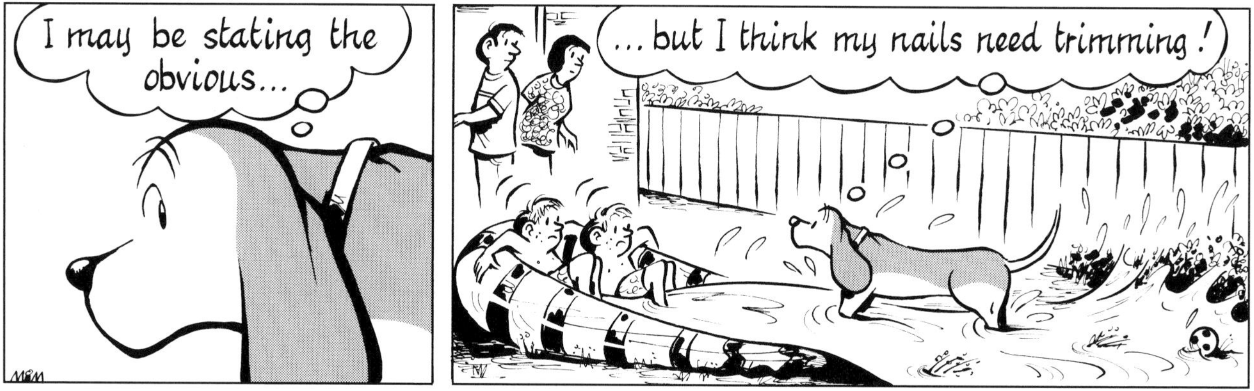
I may be stating the obvious...
MRM
... but I think my nails need trimming!

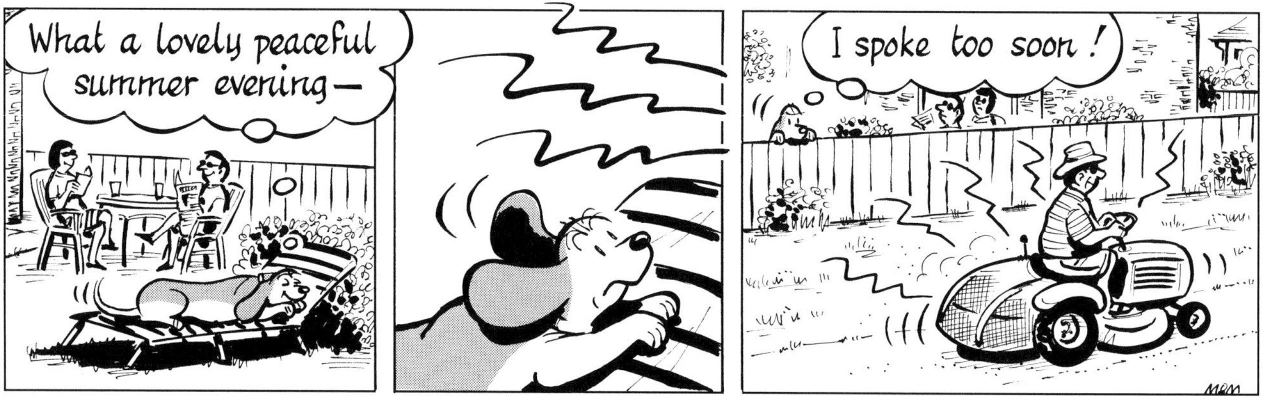
What a lovely peaceful summer evening—
I spoke too soon!
MRM

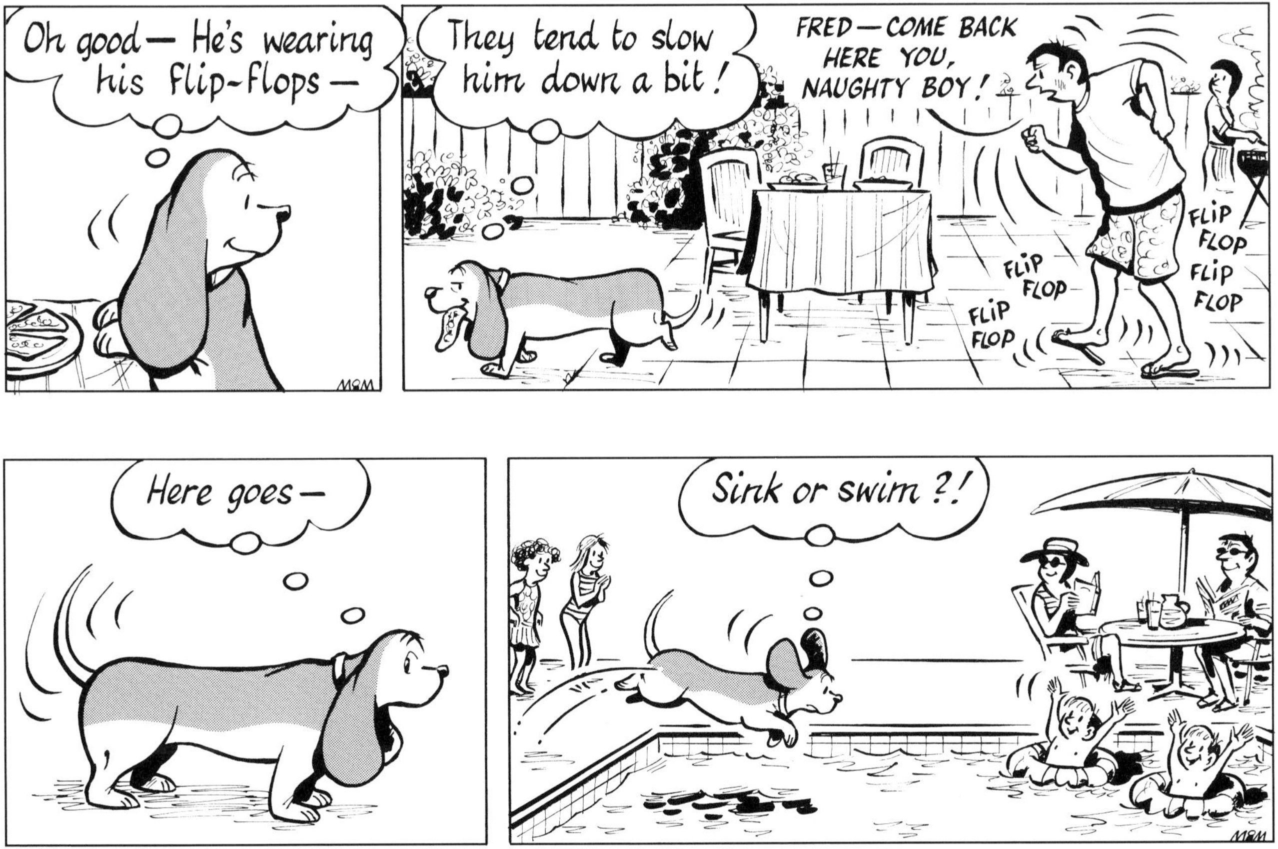
Oh good— He's wearing his flip-flops—
They tend to slow him down a bit!
FRED—COME BACK HERE YOU, NAUGHTY BOY!
FLIP FLOP
FLIP FLOP
FLIP FLOP
FLIP FLOP
FLIP FLOP
Here goes—
Sink or swim?!

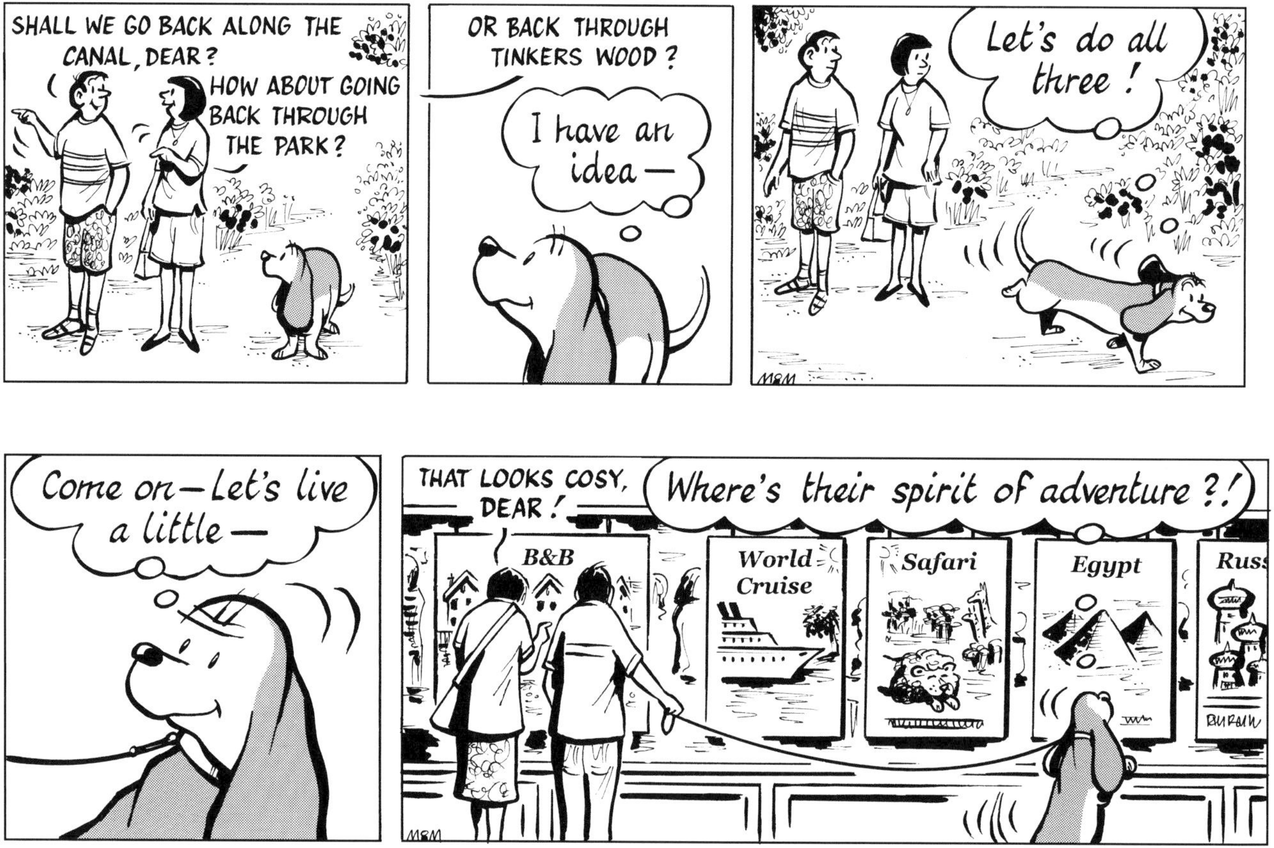
SHALL WE GO BACK ALONG THE CANAL, DEAR?
HOW ABOUT GOING BACK THROUGH THE PARK?
OR BACK THROUGH TINKERS WOOD?
I have an idea —
Let's do all three!
Come on — Let's live a little —
THAT LOOKS COSY, DEAR!
Where's their spirit of adventure?!
B&B
World Cruise
Safari
Egypt
Russ

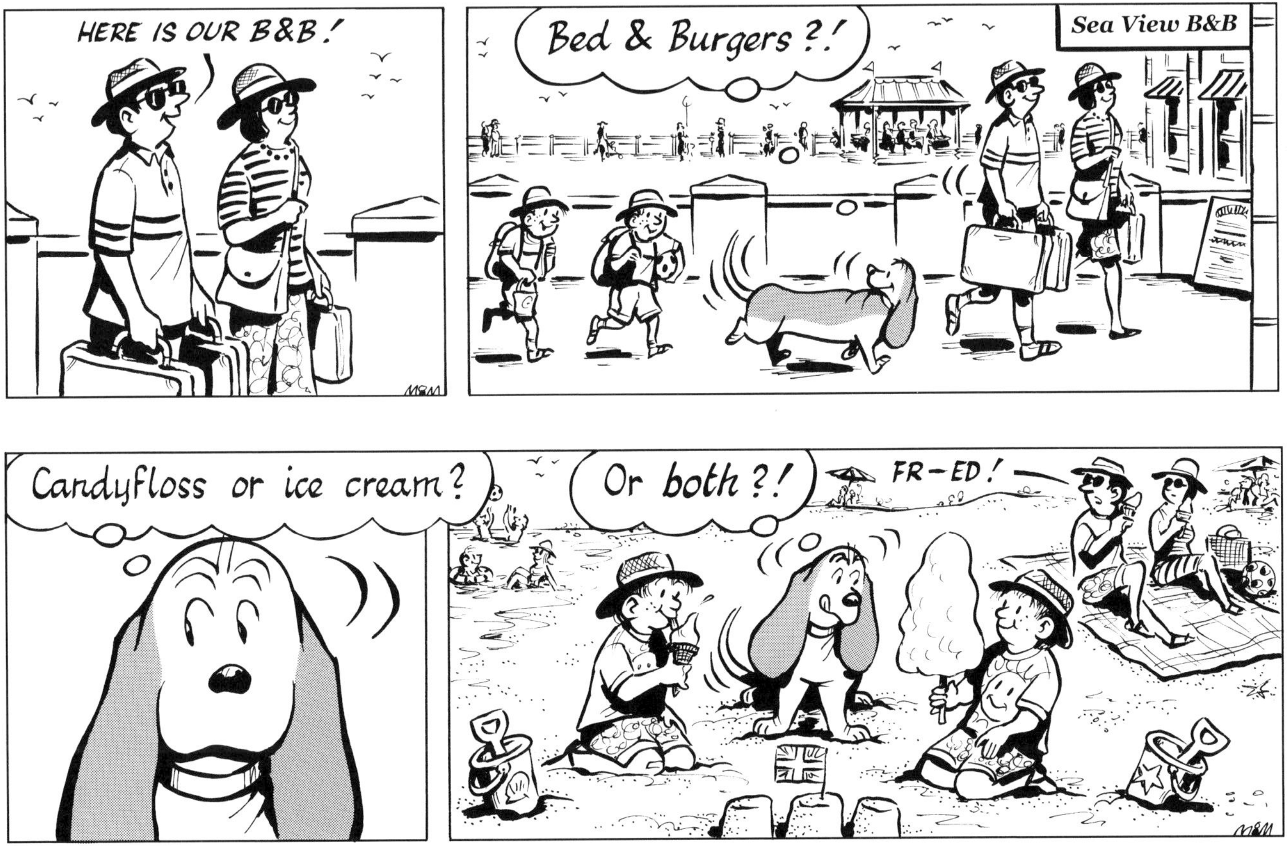
HERE IS OUR B&B!
Bed & Burgers?!
Sea View B&B
Candyfloss or ice cream?
Or both?!
FR–ED!

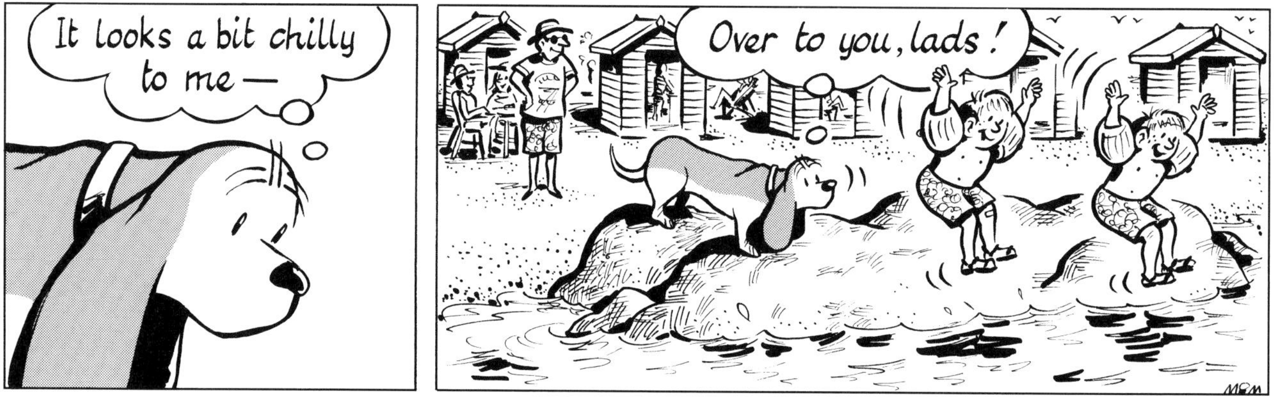
It looks a bit chilly to me—
Over to you, lads!

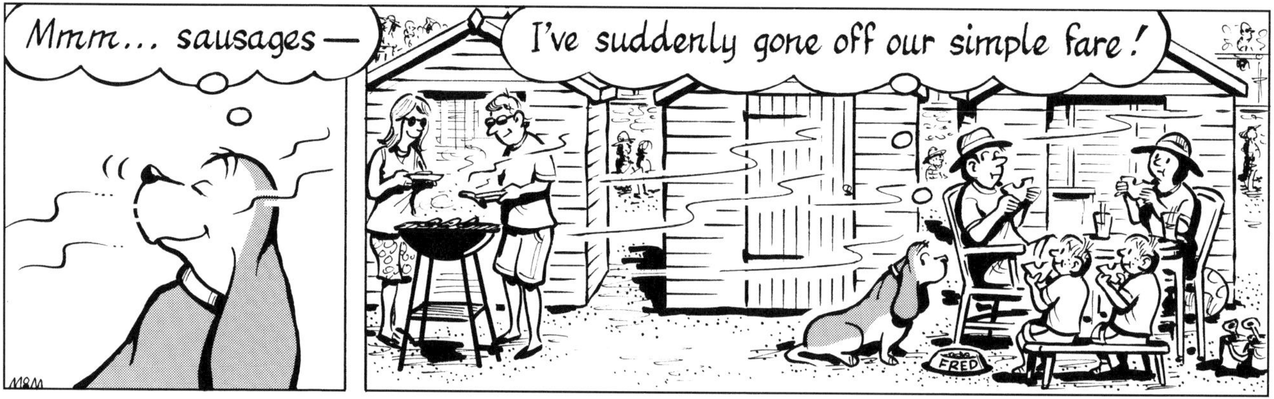
Mmm... sausages—
I've suddenly gone off our simple fare!
FRED

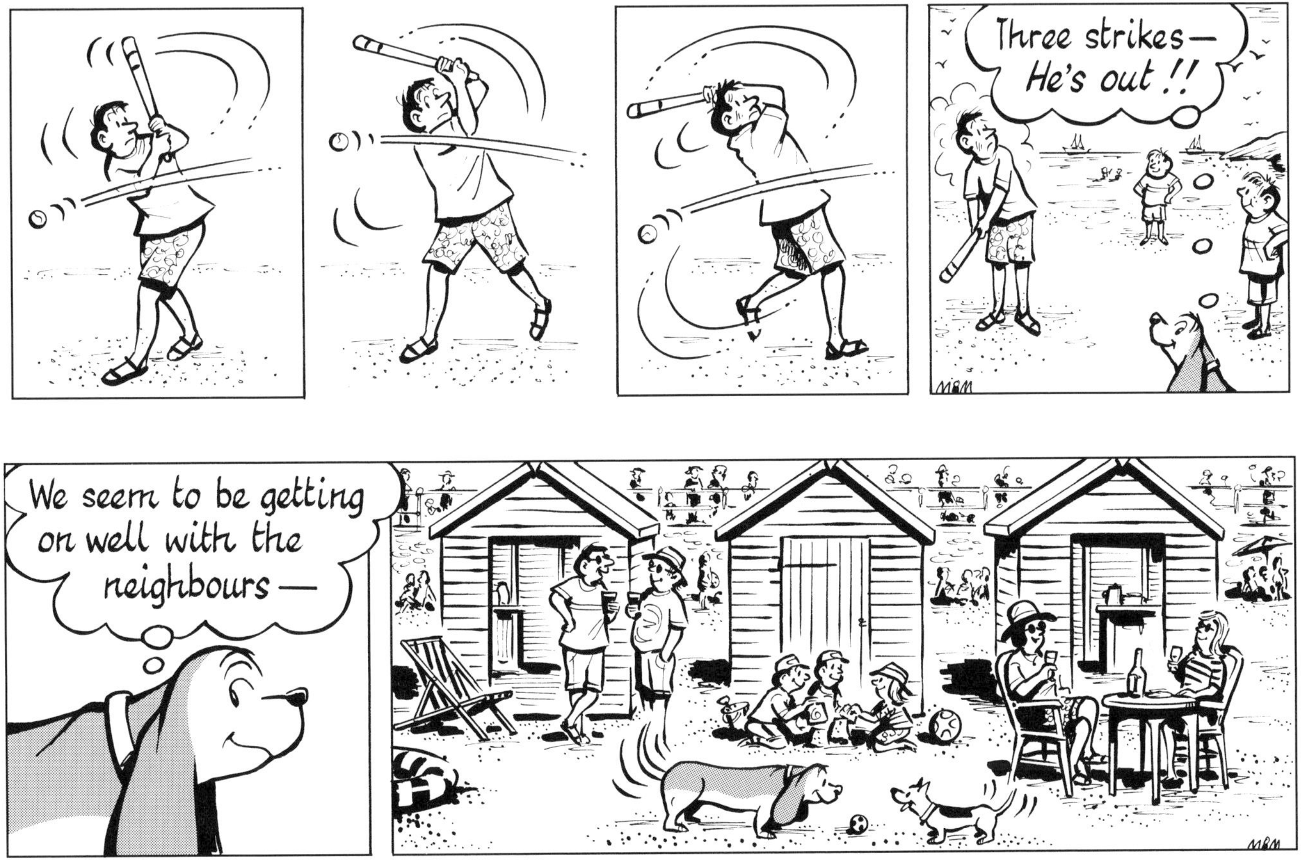
Three strikes—
He's out !!
We seem to be getting on well with the neighbours —

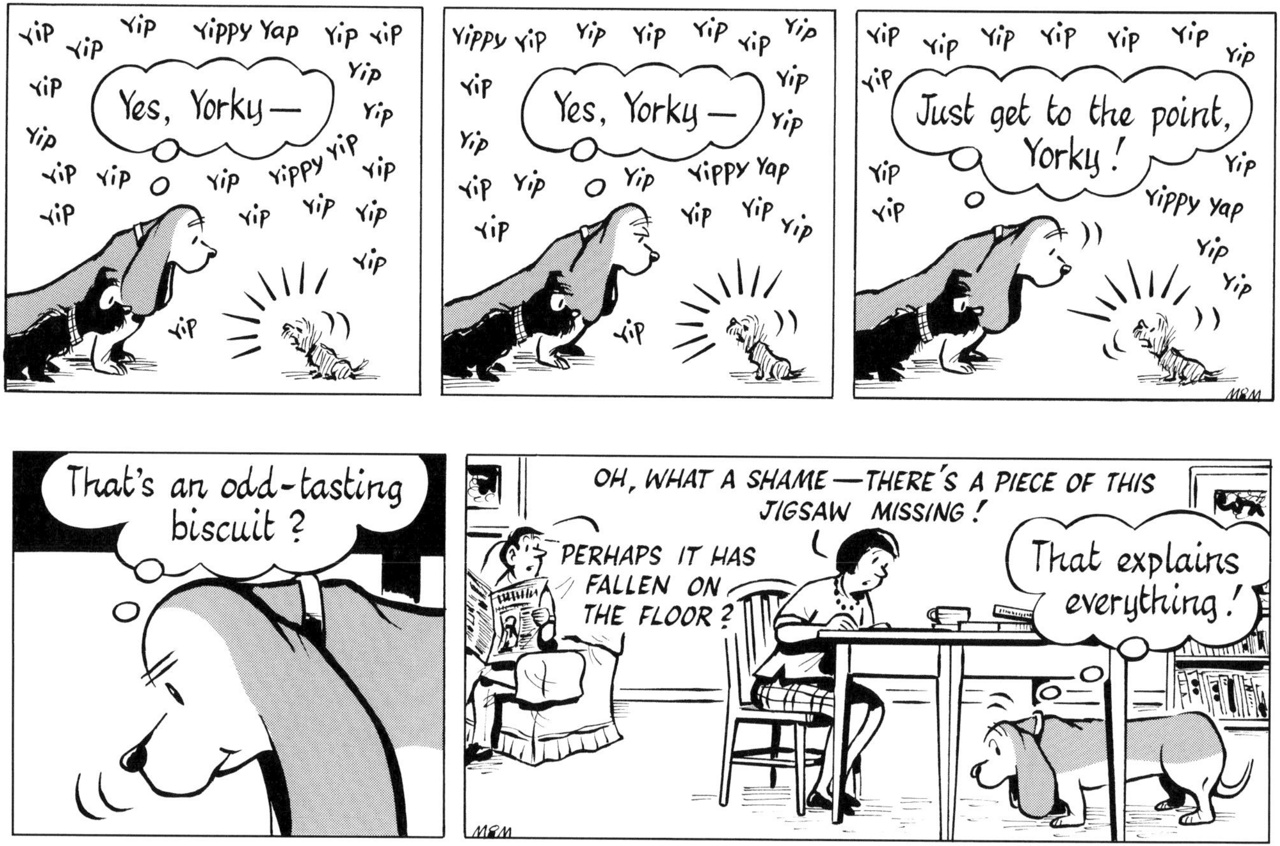

Yip Yip Yip Yippy Yap Yip Yip
Yip Yip Yip Yip
Yes, Yorky —
Yip Yip Yip Yip Yippy Yip Yip
Yip Yip Yip Yip Yip Yip
Yippy Yip Yip Yip Yip Yip Yip
Yip Yip Yip
Yes, Yorky —
Yip Yip Yip Yippy Yap
Yip Yip Yip Yip Yip
Yip Yip Yip Yip Yip Yip Yip
Yip
Just get to the point, Yorky !
Yip Yip Yip
Yippy Yap
Yip Yip
M&M
That's an odd-tasting biscuit ?
OH, WHAT A SHAME — THERE'S A PIECE OF THIS JIGSAW MISSING !
PERHAPS IT HAS FALLEN ON THE FLOOR ?
That explains everything !
M&M

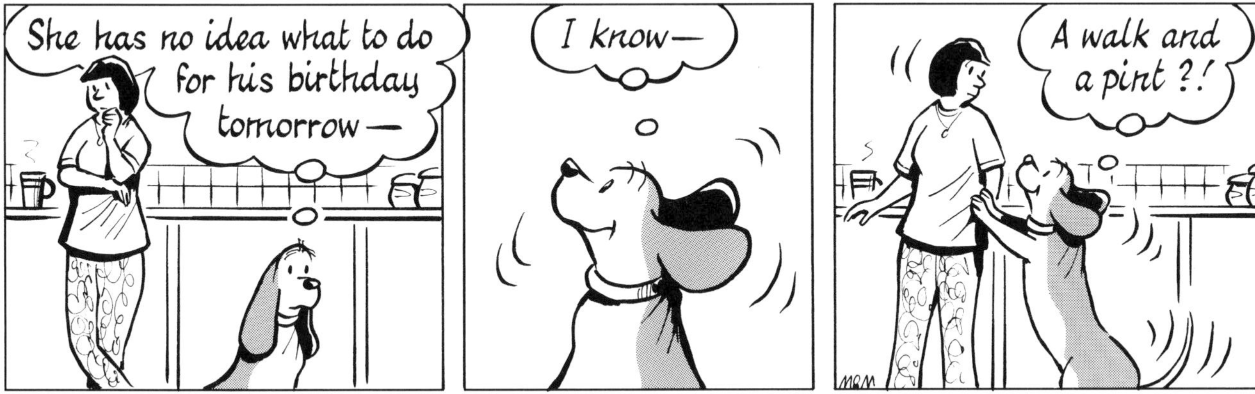
She has no idea what to do for his birthday tomorrow —
I know —
A walk and a pint ?!

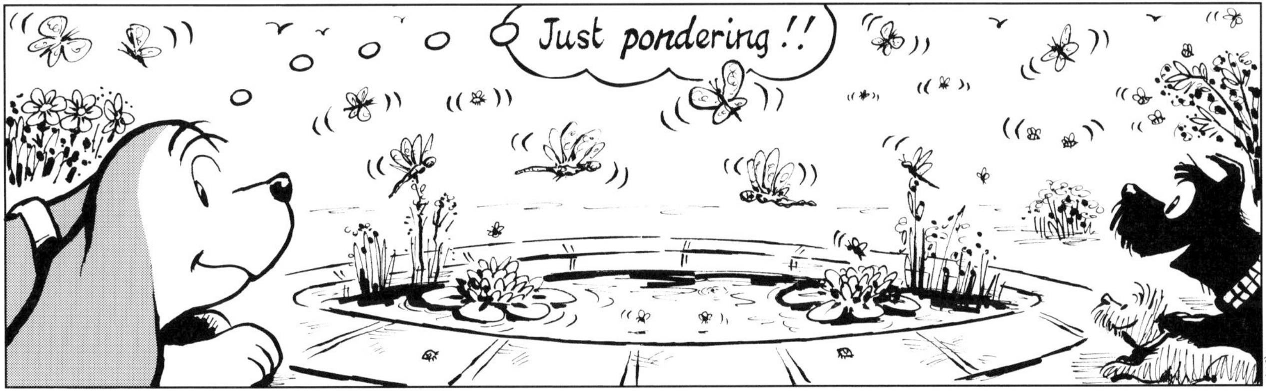
Just *pondering* !!

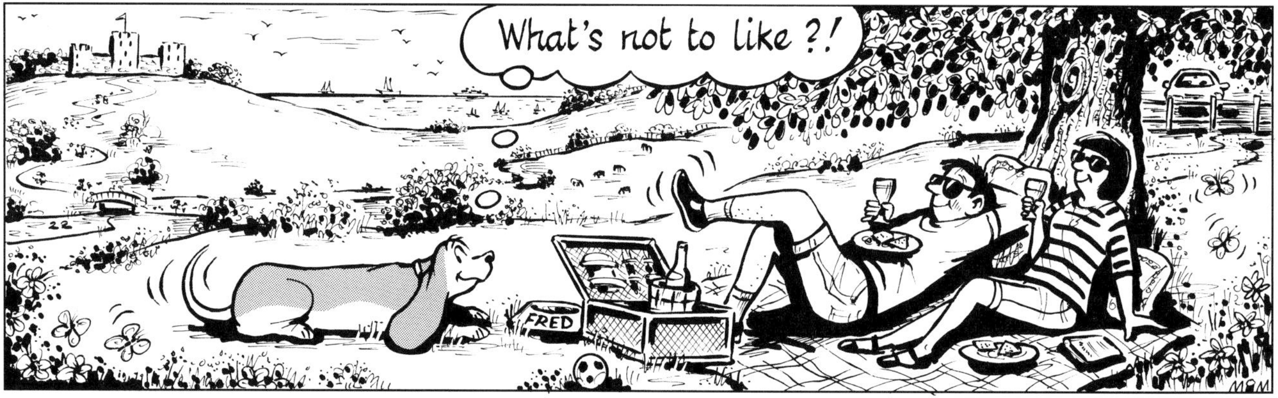
What's not to like ?!
FRED

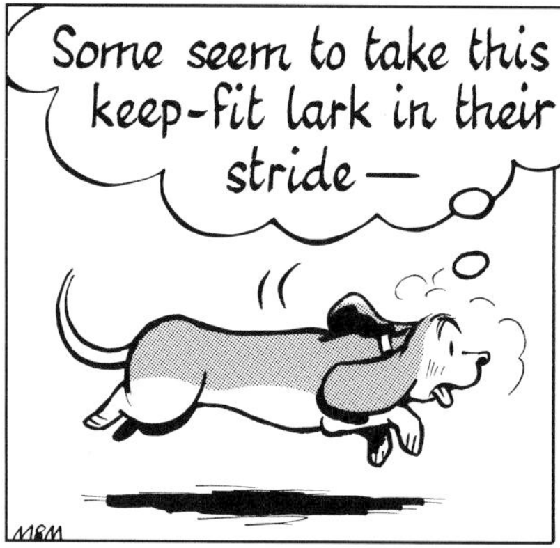
Some seem to take this keep-fit lark in their stride —

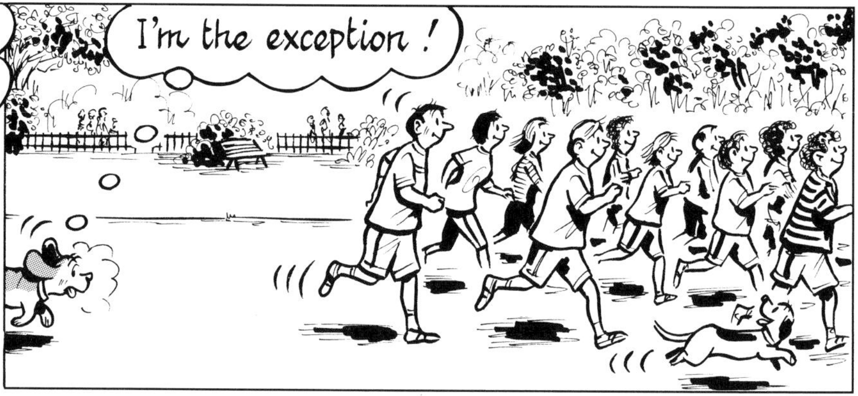
I'm the exception !

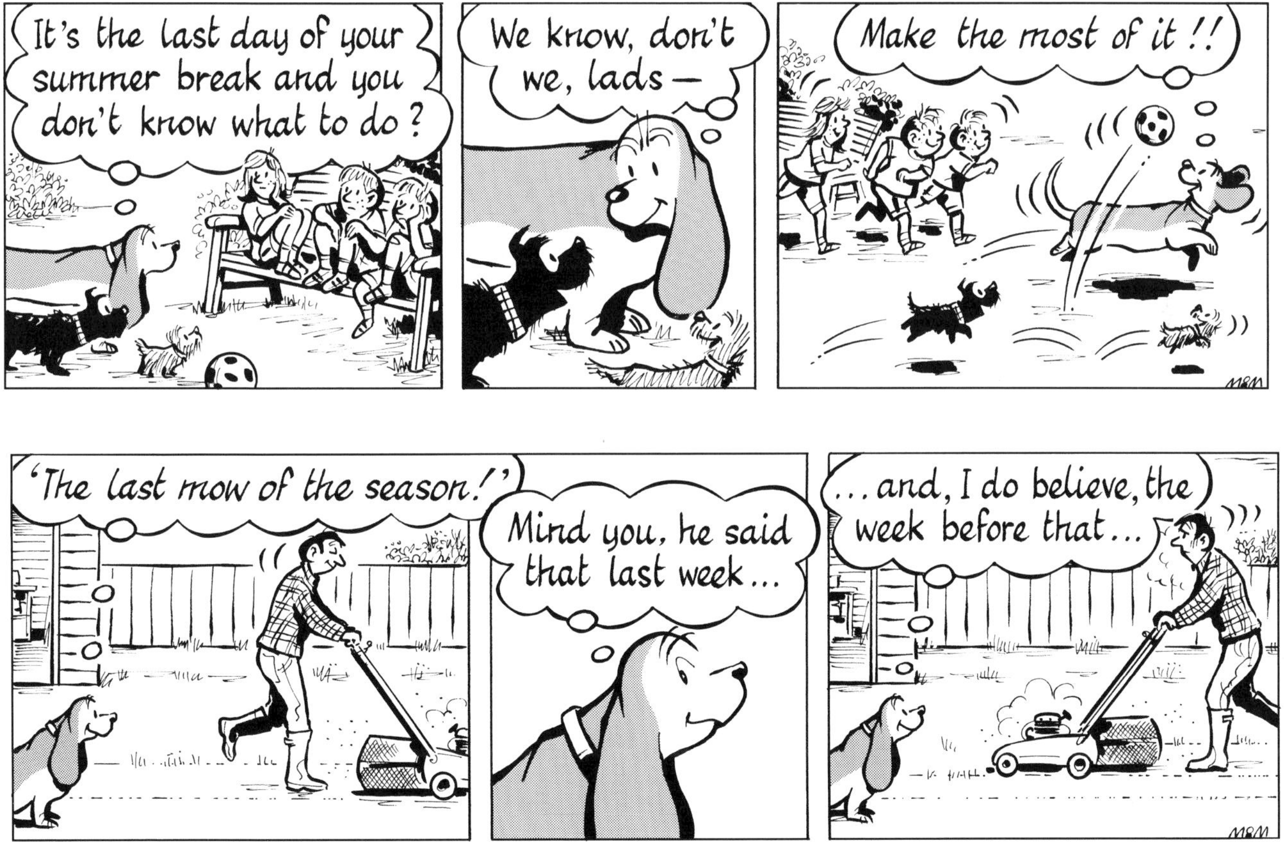
It's the last day of your summer break and you don't know what to do?
We know, don't we, lads –
Make the most of it!!
'The last mow of the season!'
Mind you, he said that last week...
...and, I do believe, the week before that...
M&M
M&M

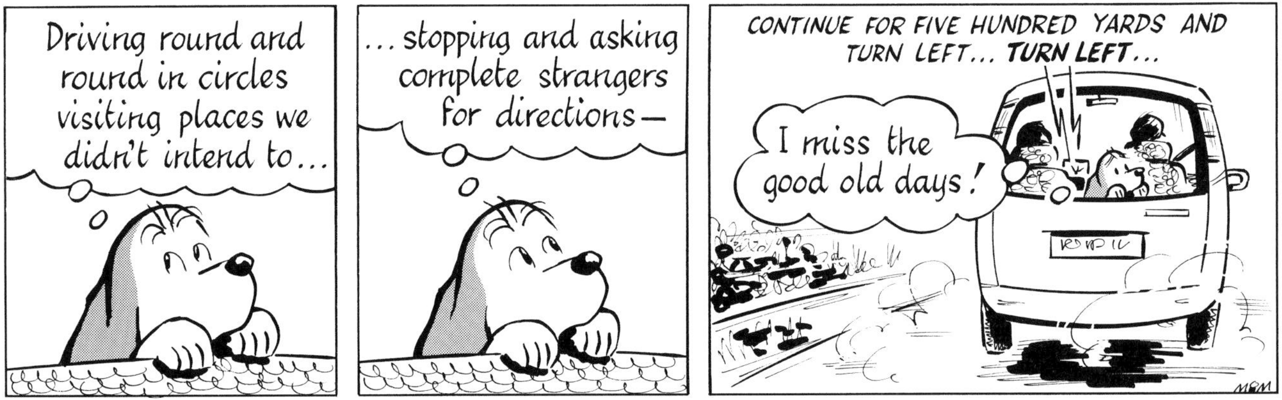
Driving round and round in circles visiting places we didn't intend to...
... stopping and asking complete strangers for directions—
CONTINUE FOR FIVE HUNDRED YARDS AND TURN LEFT... TURN LEFT...
I miss the good old days!

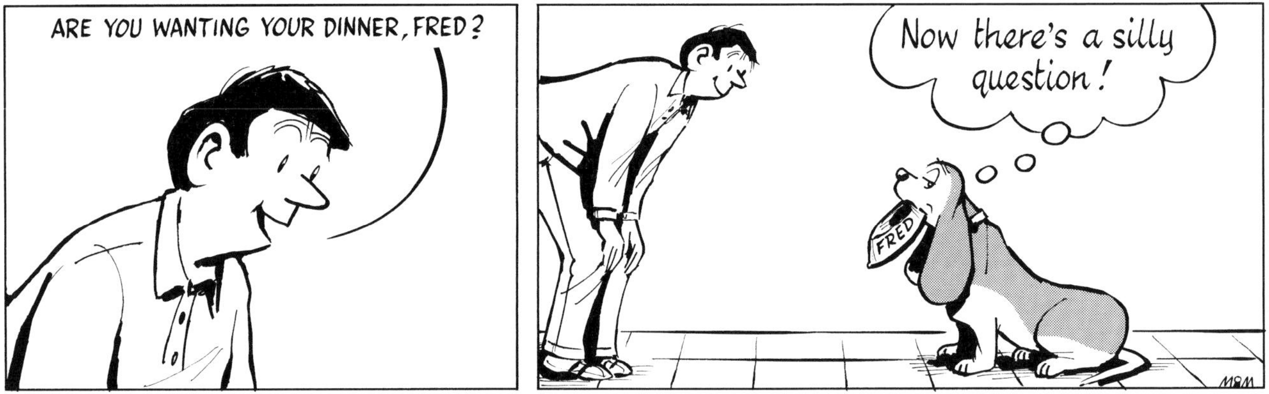
ARE YOU WANTING YOUR DINNER, FRED?
Now there's a silly question!
FRED

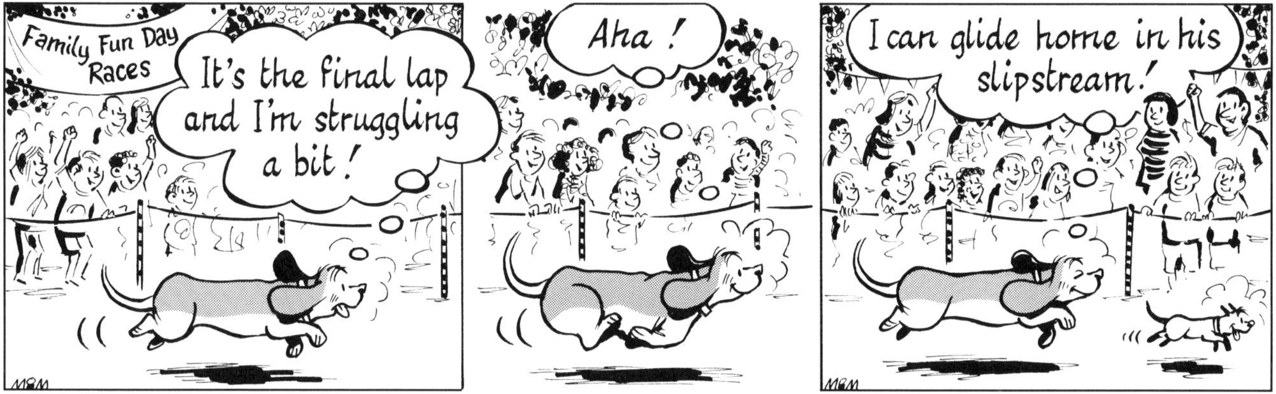
Family Fun Day Races
It's the final lap and I'm struggling a bit!
Aha!
I can glide home in his slipstream!

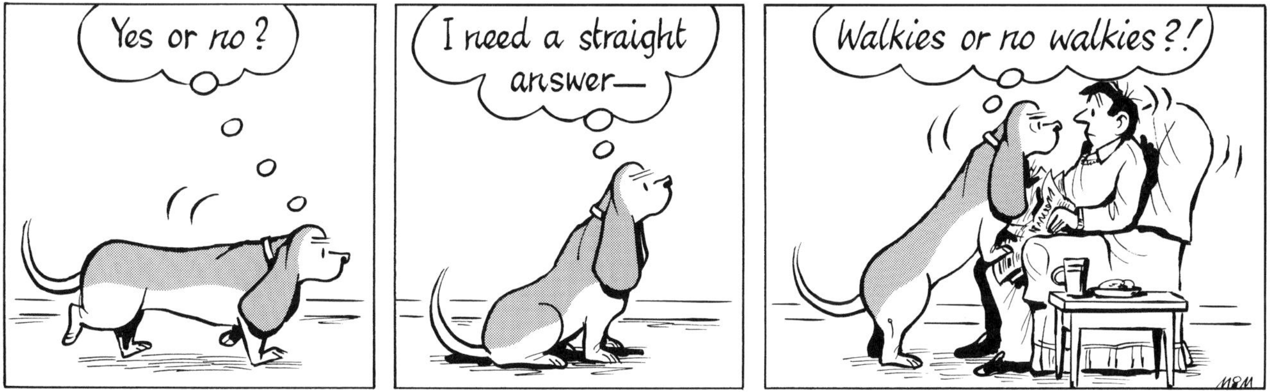
Yes or no?
I need a straight answer—
Walkies or no walkies?!

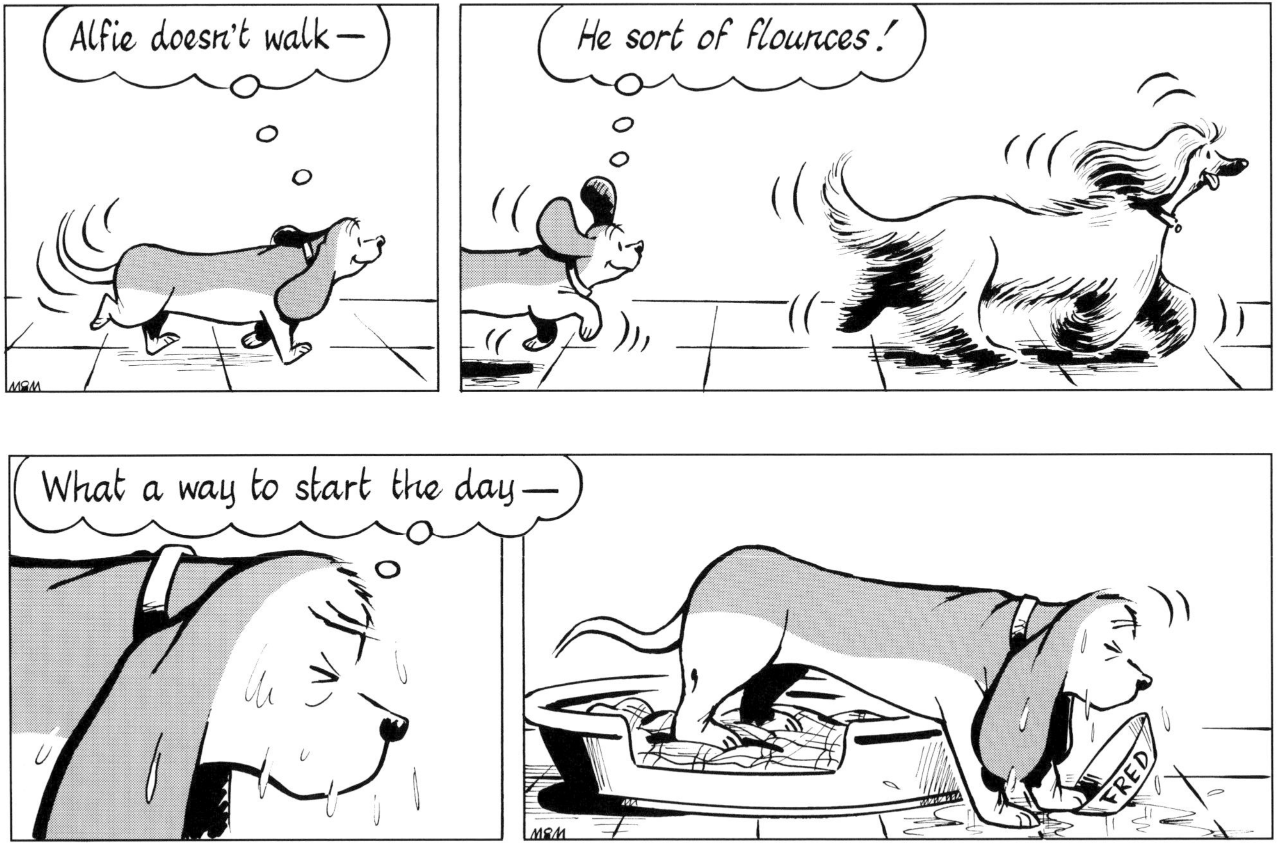
Alfie doesn't walk—
He sort of flounces!
What a way to start the day—
FRED

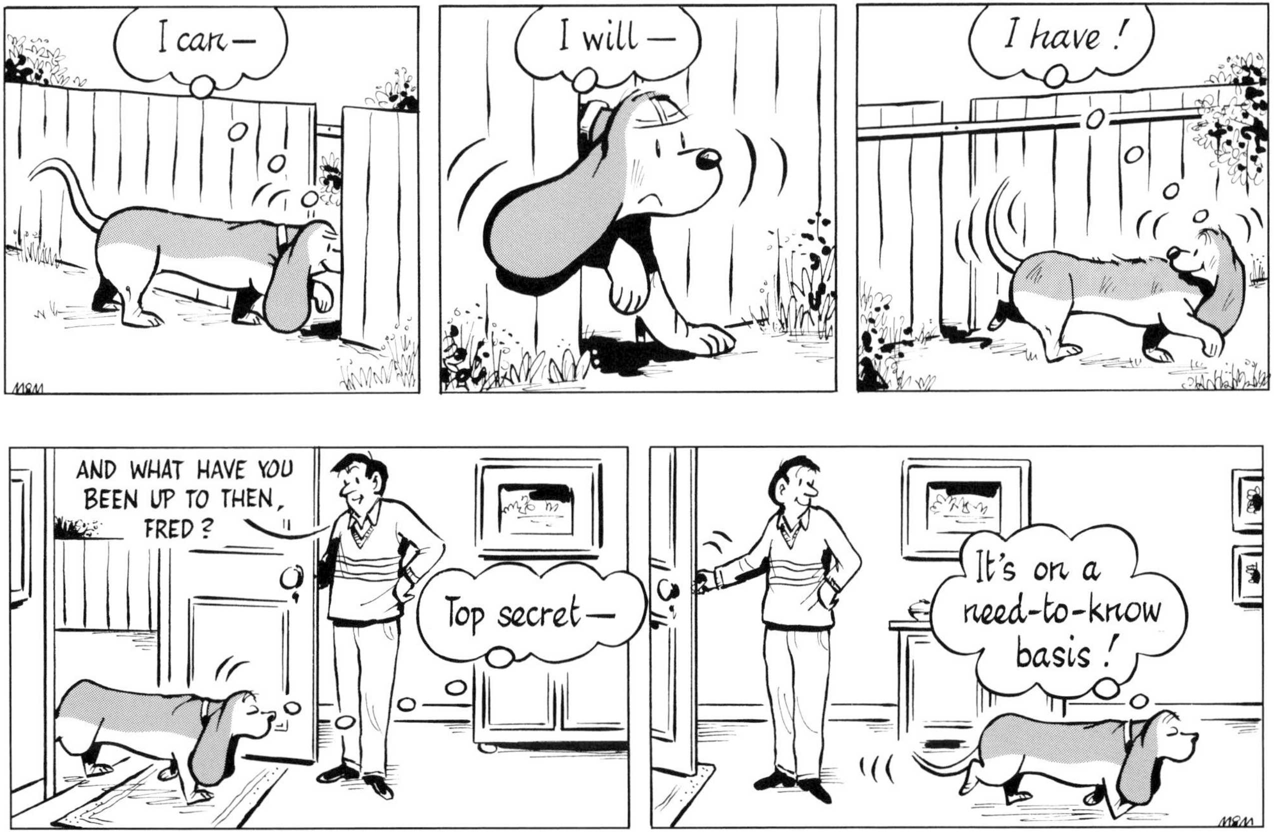
I can—
I will—
I have!
AND WHAT HAVE YOU BEEN UP TO THEN, FRED?
Top secret—
It's on a need-to-know basis!

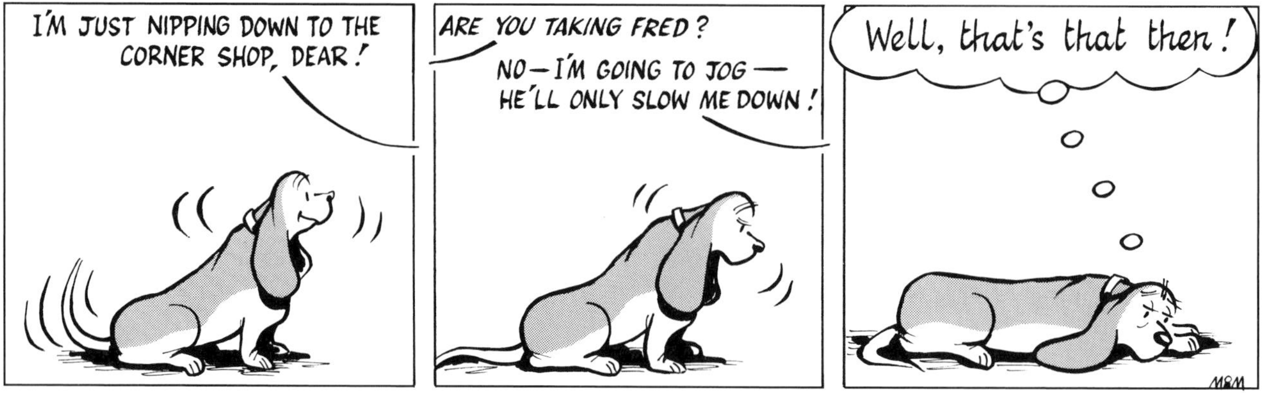
I'M JUST NIPPING DOWN TO THE CORNER SHOP, DEAR!
ARE YOU TAKING FRED?
NO—I'M GOING TO JOG—HE'LL ONLY SLOW ME DOWN!
Well, that's that then!

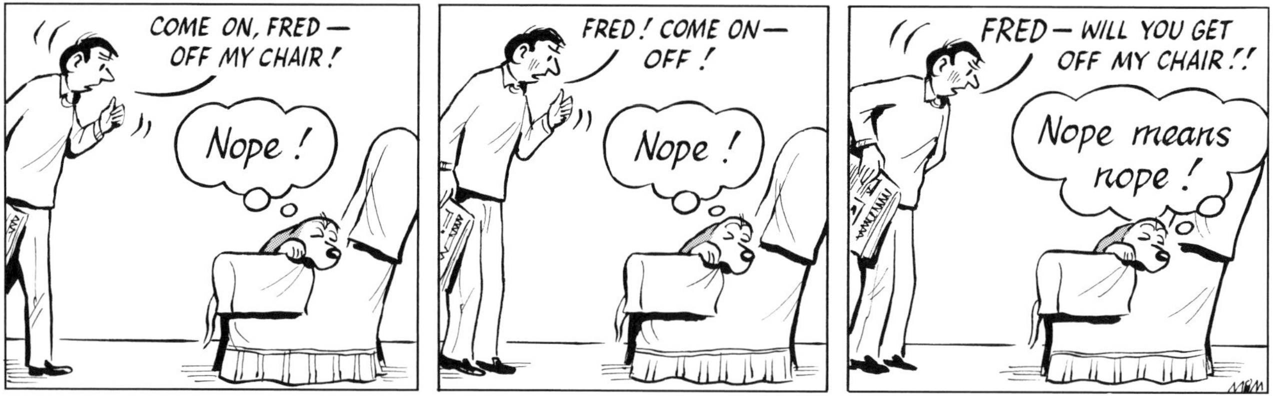
COME ON, FRED—OFF MY CHAIR!
Nope!
FRED! COME ON—OFF!
Nope!
FRED—WILL YOU GET OFF MY CHAIR!!
Nope means nope!

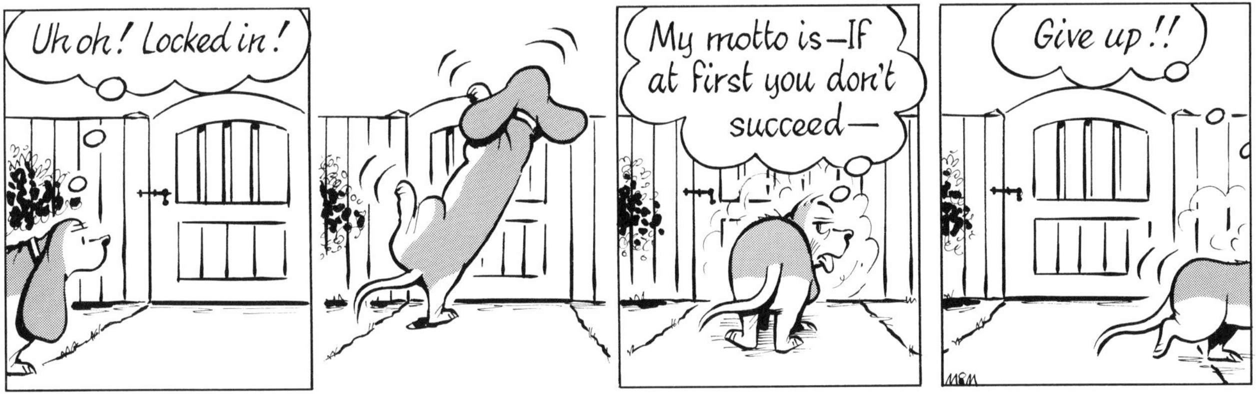
Uh oh! Locked in!
My motto is—If at first you don't succeed—
Give up!!
M&M

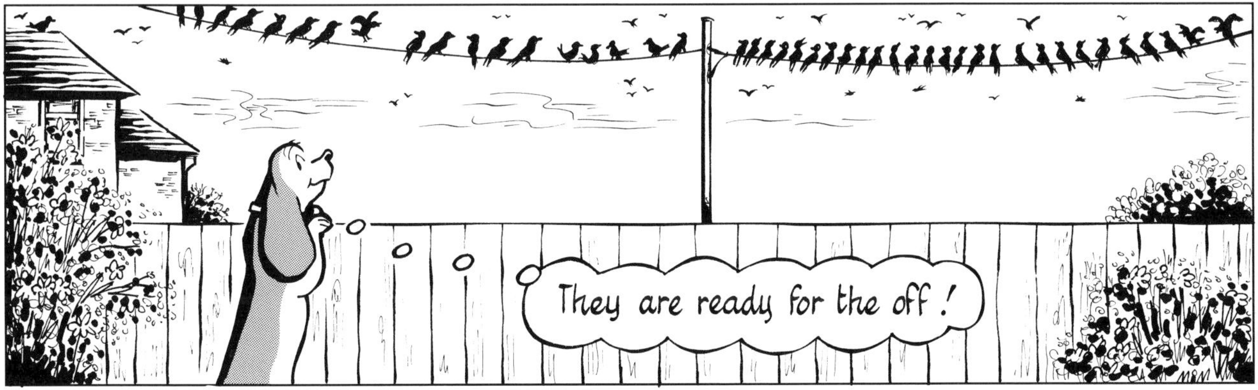
They are ready for the off!
M&M

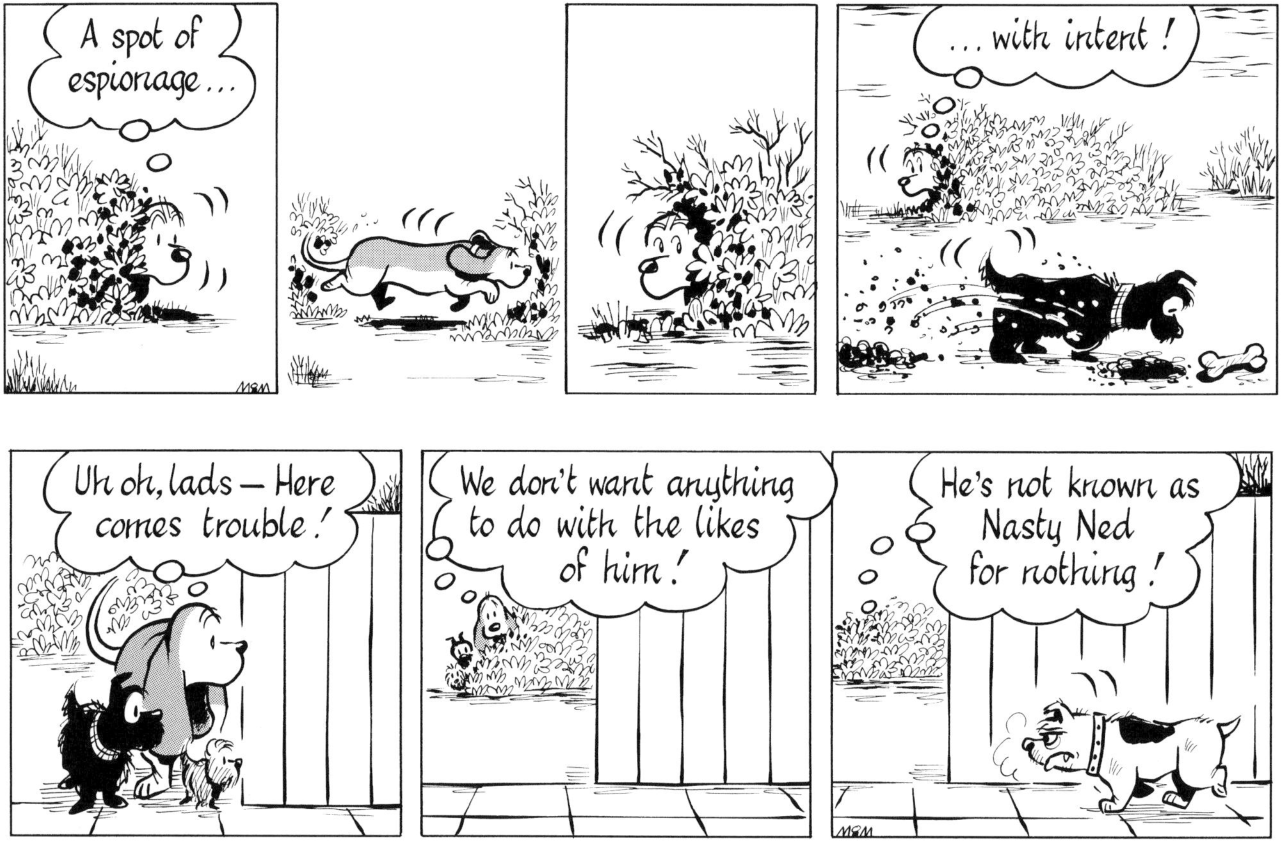
A spot of espionage . . .
. . . with intent !
Uh oh, lads – Here comes trouble !
We don't want anything to do with the likes of him !
He's not known as Nasty Ned for nothing !

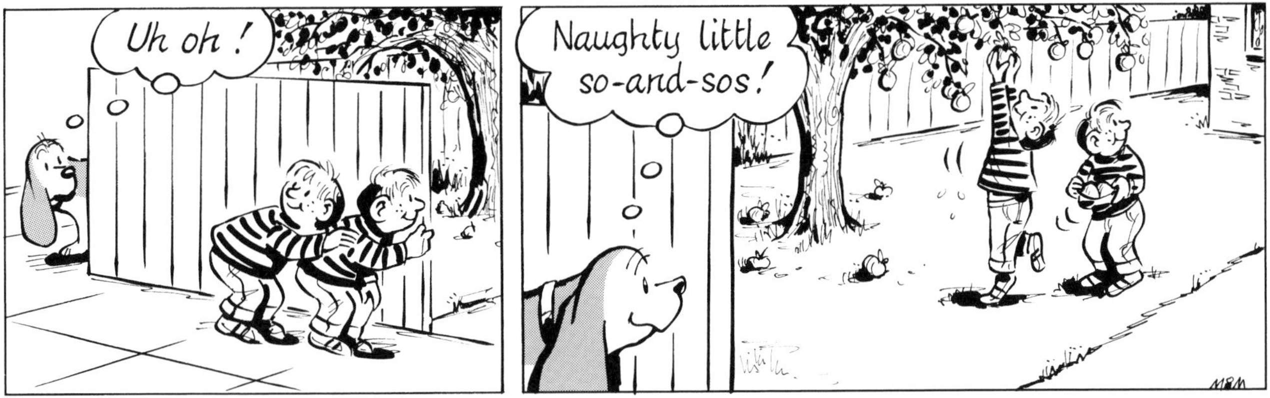
Uh oh !
Naughty little so-and-sos !
MGM

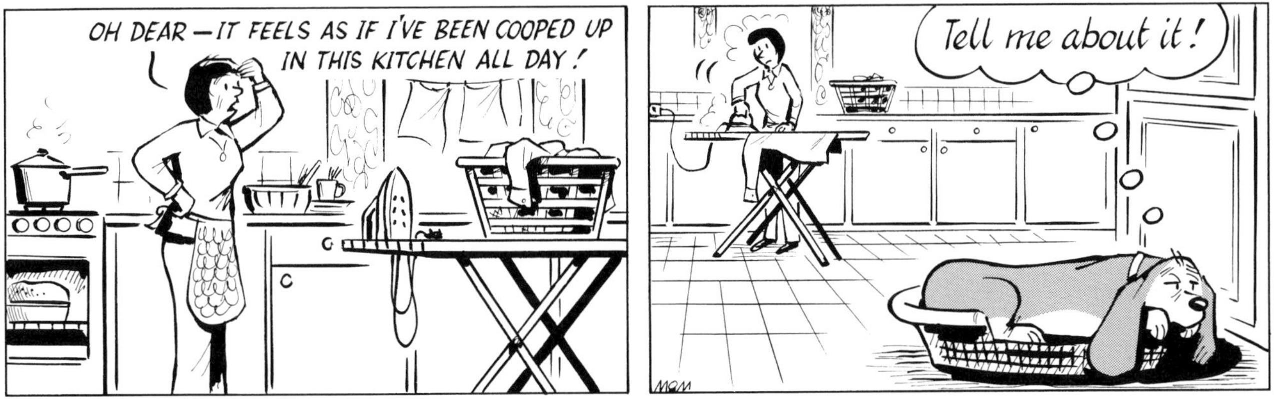
OH DEAR—IT FEELS AS IF I'VE BEEN COOPED UP IN THIS KITCHEN ALL DAY !
Tell me about it !
MGM

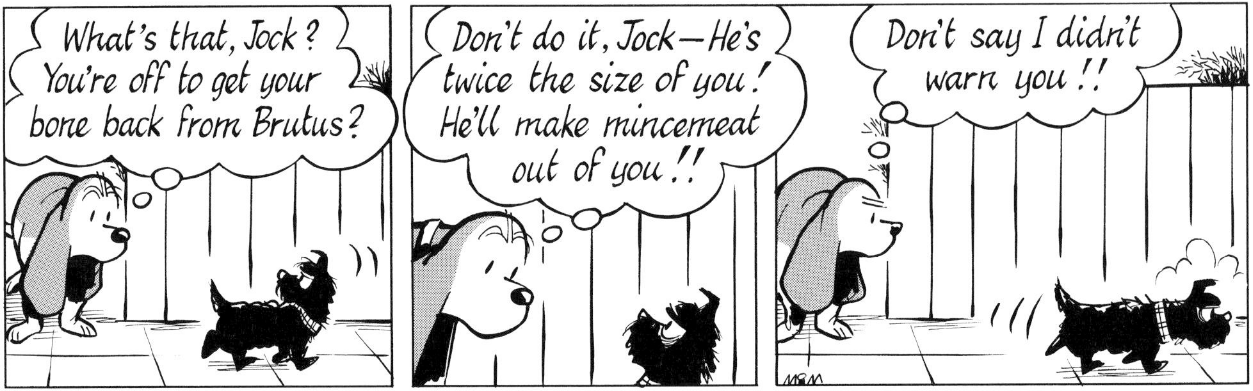
What's that, Jock? You're off to get your bone back from Brutus?
Don't do it, Jock—He's twice the size of you! He'll make mincemeat out of you!!
Don't say I didn't warn you!!

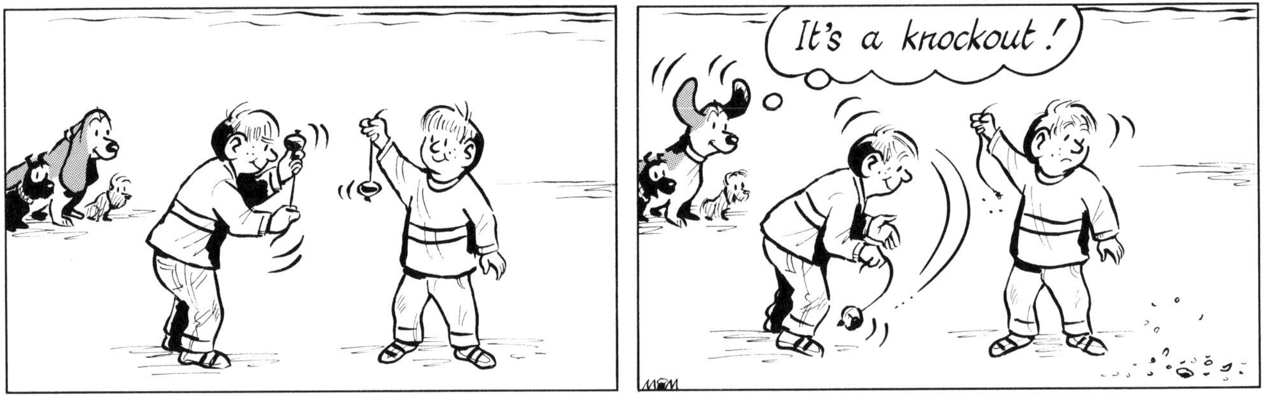
It's a knockout!

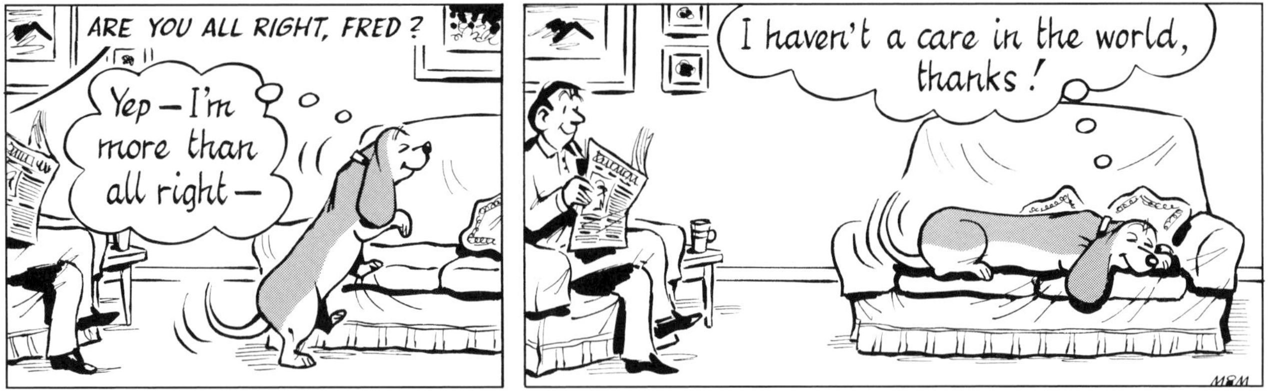
ARE YOU ALL RIGHT, FRED ?
Yep — I'm more than all right —
I haven't a care in the world, thanks !

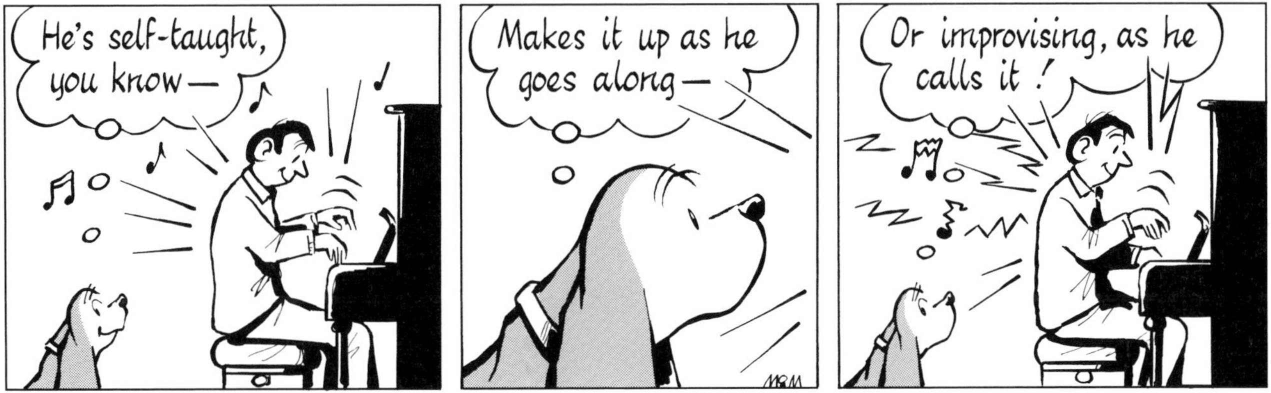
He's self-taught, you know —
Makes it up as he goes along —
Or improvising, as he calls it !

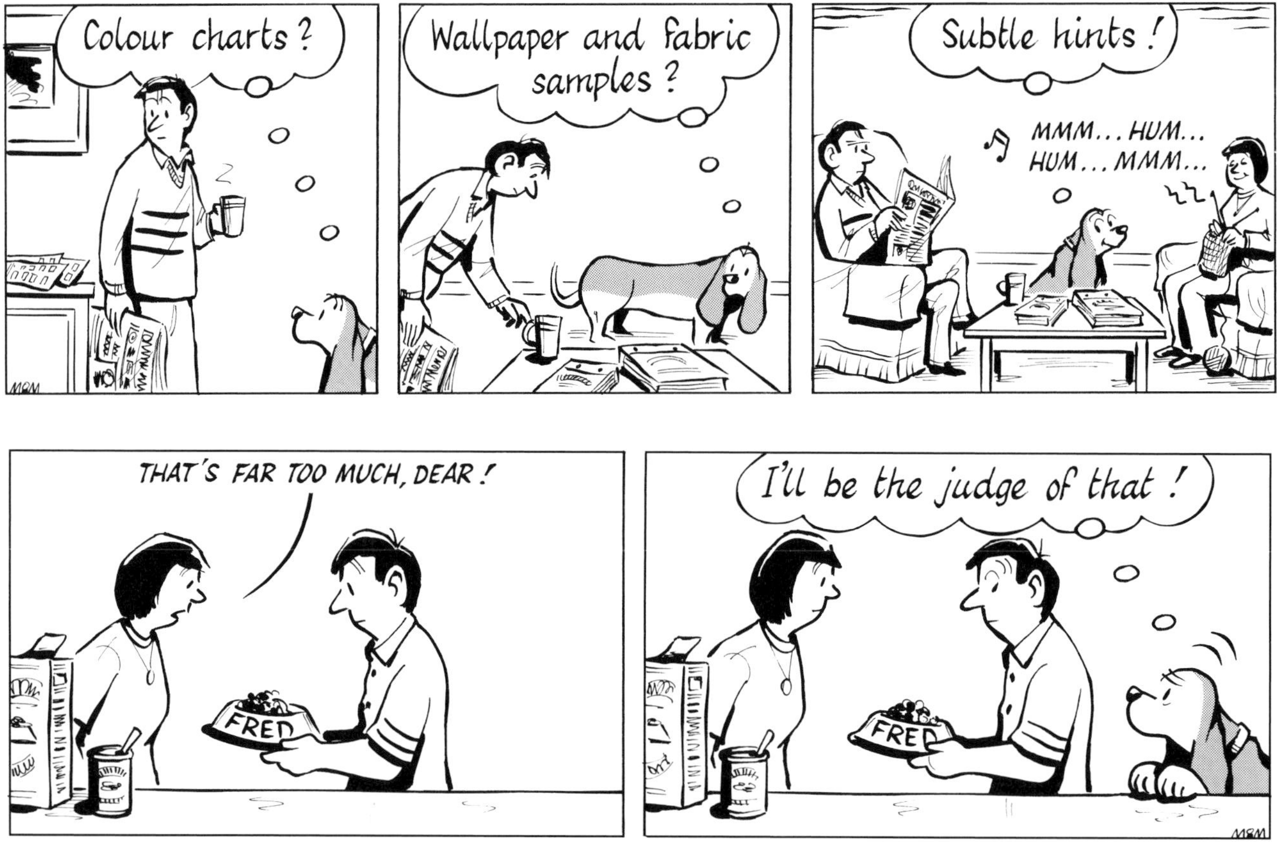
Colour charts?
Wallpaper and fabric samples?
Subtle hints!
MMM... HUM... HUM... MMM...
THAT'S FAR TOO MUCH, DEAR!
FRED
I'll be the judge of that!
FRED

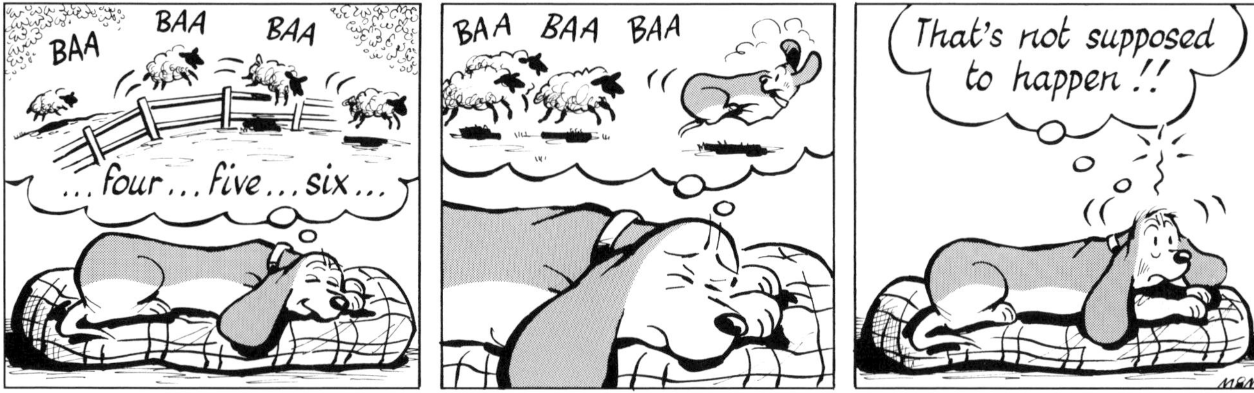
BAA
BAA
BAA
...four...five...six...
BAA BAA BAA
That's not supposed to happen!!
MRM

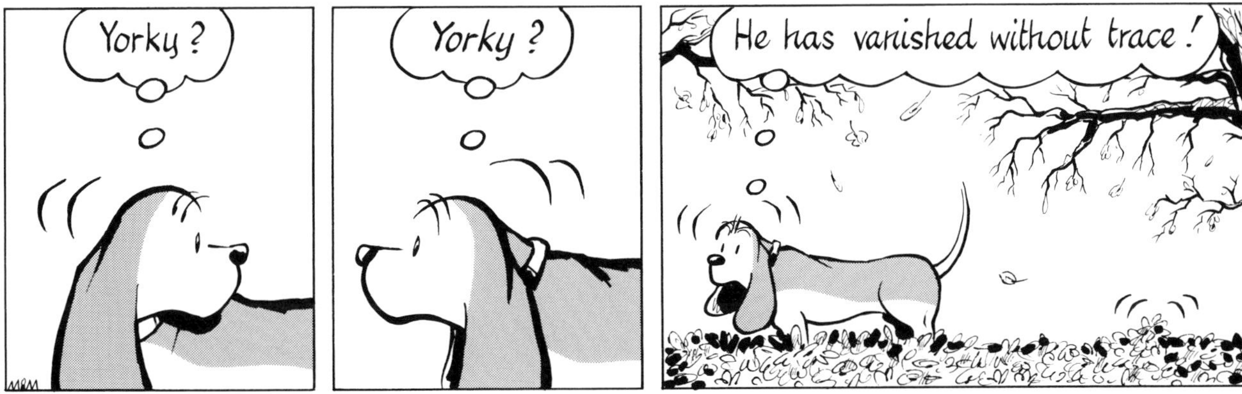
Yorky?
Yorky?
He has vanished without trace!
MRM

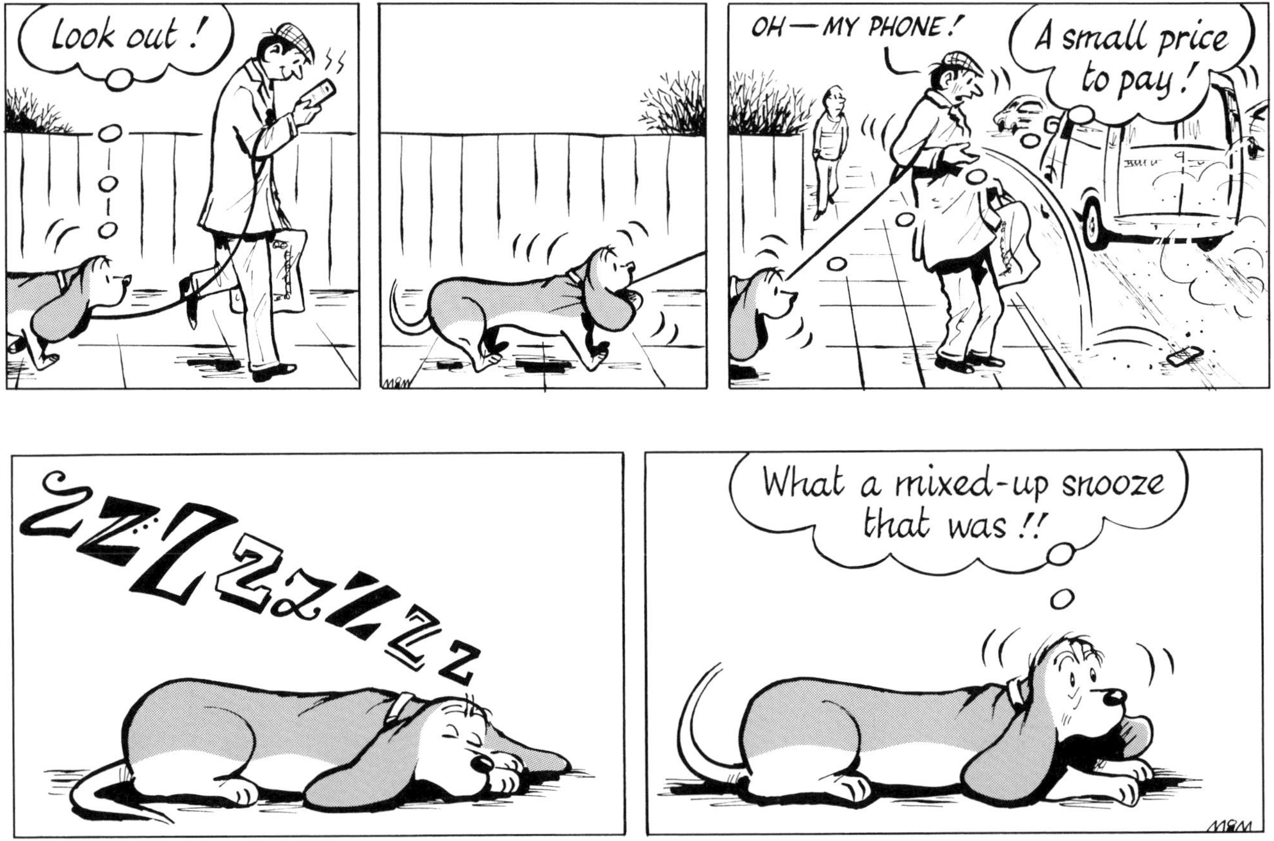

Look out !
OH — MY PHONE !
A small price to pay !
What a mixed-up snooze that was !!

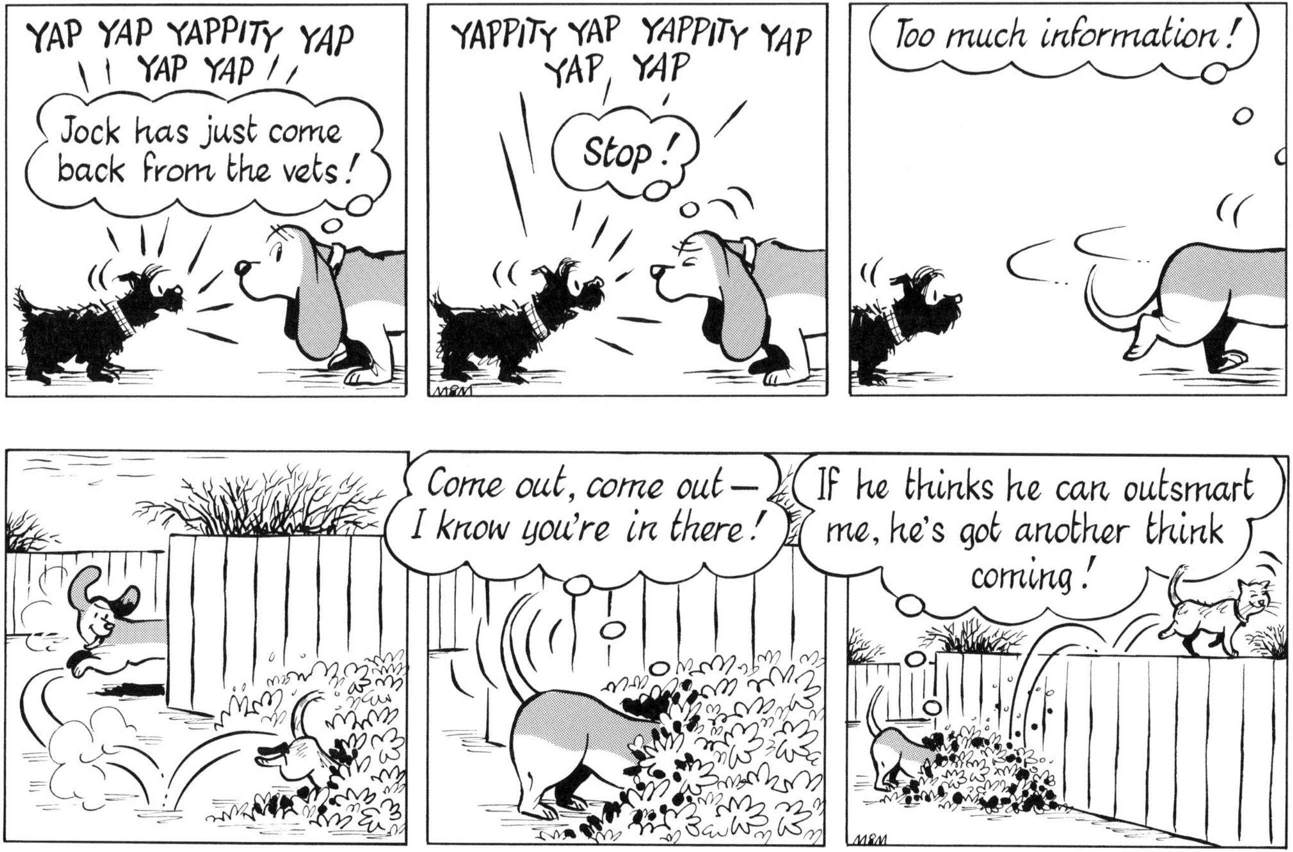
YAP YAP YAPPITY YAP
YAP YAP
Jock has just come back from the vets!
YAPPITY YAP YAPPITY YAP
YAP, YAP
Stop!
Too much information!
Come out, come out — I know you're in there!
If he thinks he can outsmart me, he's got another think coming!

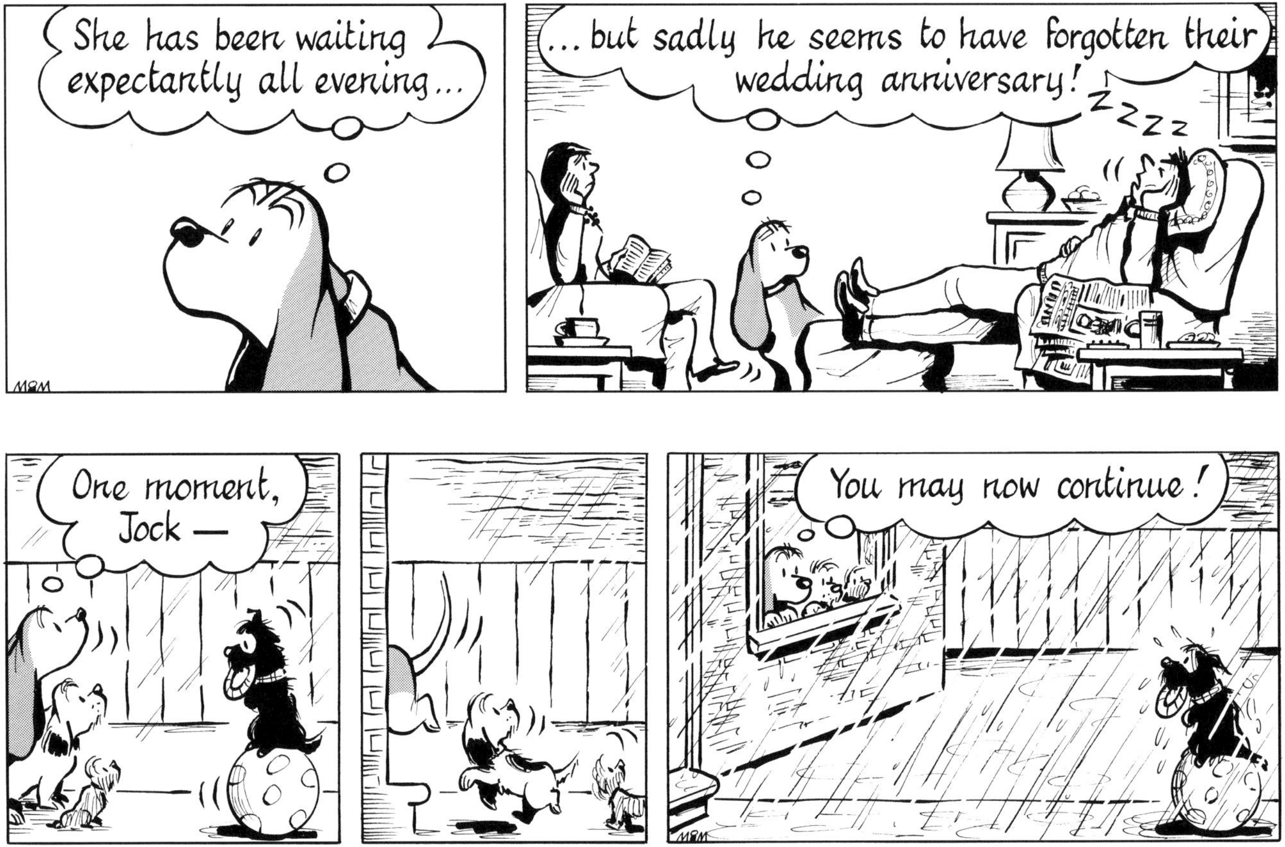
She has been waiting expectantly all evening...
MSM
... but sadly he seems to have forgotten their wedding anniversary!
ZZZZ
One moment, Jock —
You may now continue!
MSM

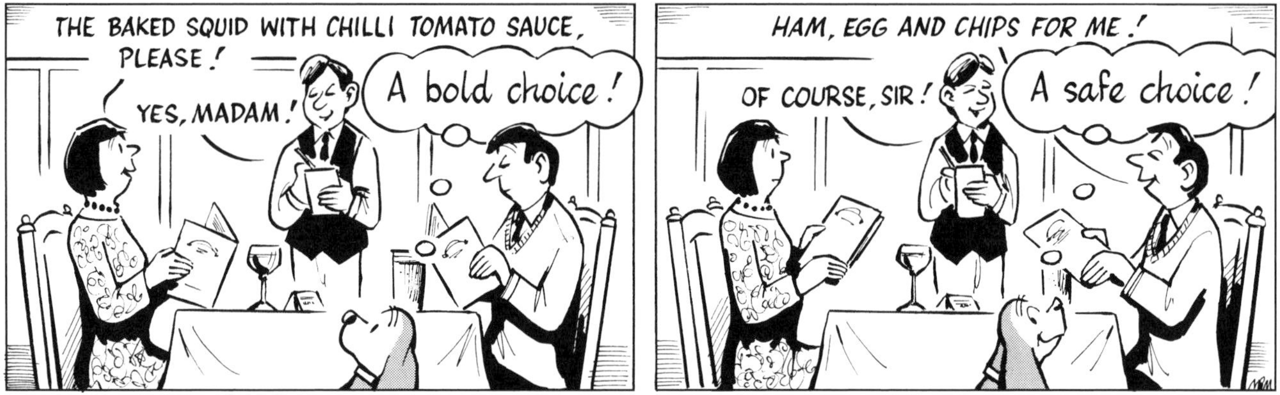
THE BAKED SQUID WITH CHILLI TOMATO SAUCE, PLEASE!
YES, MADAM!
A bold choice!
HAM, EGG AND CHIPS FOR ME!
OF COURSE, SIR!
A safe choice!

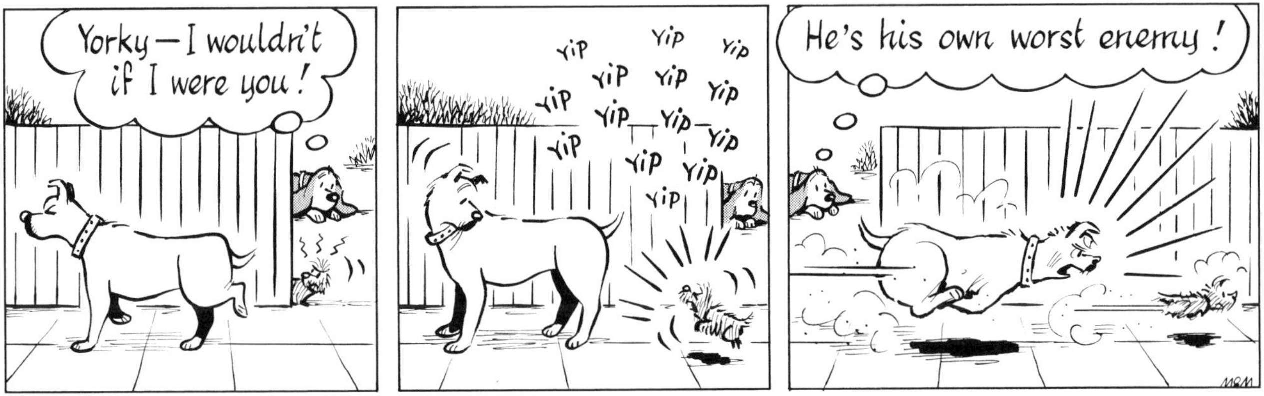
Yorky — I wouldn't if I were you!
YIP YIP YIP YIP YIP YIP YIP YIP YIP YIP YIP YIP YIP YIP
He's his own worst enemy!

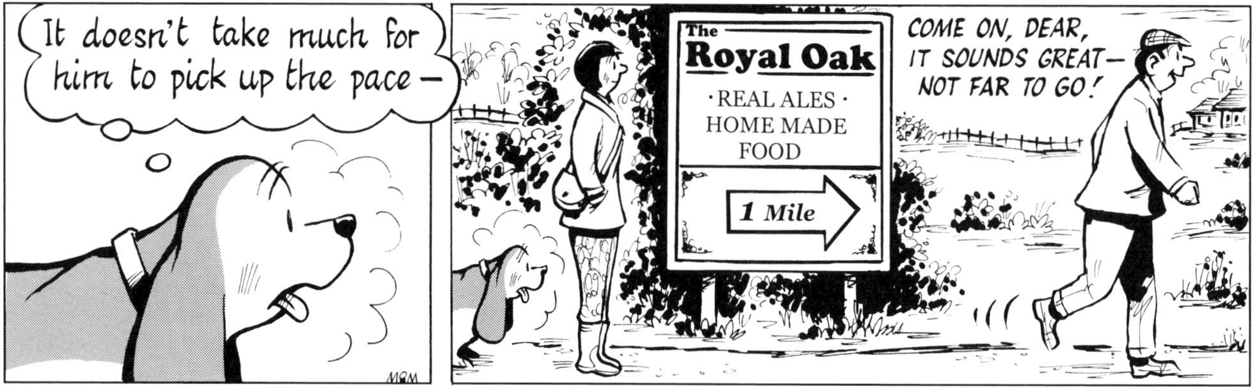
It doesn't take much for him to pick up the pace –
The Royal Oak
· REAL ALES ·
HOME MADE FOOD
1 Mile
COME ON, DEAR, IT SOUNDS GREAT – NOT FAR TO GO!

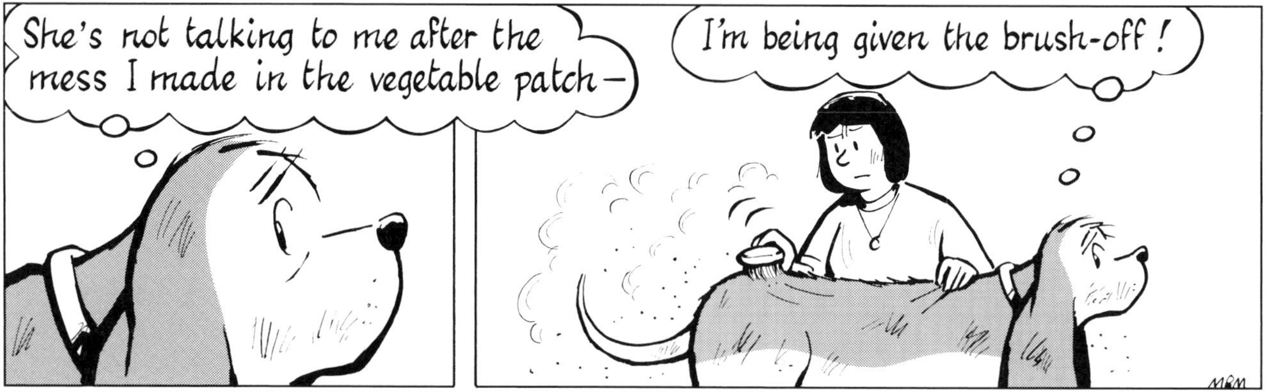
She's not talking to me after the mess I made in the vegetable patch –
I'm being given the brush-off!

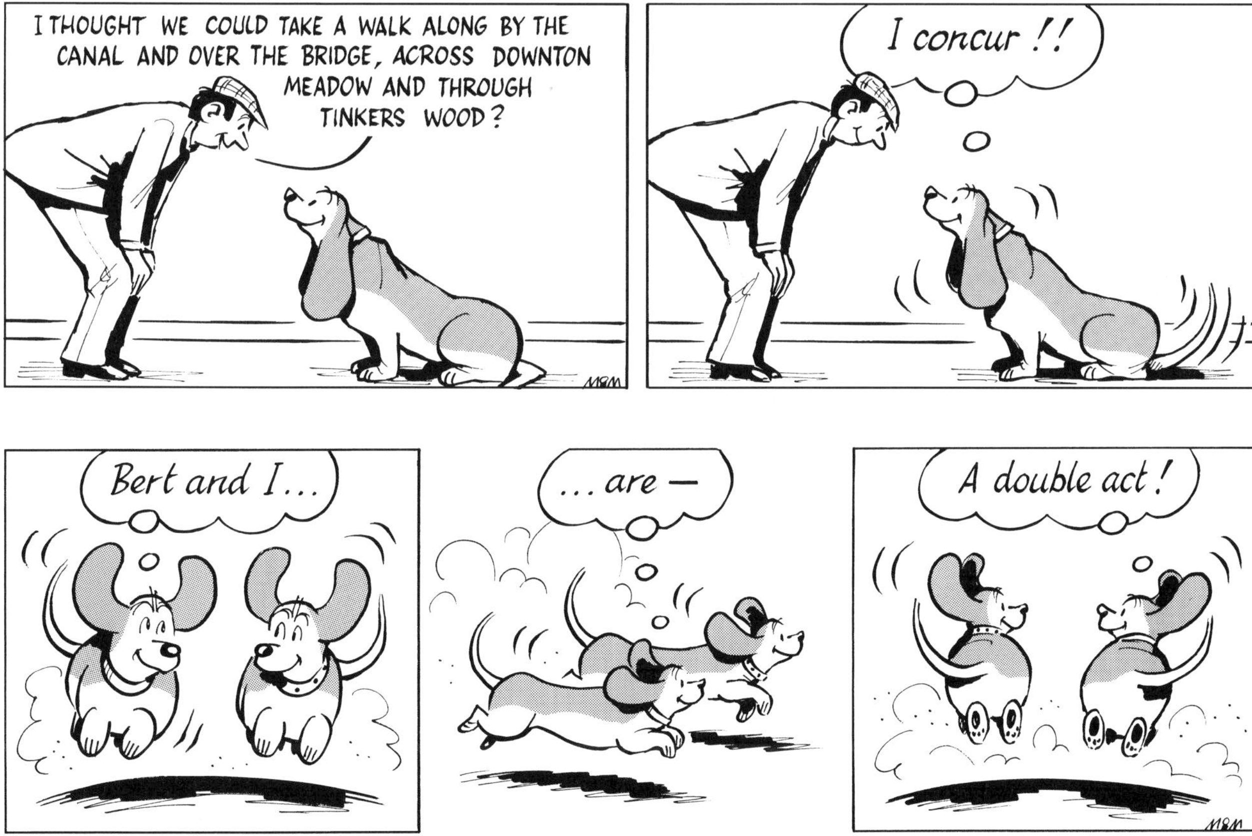
I THOUGHT WE COULD TAKE A WALK ALONG BY THE CANAL AND OVER THE BRIDGE, ACROSS DOWNTON MEADOW AND THROUGH TINKERS WOOD?
I concur !!
Bert and I...
... are –
A double act !

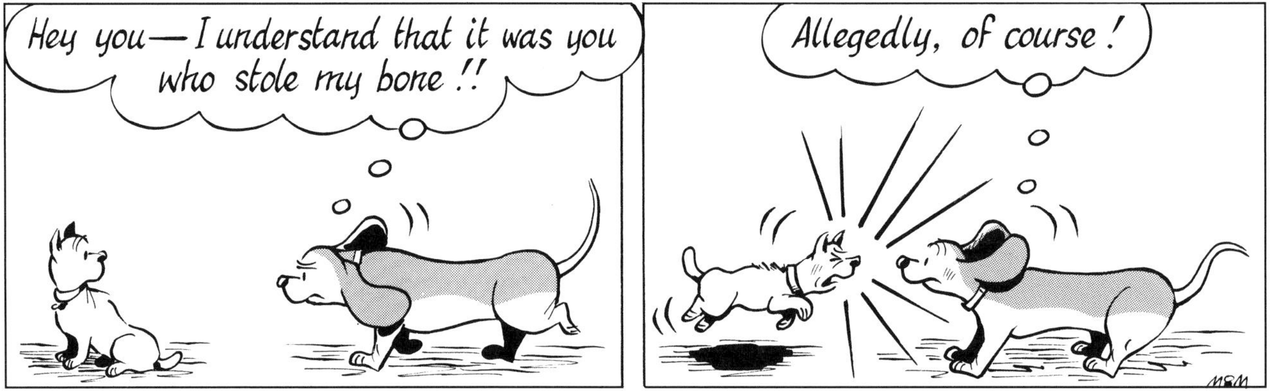
Hey you — I understand that it was you who stole my bone !!
Allegedly, of course !

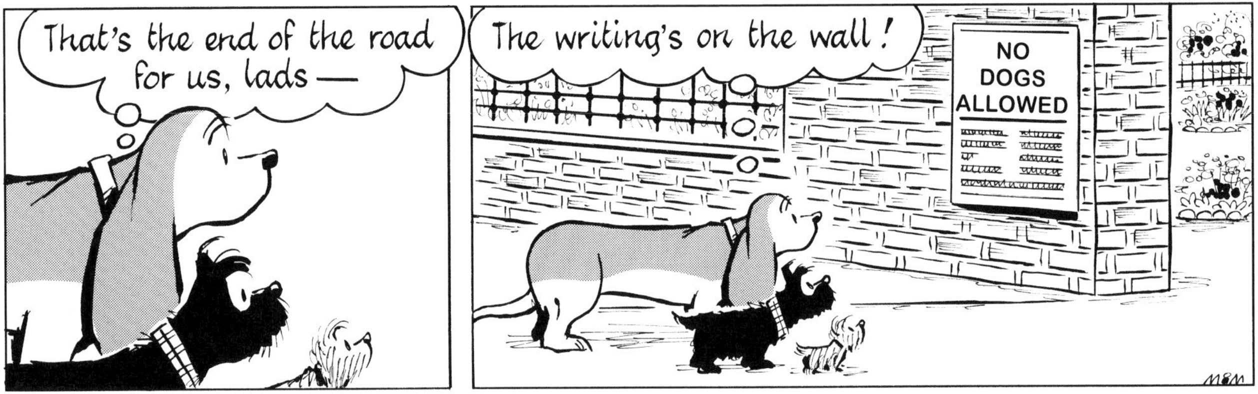
That's the end of the road for us, lads —
The writing's on the wall !
NO DOGS ALLOWED

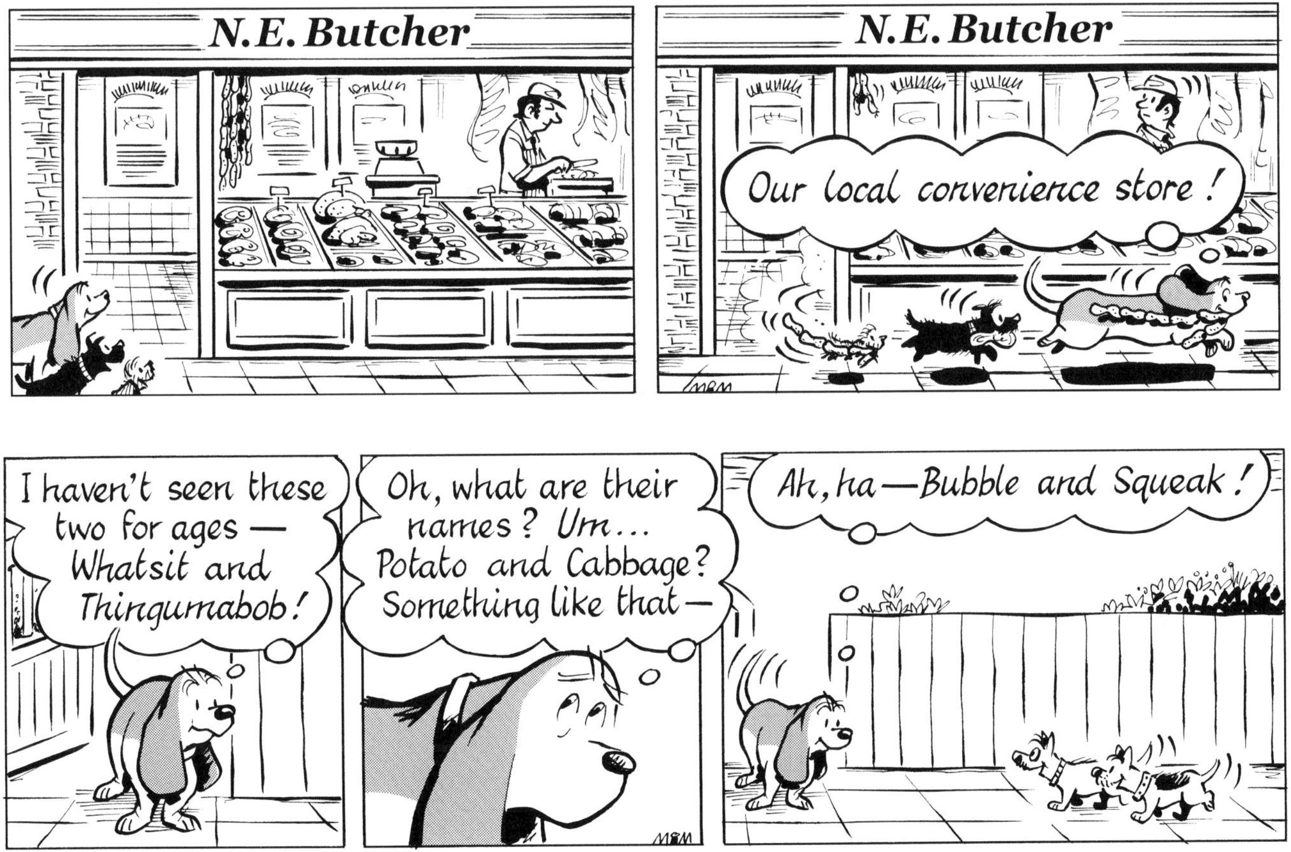
N.E. Butcher
N.E. Butcher
Our local convenience store!
I haven't seen these two for ages — Whatsit and Thingumabob!
Oh, what are their names? Um... Potato and Cabbage? Something like that —
Ah, ha — Bubble and Squeak!

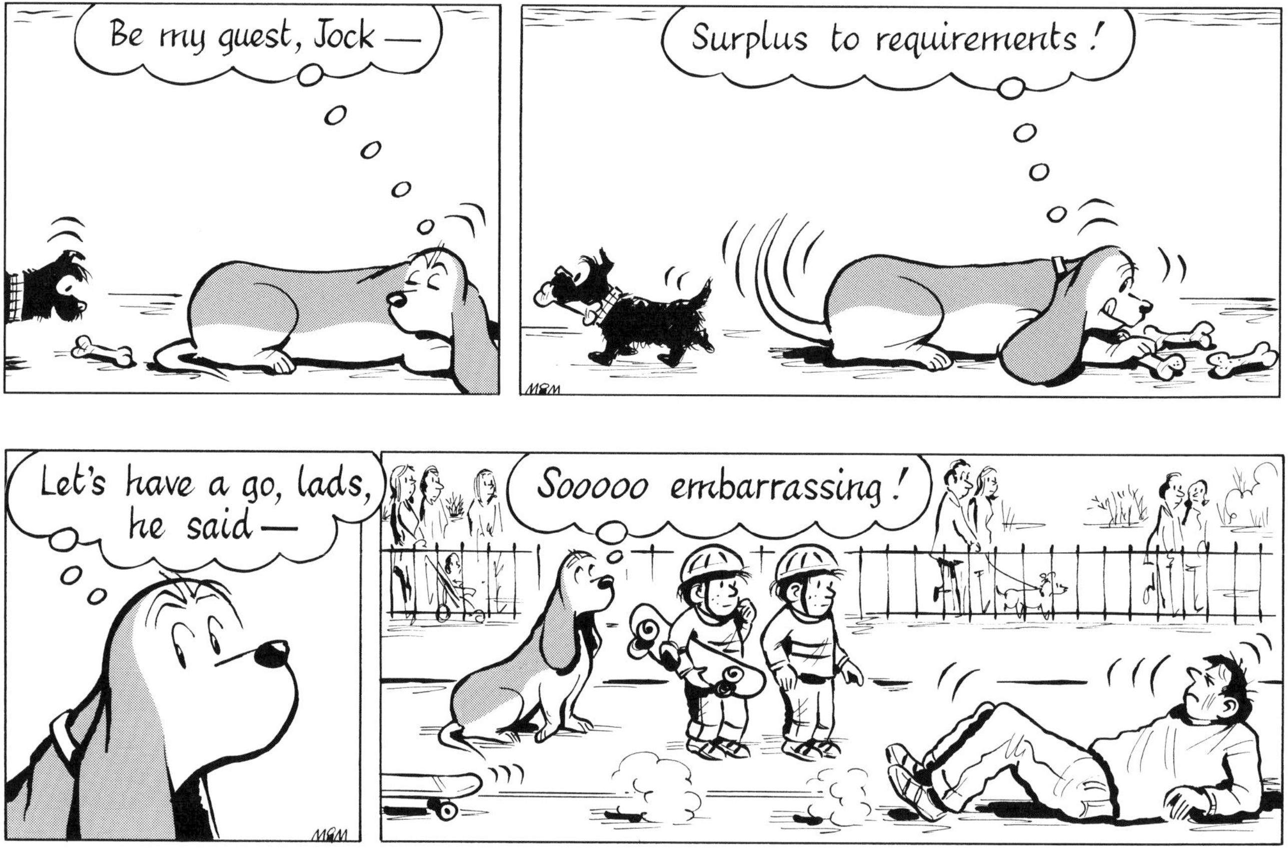
Be my guest, Jock —
Surplus to requirements!
Let's have a go, lads, he said —
Sooooo embarrassing!

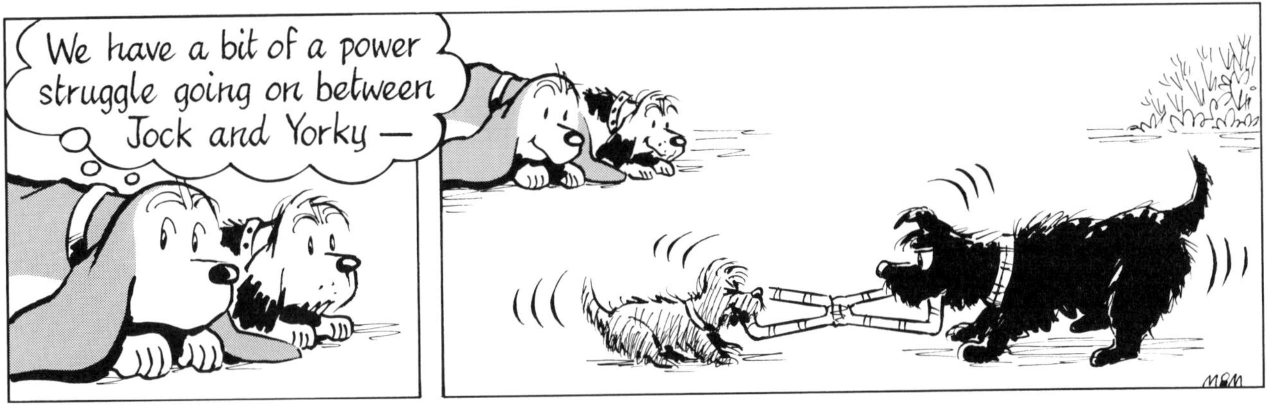
We have a bit of a power struggle going on between Jock and Yorky —
MRM

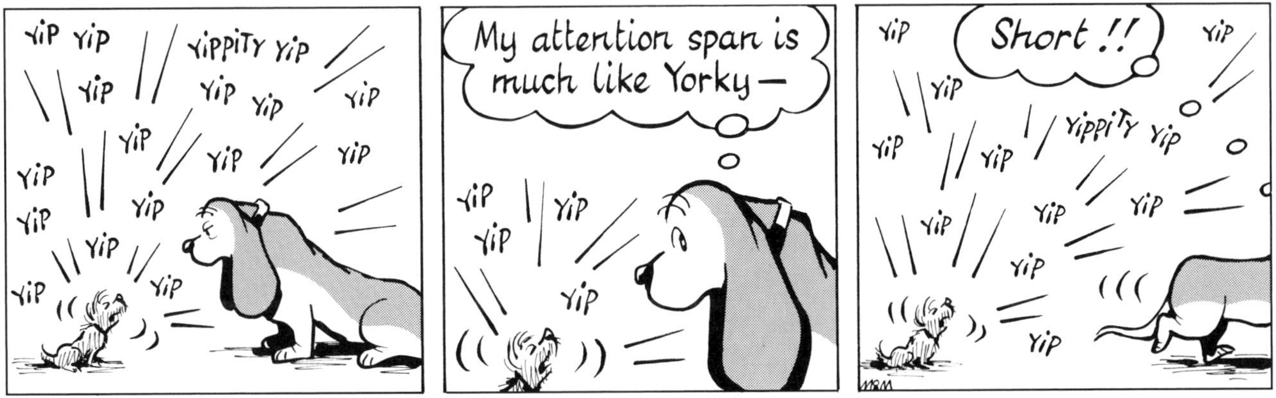
YIP YIP
YIPPITY YIP
YIP YIP YIP YIP YIP YIP YIP YIP YIP YIP YIP YIP YIP
My attention span is much like Yorky —
YIP YIP YIP YIP
Short !!
YIP YIP YIP YIP
YIPPITY YIP
YIP YIP YIP YIP YIP
MRM

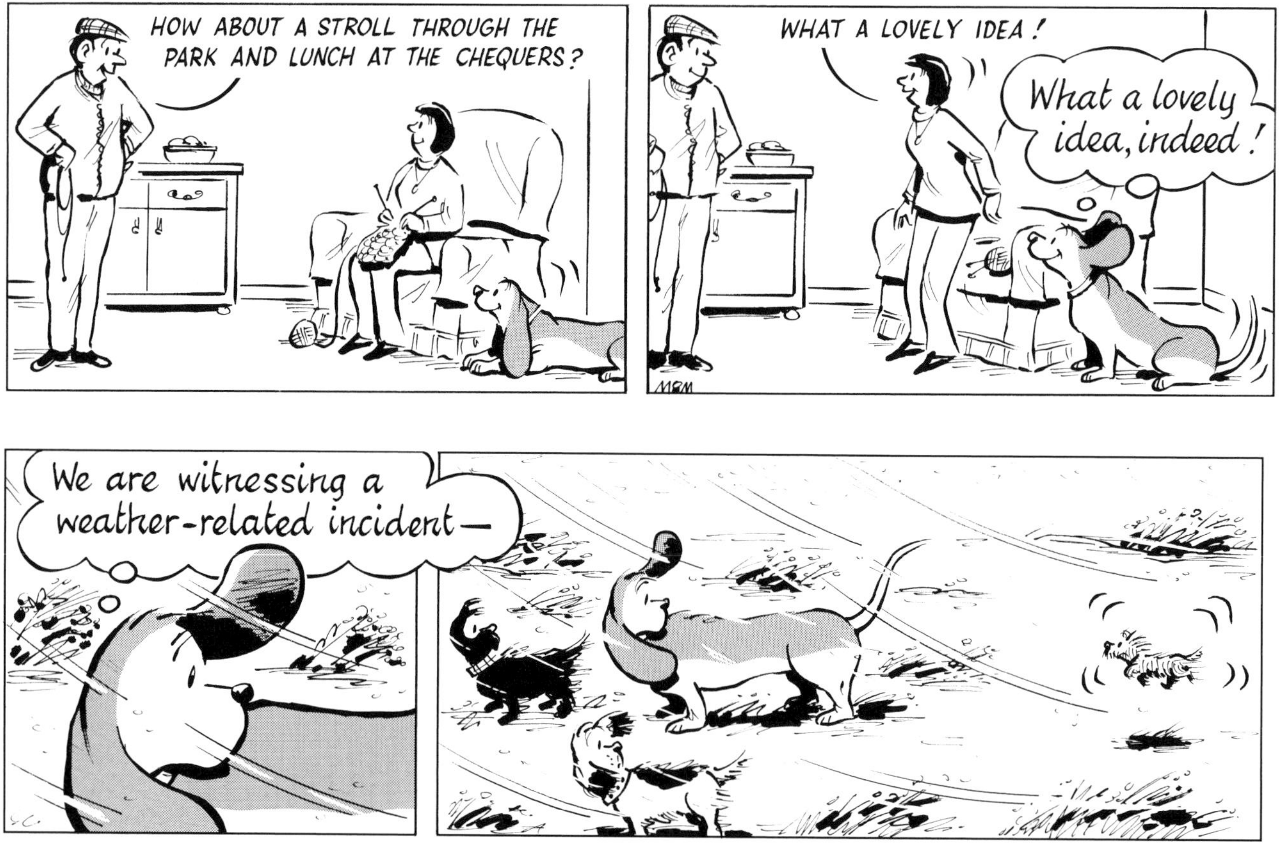
HOW ABOUT A STROLL THROUGH THE PARK AND LUNCH AT THE CHEQUERS?
WHAT A LOVELY IDEA!
What a lovely idea, indeed!
We are witnessing a weather-related incident—

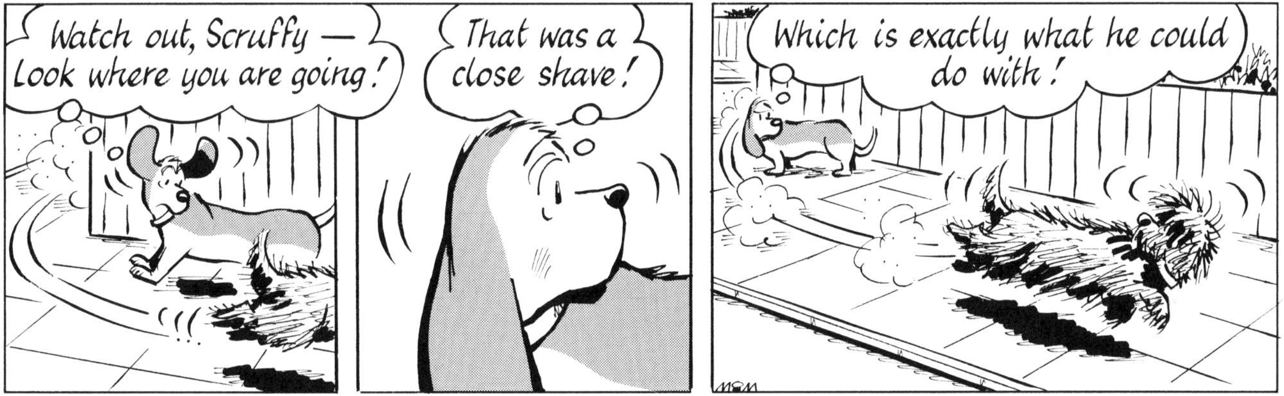
Watch out, Scruffy — Look where you are going!
That was a close shave!
Which is exactly what he could do with!
M&M

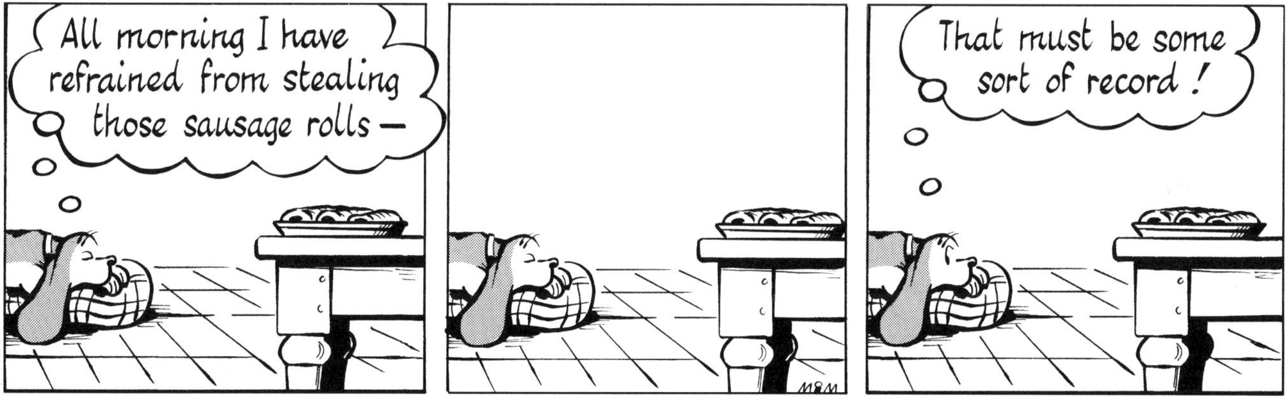
All morning I have refrained from stealing those sausage rolls —
M&M
That must be some sort of record!

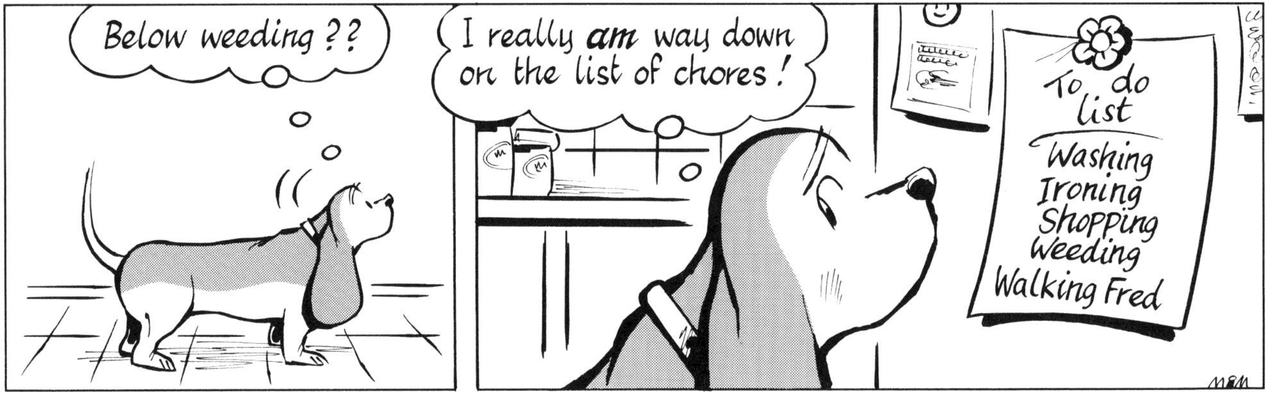
Below weeding??
I really am way down on the list of chores!
To do list
Washing
Ironing
Shopping
Weeding
Walking Fred

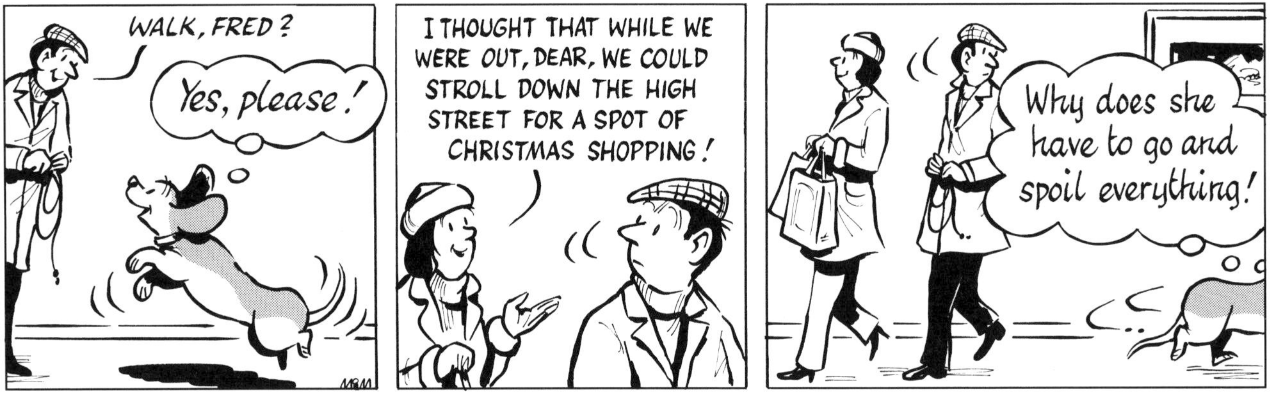
WALK, FRED?
Yes, please!
I THOUGHT THAT WHILE WE WERE OUT, DEAR, WE COULD STROLL DOWN THE HIGH STREET FOR A SPOT OF CHRISTMAS SHOPPING!
Why does she have to go and spoil everything!

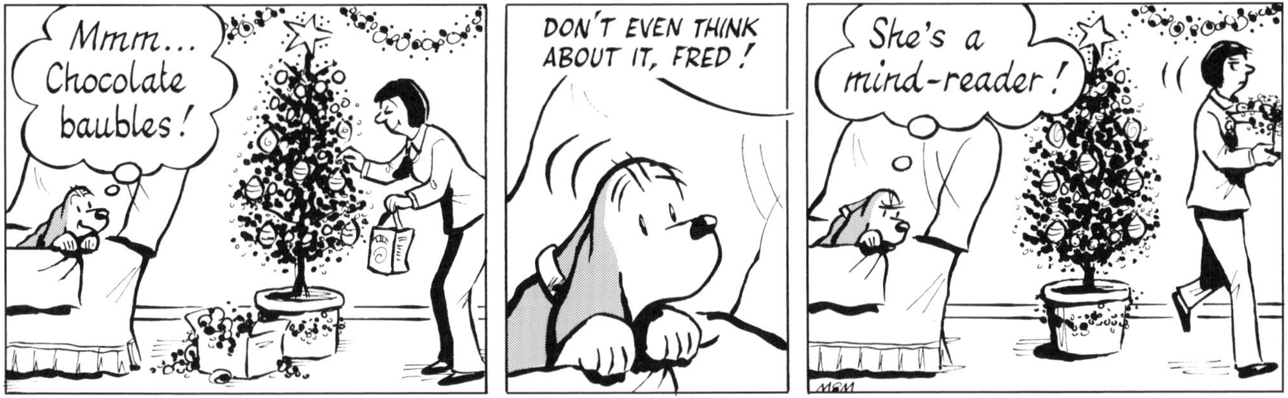
Mmm... Chocolate baubles!
DON'T EVEN THINK ABOUT IT, FRED!
She's a mind-reader!

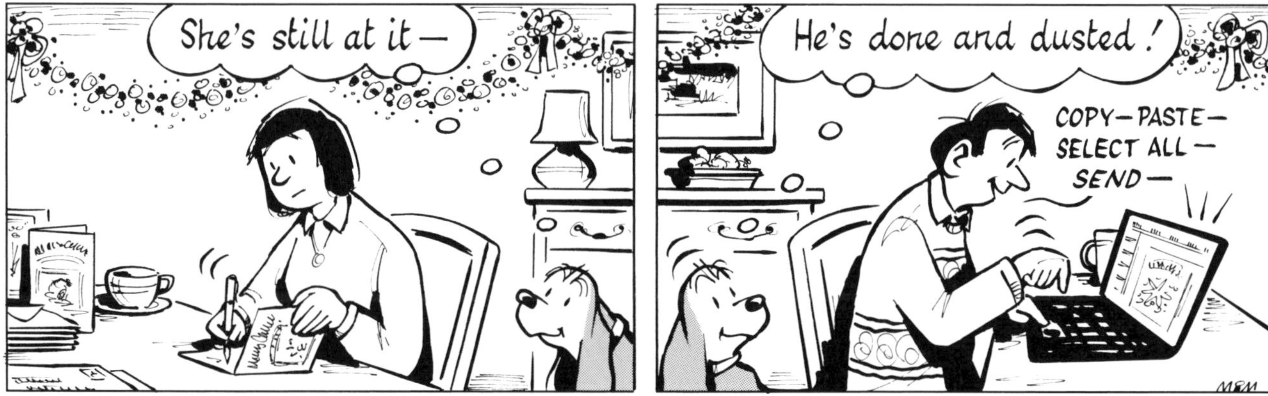
She's still at it—
He's done and dusted!
COPY—PASTE—SELECT ALL—SEND—

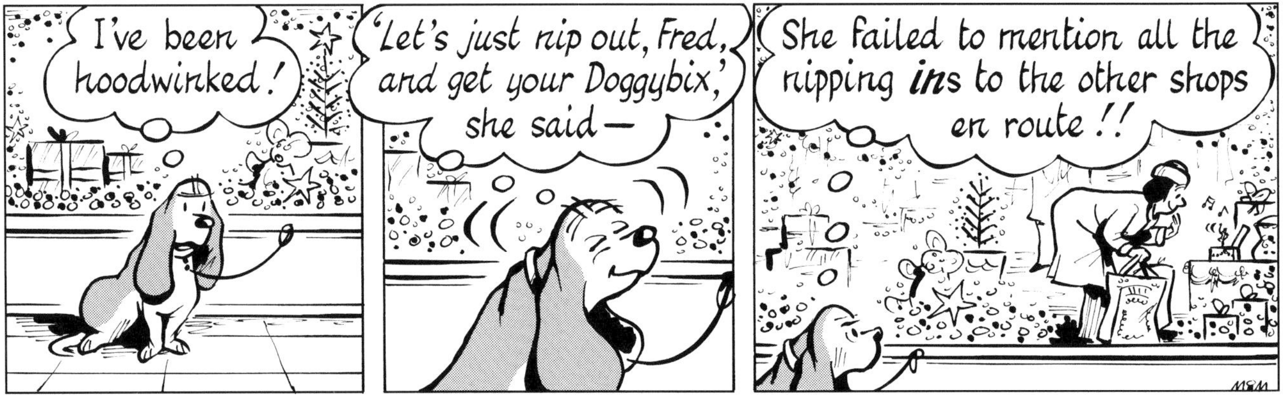
I've been hoodwinked!
'Let's just nip out, Fred, and get your Doggybix,' she said—
She failed to mention all the nipping ***ins*** to the other shops en route!!

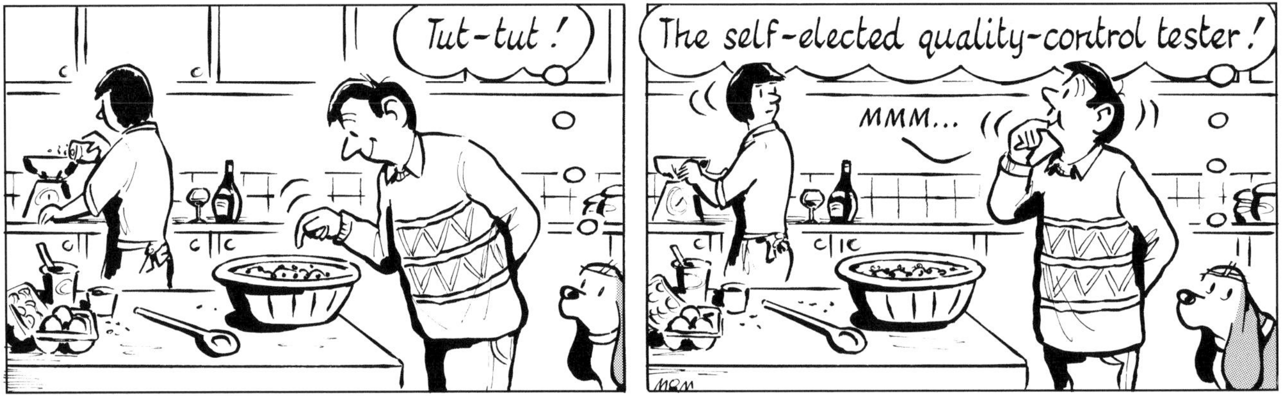
Tut-tut!
The self-elected quality-control tester!
MMM...

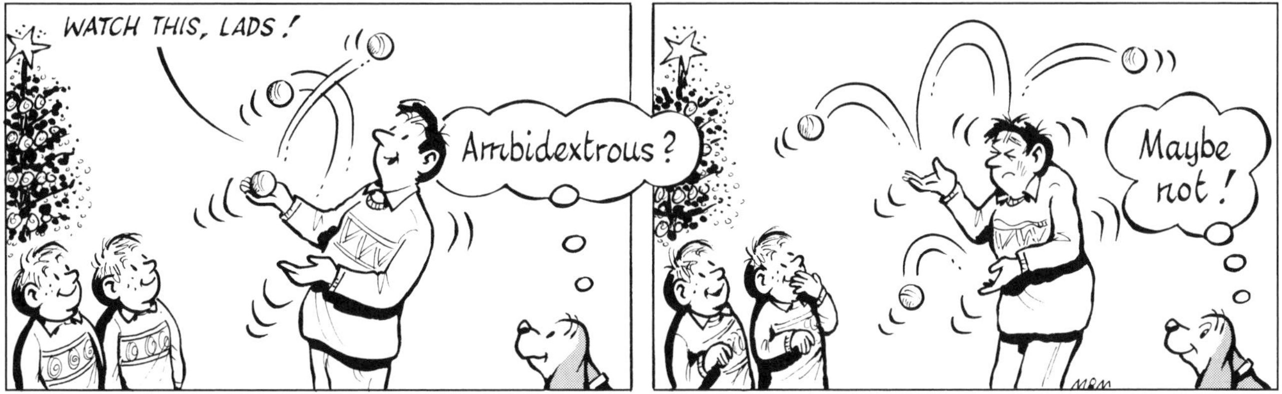
WATCH THIS, LADS!
Ambidextrous?
Maybe not!

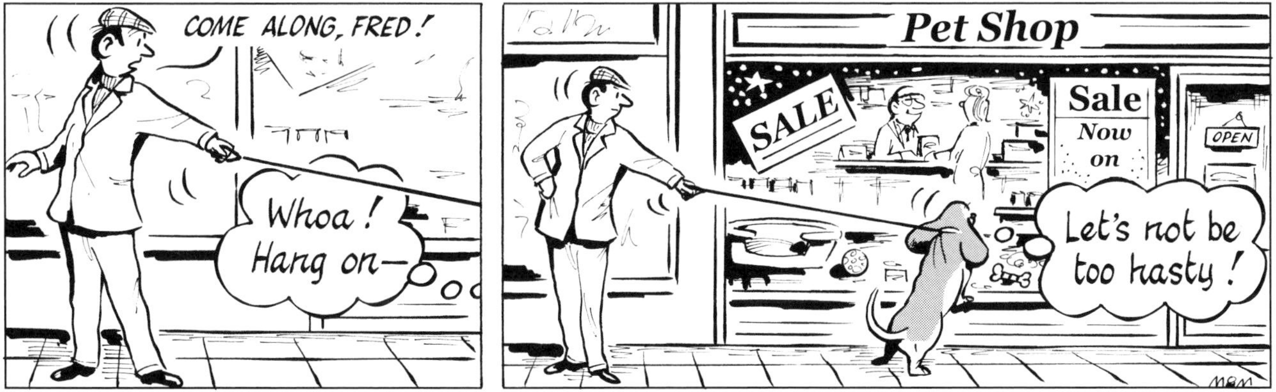
COME ALONG, FRED!
Whoa! Hang on—
Pet Shop
SALE
Sale Now on
OPEN
Let's not be too hasty!

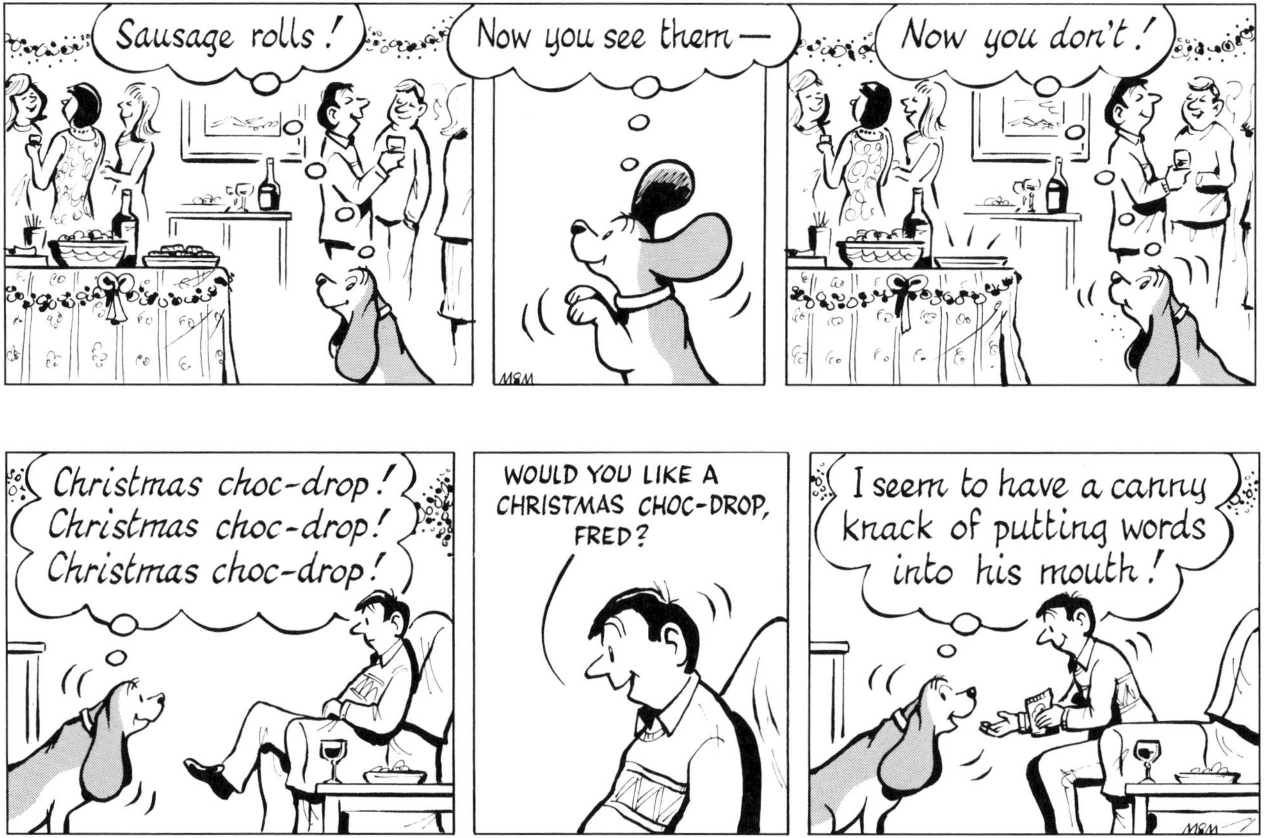
Sausage rolls!
Now you see them—
Now you don't!
Christmas choc-drop! Christmas choc-drop! Christmas choc-drop!
WOULD YOU LIKE A CHRISTMAS CHOC-DROP, FRED?
I seem to have a canny knack of putting words into his mouth!

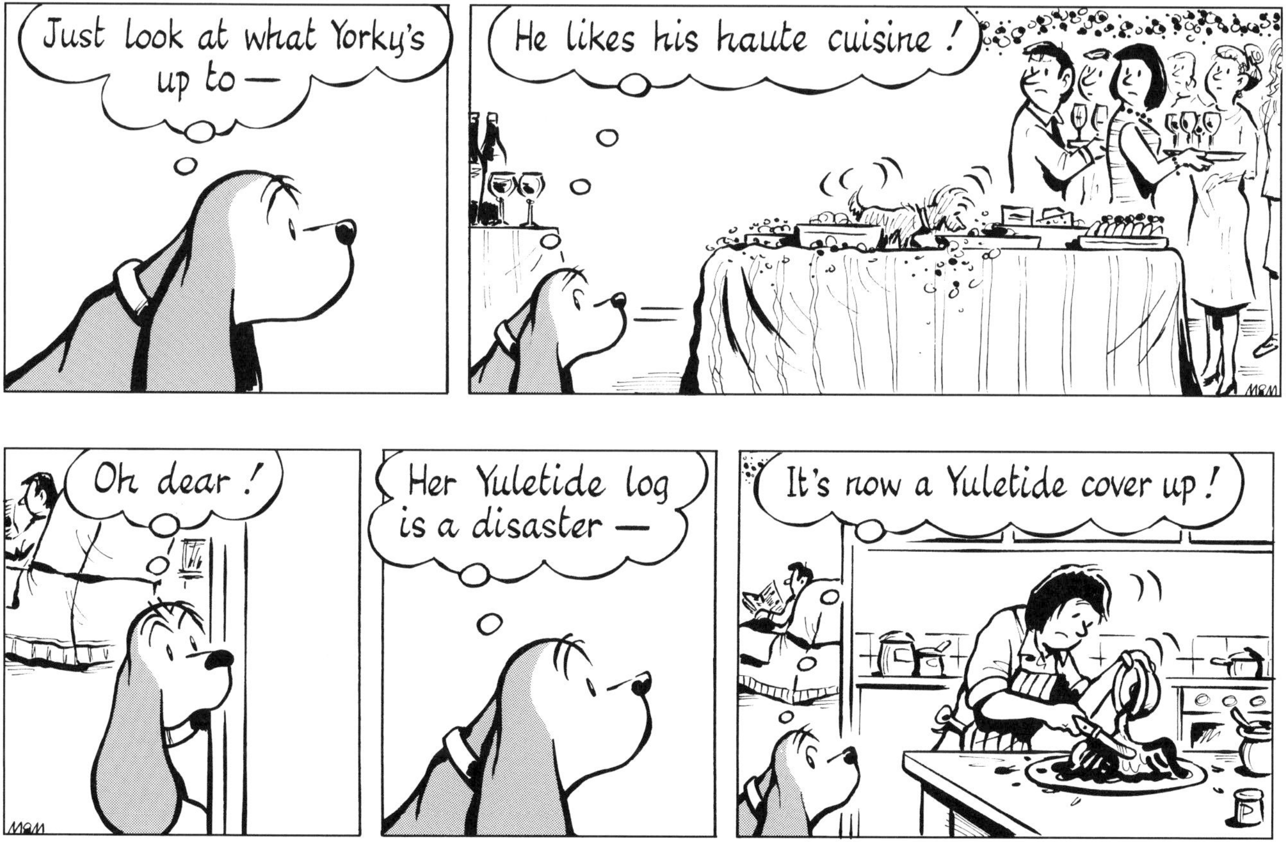
Just look at what Yorky's up to —
He likes his haute cuisine !
Oh dear !
Her Yuletide log is a disaster —
It's now a Yuletide cover up !

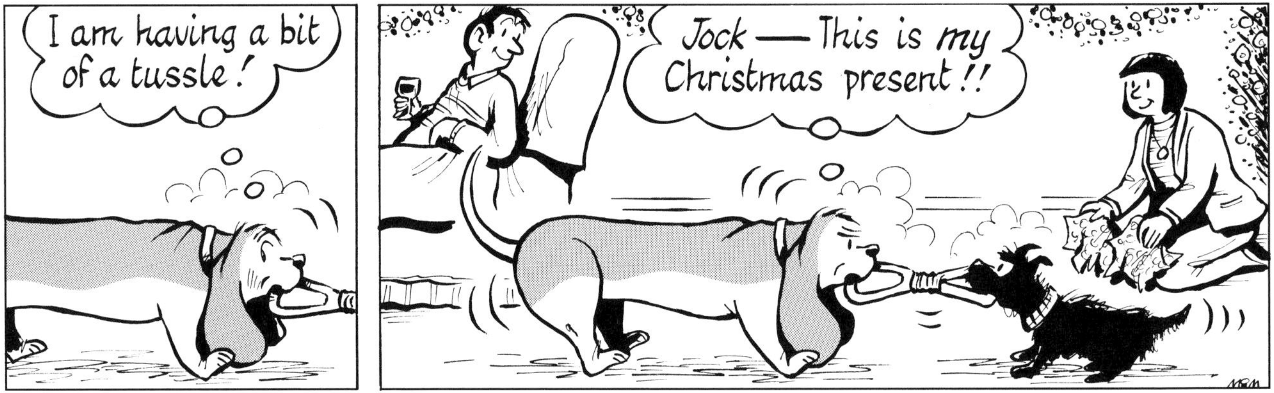
I am having a bit of a tussle!
Jock — This is my Christmas present!!
MBM

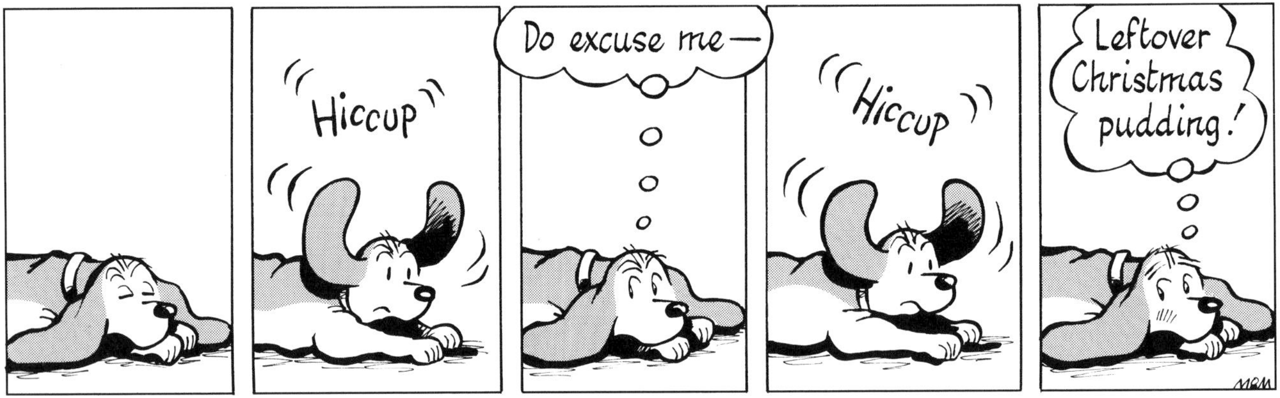
Hiccup
Do excuse me —
Hiccup
Leftover Christmas pudding!
MBM